The Changing Scenes of Life

By the same author:

The Story of the Arab Legion
A Soldier with the Arabs
Britain and the Arabs
War in the Desert
The Great Arab Conquests★
The Empire of the Arabs
The Course of Empire
The Lost Centuries
A Short History of the Arab Peoples★
The Middle East Crisis
Syria, Lebanon, Jordan
The Life and Times of Muhammad
Peace in the Holy Land
Soldiers of Fortune
The Way of Love
Haroon al Rasheed
Into Battle: A Soldier's Diary of the Great War
Arabian Adventures
A Purpose for Living

★Published by Quartet Books

DA
69.3
G56
A33
1983

The Changing Scenes of Life

An Autobiography

John Bagot Glubb

Quartet Books
London Melbourne New York

First published by Quartet Books Limited 1983
A member of the Namara Group
27/29 Goodge Street, London W1P 1FD

Copyright © 1983 by Sir John Glubb

British Library Cataloguing in Publication Data

Glubb, John Bagot
    The changing scenes of life.
    1. Glubb, John Bagot 2. Near East–Biography
    I. Title
    956'.03'0924   DS61.52.G/

    ISBN 0-7043-2329-X

Typeset by MC Typeset, Rochester, Kent
Printed and bound in Great Britain by Mackays of Chatham, Kent

Contents

Illustrations

Maps

Maps on pp. 31, 40, 45, 69, 76, 92 reproduced by kind permission of Cassell Ltd.

The Changing Scenes of Life

1
Our Fathers that Begat Us

The name Glubb was probably derived from the early Britons, before the invasions of the Anglo-Saxons or the Danes. The first Glubb personally recorded in history was a Henry Glubb, who was Member of Parliament for Okehampton in 1313, in the reign of Edward II.

My great-great-grandfather, Thomas Glubb, was born in April 1725 and settled at Nether Stowey in Somerset and, on 30 December 1756, married Elizabeth Conyngham or Cunningham. The Cunninghams were said to have descended from the eighth Earl of Glencairn. In 1715, seeing their clan cut to pieces at the Battle of Sheriffmuir when fighting for the Pretender, these Cunninghams fled from Scotland and hid themselves at Okehampton in Devon.

Peter Goodman Glubb was the son of Thomas Glubb of Nether Stowey and his wife, Elizabeth Cunningham. He became a lawyer at Liskeard in Cornwall in 1783. His eldest son Peter Glubb followed him in his legal business in Liskeard. His second son, John Matthew Glubb, graduated in Second Class Honours from Exeter College, Oxford, in 1814, and was for seventeen years Rector of St Petrox, Dartmouth, in Devonshire. Later he was for thirty-five years Rector of Shermanbury in Sussex, where he also became Rural Dean and Diocesan Inspector of Schools.

Meanwhile, other Glubbs had scattered over the world. One was killed in India, another in the Peninsular War, a third in South Africa.

Both the sons of Rev. John Matthew Glubb left the country rectory of Shermanbury to join the Honourable East India Company's service in 1847. The eldest, John Matthew, joined the 38th Bengal Light Infantry, but was later transferred to the Sappers and Miners. He was severely wounded in six places when leading a storming party at Futtehpore Sickree – it was always the privilege of the senior engineer subaltern present to lead the storming party up the breach in a city wall. In 1864 he married Mary Sarah Catherine Whittington. He survived his service in India and returned to live in Bedford. His son became rector of Gerrards Cross, the church in which Gray is alleged to have written the *Elegy in a Country Churchyard*.

The second son, Orlando Manley, was my grandfather. He joined the 37th Bengal Light Infantry, in the East India Company's army, and was private secretary to the Lieutenant Governor of Bengal. He took part in the Second Sikh War, 1848–9, becoming a captain in the Bengal Staff Corps.

On 2 October 1856, at Calcutta, he married Frances Letitia Kelly, the daughter of Captain John Kelly, of New Park, Co. Longford, who was an officer in the 87th Royal Irish Fusiliers. His father had lost a leg in the Peninsular War and returned to Brighton.

Here one day, as he was stumping with a wooden leg along the street, he saw a carriage and pair galloping wildly towards him. The coachman had fallen off the box, the reins were dragging loose, and a panic-stricken lady was screaming in the carriage. Old Kelly hopped into the street and threw himself at the heads of the horses. They swung him off his feet but he held on to their bridles and, by his weight dragging along, brought them to a standstill. He handed them over to the coachman, who had meanwhile arrived, took off his hat and bowed to the lady, and hobbled off on his wooden leg.

To return to the marriage of Frances Letitia Kelly and Orlando Manley Glubb in 1856, in Calcutta. Fannie and Manley Glubb were deeply in love, as the many letters still in my possession amply prove. Only a matter of weeks after their wedding, the Mutiny of the Bengal Army began.

It was decided to disarm the 37th Bengal Native Infantry. On 4 June 1857, the regiment was paraded on the barrack square for this purpose, while Fannie Glubb looked on from the window of their quarter. Only the company commanded by Manley Glubb obediently grounded their arms at his orders and marched off. The other companies of the regiment opened fire on their officers before they could be disarmed.

After the mutiny, Manley Glubb was made assistant military secretary of the North-West Province, and soon after he was gazetted as District Superintendent of Police, First Grade, at Meeruth, with the command of 1,200 foot and 300 mounted constables. This district was the largest in the North-West Province and on him devolved the arduous task of enforcing the police regulations, where anarchy and confusion still reigned as a result of the recent mutiny. He was thanked by the government for his services in restoring order. Copies of his regulations were sent to all the other superintendents of police in the province with orders to apply them in their respective districts.

In order to hold these different appointments, he had passed examinations in the higher standard in Persian and Hindustani and one in English law, including its adaptation to the Indian Penal Code.

The aftermath of the mutiny was a period of great strain to Fannie and Manley. By this time they had two children, the elder of whom was my father. Fannie and the children had to be deposited somewhere in safety, while Manley was constantly away on his duties, endlessly on the move in his efforts to restore law and order.

May 12th

My darling Fan,
I shall send you a very few lines only to tell you that I have arrived here in safety, and purpose going on to Allahabad. The road for some thirty miles was most unsafe and I felt very glad when I was out of danger. We met with no interruption but it was evident from the manner of the people on the road that they thought the rebels might make their appearance at any moment. I thought a great deal of you, my pet, and of our little ones and of the misery you would endure if anything happened to me.

I am very glad you did not come with me. The heat was intense. Ever my most dear wife, yours most fondly,

Manley

My darling Fan,

I arrived here yesterday evening. I thought of you and our dear little ones very frequently on the way and managed to alarm myself and fancy you were ill. I was relieved however on being told at the C.S. office that no message had arrived for me for I concluded that if anything had occurred to you Mrs Stephenson would surely have sent a telegram.

Let me know how you are and how the children are getting on. Do not exert yourself too much, my pet. Your little strength must be carefully preserved for expenditure at Allahabad. I miss you all very much. Goodbye my darling Fan. Take care of yourself. Kiss the little ones for me and do not allow Louie to forget to say pa-pa-pa. Your very fondly attached husband,

Manley

But the devoted love match of Fannie and Manley was not long to endure. In August 1861, they were living in Meeruth, but Fannie was staying not far away with friends to give the children a change.

Below is an account of Manley's death, contained in a letter written immediately after the event by his elder brother, John Matthew Glubb, who was present.

On the night of the 25th August, 1861, Dunbar of his old regiment had dinner with Manley, and just as he was going poor Manley said, 'I am not right in my insides tonight, but I shall take some ginger and that will make me right again.' Dunbar came over in the morning to ride with him, when he again complained that something was wrong. They both then went to Dr Cutcliffe but he was out. Upon this they went to Corbyn's and asked him for a dose. The latter told him it was nothing and that the medicine he gave him would make him right. He took the dose and then went to the office (this was about 8 a.m.).

He could not keep the medicine down, but he remained and did the office work. About 10 a.m. he felt worse and went home and took to his bed. Dunbar came over to see him about 11 a.m. and found him very ill in bed. He had been very sick many times. He sent for Dr Cutcliffe who at once said it was cholera, and told Manley so. Manley asked if he were in danger and being told 'yes' said, 'Send for my wife if I am in danger, but do not frighten her for nothing.'

Up to 3 p.m. the doctor thought he would recover but at that hour he sent a message to Fannie to bring her in. At 4 o'clock he was much worse. He got weak very soon and about four hours after he was taken ill was so changed that Ogilvie (of the 48th) told me he would not have known him. The weakness was so great that he could not speak. He asked several times if she was come and desired the doctor in case of his death to take her to Major and Mrs Frith's house. He spoke of death in the most calm and collected way and had not the least fear of death. He knew his end, poor fellow, was near and he obeyed without a murmur.

All those that were near him agree that they never saw the body and soul part so calmly before. About midnight, his eyes became fixed. He remained in this state until four in the morning, and then his soul went to God who gave it.

Ogilvie was just making the room straight when poor dear Fannie came. As soon as she saw them she knew the worst and said, 'Take me to him.' They did and left her with all that remained of him whom she loved so truly and so deeply. You know her well and can fancy what her grief would be.

If ever there was a case of true and sincere love, hers is one.

This letter, dated August 1861, now yellow with age, lies on my desk today.

'Darling Fannie' was my grandmother. Although she was to live for another forty-four years after the death of Manley, she wore heavy black mourning for the rest of her life. Manley had left enough money to pay her passage to England with the children, and she, at the age of twenty-four, travelled back in her loneliness in a sailing ship round the Cape, a journey lasting several months.

In England, she took refuge with her father-in-law, John Matthew Glubb, the Rector of Shermanbury in Sussex. I remember her well, with her sweet and gentle expression and her black clothes, for she did not die until 1904, when I was seven.

It may perhaps be thought unnecessary to include this description of the death of my grandfather, for we all have to die. But I have done so because the story is so vividly told by someone who was present. It also illustrates something of the precarious nature of life in India in the mid-nineteenth century, before the invention of modern drugs and inoculations. In those days, a young man at the height of his physical strength might at any time be dead within twenty-four hours.

I can well remember an epidemic of cholera at Nasiriya in lower Iraq in 1922, and the continual funeral processions on foot carrying the corpses out for burial, followed by weeping women.

My father first went to a preparatory school in Brighton and then gained a scholarship into Wellington. In 1875, he passed third into the Royal Military Academy at Woolwich. He had always been bent upon being a soldier, but few officers in those days could live on their pay. As his widowed mother could not help him financially, he was commissioned into the Royal Engineers, where it was possible for an officer to live on his pay. His first commission lies on my desk while I write these words. 'Victoria by the Grace of God . . . to our trusty and well-beloved Frederic Manley Glubb . . . Given at our Court at St James's the seventh day of May, 1878.'

Frederic Manley Glubb was a young subaltern not entirely unsusceptible to the usual gaieties and frivolities. He was an accomplished dancer, and I have found among his early papers 'a prescription for nervousness at amateur theatricals. Take a glass of port behind the scenes at the beginning of each act.'

But his real passion was horses, and was to remain so all his life. His love of horses was to play a great part in his life and, to a lesser extent, in mine. He was small, light and athletic and was soon in great demand as a jockey in garrison race meetings. The only silver cups and trophies which have ever adorned my sideboard were all won by my father's riding prowess. 'Bermuda Spring Meeting 1883, Won by Mr Glubb's Missy', 'Malta Spring Meeting 1885. Polo pony race won by Mr Glubb's Real Jam', 'Malta Winter Race Meeting 1885. Hurdle Race won by Mr Glubb's Cherry Brandy'; and so the list goes on. As my father was living on his pay, it was by no means easy for him to keep horses. His letters to his mother are full of long accounts of how he picked up lame horses, vicious horses or old screws – any horse with some bad quality which made it cheap and to which he could then devote his time and pleasure to cure and train.

In 1887, he had been posted from Aldershot to the Curragh, the largest garrison in Ireland in those days. Here his future (and mine, for that matter) was to be decided, for it was here that he met Miss

Frances Letitia Bagot, the daughter of Bernard William Bagot Esq., of Carranure.

If the Glubbs were ancient British Celts, the Bagots were Norman conquerors. The name and coat of arms of the Bagots appear on the Battle Abbey Roll, which claims to be the list of the principal Knights in Arms at the Battle of Hastings. But the Bagot claim to have come over with the Conqueror is further substantiated by Domesday Book, which records the grant of lands to the Bagots at Bramshall in Staffordshire in 1086. Hervey Fitz Bagot, possibly the son or grandson of the Battle of Hastings warrior, was living in 1160, when he held Three Knight's fees of old feoffment from his feudal overlord, Robert de Stafford, whose daughter he married. The family still survives at Blithfield, in the County of Stafford.

In 1170, Richard de Clare, Second Earl of Pembroke, nicknamed Strongbow, crossed to Ireland to help Dermot MacMurrough, King of Leinster, who had been evicted from his dominions. Henry II, King of England, as his liege lord, granted Strongbow lands in Wexford, Waterford and Dublin.

One of the Staffordshire Bagots went in Strongbow's army and founded the Irish branch. The family attained a certain position in Ireland, for in 1495 we find a record of Patrick Bagot of Bagotstown Castle in the County of Limerick. Two hundred years later, an Edward Bagot was High Sheriff for County Kildare and King's County. The family nearly ruined itself by supporting Charles I in the Civil War and the Jacobite cause after the exile of James II. My grandfather was Bernard William Bagot of Carranure House, in the County of Roscommon.

My maternal grandmother was Josephine Isabella, the daughter of Joseph Holmes Esq., of Colgher House, in the County of Sligo. At the beginning of the nineteenth century, a William Holmes had been prominent in London political life. He was a Member of Parliament for Hazlemere and held the position of Treasurer of the Ordnance in the governments of Lord Liverpool and the Duke of Wellington. He is alleged to have held the unique distinction of being the only member of the Duke of Wellington's government who ever dared to vote against the openly expressed wishes of his formidable chief . . . Evidently a man of character, Mr William Holmes.

He was also, in his time, a close friend of General Picton.

Tradition relates that the night before Picton sailed for Belgium to take part in the Waterloo campaign, he dined in London with William Holmes. After dinner, his little son was allowed to come down to pay his respects to the guest but, in doing so, upset a glass of red wine over the General's white knee-breeches. It was the day of white buckskin breeches which lasted a lifetime and Picton does not appear to have had a second pair with him – in any case he was sailing at midnight. So the General set out for the war with his breeches already stained a deep red. Perhaps it was an omen. A few days later he was killed while commanding his division at Waterloo and his gallant blood was mingled with the wine-stains on his white breeches.

As a child, I used to say facetiously to my mother that the Bagot crest was a goat looking through a napkin ring, although I really imagined that the armorial beast in question was probably intended to be a deer. It was only after I was grown up that I turned idly one day to the name of Bagot in Burke's *Peerage,* and found the crest actually described as 'out of a ducal coronet a goat's head argent'. What is more, the arms had as supporters two goats argent. So I had been right about the goat after all. But why this obsession for goats? It is true that there were plenty of goats in Roscommon, but this coat of arms was shared equally by the Staffordshire branch.

I had originally been told that a certain Richard Bagot had been a veteran crusader and had brought a flock of goats with him on the ship, when he returned from Palestine by sea, a common way of providing fresh milk and meat on a sea voyage.

It appears, however, that the goats are of a black-necked breed found in the Rhône valley, and called Schwarzhals. Richard II (1377–99) is believed once to have spent a Christmas at Lichfield, during which he enjoyed some good hunting in Bagot's park. He enjoyed himself so much that he presented the flock of Schwarzhals goats to Sir John Bagot. Presumably the Bagots were so flattered by the royal gift that they adopted a goat's head as their crest and two goats as supporters to their coat of arms.

The Bagot goats still survive and some are being cared for by the Rare Breeds Survival Trust. There is a Bagot Goat Society, which also cares for them. I am indebted for these details to Nancy Lady Bagot, who still lives at Blithfield in Staffordshire.

The point which has always impressed me about these old worthies

– Glubbs, Kellys, Bagots or whoever they were – is their simple outlook. They did their duty as it appeared to them, without doubts or philosophizing. Today, by contrast, we question everything, debate, discuss and talk – and in the end do nothing. Excessive intellectualism is one of the sure signs of decadence, as simple devotion to duty and service is the hallmark of national greatness.

2

The Delectable Island

My father and mother were married quietly in Dublin in 1889 and left almost immediately for Hong Kong, whither my father had been transferred. They remained three years in the Far East, visiting also China and Japan. My sister, Gwenda, was born in 1894, after their return to England. I myself was born on 16 April 1897, at Preston in Lancashire, though, three weeks after my birth, my father was posted to the Portsmouth area, and we moved to Netley, on Southampton Water.

Meanwhile, however, more serious matters were afoot, unknown to me in the nursery. The South African War had broken out and my father was fretting with anxiety lest it be over before he could go. He had already been twenty-two years in the army and had never been on active service. In January 1899, he wrote to his mother that he had still received no orders, adding bitterly, 'I suppose I shall always be only a peacetime soldier.'

At last the orders came, and in February 1900 he sailed on the S.S. *Goorkha* for South Africa. But delighted as he was to go, there was still that horrible ordeal of saying goodbye, the dread and horror of the life of the soldier's wife.

Writing from Aldershot, where he had gone to collect a draft of reinforcements for South Africa, he said in a letter to his mother,

My dear old lady,
You know I think how I have always longed for active service,

though no one ever really could quite know except myself – but still it is a great wrench going. The little wife has been so plucky, and went off today as cheery as possible, but I know she has felt it and will feel it terribly, and I grieve for the anxiety she and you will feel.

Then he added characteristically – for he was a very keen soldier – 'I hope there will be some fighting left for me.'

But although my mother seemed to him to go off so cheerily after saying goodbye to him, she wrote a less reassuring letter to his mother. 'I suppose in time one will get used to the dreadful ache of separation,' she wrote from Netley. 'At least he has got what he wished for so much. This has been such a fine day here and the sea so smooth. I do hope it will last this week. I do want it to be nice for *him*.' What a world of longing seems to be conveyed in that wish – 'I do want it to be nice for *him*.'

My father's letters from South Africa often make spirited reading. Writing on 6 April from Elandslaagte, he said,

Yesterday morning we had a rude awakening. We had had breakfast and I was going on parade, when suddenly there was a sort of shrieking scream through the air just overhead – and a great cloud of dust right in the middle of our camp. Those blessed Boers had got up guns on the hills round, and proceeded to give us a lively time for a bit. I got my men out in the veldt lying down, and then with three or four sappers, I got my mules inspanned, which was not an easy job. Finally a few sappers and I tied them in somehow. One mule was killed and another shell burst right under a mule team but hurt no one.

My father was given command of the 17th Field Company, which had lost its commander on Spion Kop. The company was in Clery's 2nd Division, north of Ladysmith. According to the Royal Engineers' journal, the chief impression which my father made on one of his subalterns concerned the skill with which he handled the formidable divisional commander.

The 17th Field Company took part in Buller's advance through Newcastle and Laing's Nek and in the attack on Botha's pass on 8 June 1900. He spent the next four months trekking about the country east of Standerton with Clery's mobile column. There were plenty of brushes with the Boers, but their main resistance was in reality already broken. The Boers were playing at tip–and–run raids, but my father's martial enthusiasm was unabated.

'I have not had my fill of fighting yet,' he wrote from Laing's Nek (in the Boer War, units were allowed to give their locations in letters).

> Of course one is generally under fire of sorts, but one very seldom has a chance of fighting back oneself, only of letting the other fellow have a shot at you. The infantryman does the job really and gets all the knocks. My highest excitement up to now has been riding a good race, but that is not in it with facing a position which is well defended, a test of nerve and pluck and all the qualities that make a *man*.

After a year in South Africa, his mare put her foot in a hole while galloping across the veldt and turned somersault. My father broke his ankle and was invalided back to England. His war service cannot have been futile, for he was mentioned in despatches and awarded the D.S.O. The award was dated 24 January 1902, and was in the name of 'the King'. But it came in an envelope on which an economical government had crossed out 'Her' in *On Her Majesty's Service,* and had substituted 'His' in manuscript.

My father had scarcely returned from South Africa to Netley when he was posted to Mauritius in the Indian Ocean.

One day I found myself being rowed out to a ship lying in the Thames. My memories of those years are vague, but I remember being seasick in the Bay of Biscay, then the warmth and the blueness of the Mediterranean.

When we sailed for Mauritius, my grandmother – the same 'darling Fan' who had been left a widow in India after the mutiny – was dying. I have before me her farewell letter to her only son, my father, and his wife and children, my sister and myself.

Cowfold
March 5th 1903

My darlings,
I have been so delighted with your dear letters since you left us, and so pleased that your tooth and throat have been attended to

and that you my dear Fanny have picked up before the voyage has begun. I have been very weak but am feeling more rested again just waiting till my Saviour sees right to take me home. What untold mercies he has been showering upon us all. I hope you will like the book of Collects. I like the Church prayers so much and that lovely General Thanksgiving before going to bed.

Goodbye and God bless you *all* my Darlings. May God's best blessings be poured out abundantly upon you all. Your fond mother,

F.L. Glubb

All through my childhood, until our home was broken up in 1914, we had family prayers every morning and my father read that General Thanksgiving to which his mother had been so devoted. Sad to say, the Church of England has virtually abandoned that Book of Common Prayer to which the people of England had been so devoted for nearly three hundred years, and on which my contemporaries and I were brought up.

Although our ship had engines, she was fully rigged, and when the wind was favourable would hoist the sails to help the engines along. We arrived eventually in Ceylon, and walked through the bazaars in Colombo. I remember to this day the vociferations and gesticulations of the shopkeepers in the bazaars, pursuing us with souvenirs and trinkets of carved wood and ivory. We bought an elephant's foot which I still use as a doorstop in my study.

In Mauritius, we had what appeared to me then a large house and garden, at least compared to Netley. We grew our own bananas, pineapples and lychees. Outside the garden fence, the country for miles around was one vast sea of sugar cane.

My childhood was so much concerned with horses that it is natural that one of my most vivid memories is of my father's two horses, a chestnut called Rayon d'Or, and a black polo pony called Nigger.

For holidays, we went to the sea and stayed in little huts on a tiny island called Mouchoir Rouge, just off shore. The sea was perfect, as the island was surrounded by coral reefs on which broke the rollers of the Indian Ocean. Inside the reefs was a great expanse of mirror-like calm water, warm and blue and so clear that one could lean over the side of a boat and look down and down through crystal water to the luxuriant coral growing far below like a sub-marine garden. Those who have seen only European seas can form no conception of those still, clear, tropical waters.

It appears that when we were in Mauritius, I used to go about with my mouth open, a habit attributed by the doctor to adenoids. One day I was placed on a chair in my parents' bedroom, and the doctor sat down in front of me. Suddenly producing what looked like a knife and fork, he told me to open my mouth, and, before I knew what was happening, he had taken my adenoids out! Presumably surgeons had to act quickly, before the days of anaesthetics. I remember having a very painful sore throat but, in compensation, I received a toy horse and cart. The horse had a lovely soft brown hairy coat.

Mauritius was a remarkable island. It was occupied by the Dutch in 1598, when it was entirely uninhabited, and named after their *stadhalder*, Maurice of Nassau. In 1710, however, the Dutch abandoned it, but in 1721 it was occupied by the French East India Company, who established the capital at Port Louis, and used it as a naval base to fight the British in India.

Britain occupied Mauritius in 1810 as a crown colony. The economy depended almost entirely on sugar. Port Louis is a deep-water harbour and an ideal naval base to protect the vital sea route from the Persian Gulf and India round the Cape of Good Hope. In 1968, when Britain was in the process of ridding herself of her possessions, Mauritius was made independent. The island would probably have been safer and more prosperous as a British colony. There was no reason for making it independent, except that Britain at that time was in a mood for giving up everything. There was no native population, the island having been uninhabited when first occupied by Europeans. The population was subsequently imported as labour from Africa and later from India. There were also many Chinese.

There was no native language and the people spoke a kind of pidgin French. One day my sister and I were paddling in a running stream near our house. In the process we stirred up some mud. Some Mauritian women arrived to fill up their water jars and were annoyed to find the water so cloudy. Pointing at the water, they cried at us indignantly, '*De l'eau malade! de l'eau malade!*'

There were also in Mauritius many old French families which had been there since the time when the island was a French colony, before 1810. We used to play with their children and we had a French Mauritian governess called Inès Gallet. It was thus that I acquired my first knowledge of French.

After three years in Mauritius, we returned to England by way of the Cape. I still remember Table Bay and a visit we paid to the house of Cecil Rhodes. I was just eight years old.

From Cape Town to England, we sailed in what seemed to me a very large ship called the *Armadale Castle*, of the Union Castle Line. This one was a real steamship and did not use masts and sails as we had done when going out through the Suez Canal three years before.

The captain was a religious man and used to take Sunday School in his cabin for the children. He taught us to sing:

> Count your blessings, name them one by one:
> Count your blessings, see what God has done.
> Count your blessings, name them one by one,
> And it will surprise you what the Lord has done.

I have remembered that chorus all my life, but I have not always lived up to it. Presumably it is easier to go on grumbling.

We readily accept our blessings as a matter of course, and rarely stop to count them, though we are ready enough to express our dissatisfaction with anything which displeases us. Unlike millions of others in this strife-torn world, I have enough food to eat and clothes to wear. I can have a hot bath every day, an unheard-of luxury to most of the dwellers upon earth. And so I could go on. The list of my blessings is endless, if only I sometimes stopped to count them.

3

Horses and Soldiers

When we arrived back in England, my father was stationed at Aldershot. We rented a house called 'Lincroft', in Alexandra Road, Farnborough. I went back forty years later and found the old house much as it had been, but its name had been changed.

I was sent as a day boy to a dame school about two hundred yards up the road, run by a lady called Miss Linton. Opposite our house was a large building, which I think belonged to Dr Barnado's.

My chief memory of Miss Linton is of her standing in front of the class, teaching us to repeat by heart George Herbert's poem:

> Teach me, my God and King,
> In all things Thee to see,
> And what I do in anything
> To do it as for Thee.
>
> A servant with this clause
> Makes drudgery divine,
> Who sweeps a room as for Thy laws,
> Makes that the action fine.

When she reached the word 'clause', she would refresh our memories by holding up a skinny hand with the fingers apart and bent like a claw.

I was now eight years old and my father thought it was time I became a horseman. I started on a Shetland pony, but presumably I made satisfactory progress, as I was promoted to a white pony called Nobby. My father had a bay mare called Gay Lass which he used to ride and which also went in harness in a dog-cart; Nobby went in a governess cart, so we had two vehicles.

Nobby was really too big for me and I could not hold him. When going out riding with my father, Nobby would behave sedately on the way out but, as soon as we turned for home, he would start to play. When we were trotting along, side by side, he would suddenly break into a gallop and dash on ahead up the road, throwing a succession of bucks. (My mother once described this performance by saying that he went off 'in shtanding leps like the devil went through Athlone!')

If my father had galloped after Nobby, a wild race would have ensued, so he merely trotted on quietly, shouting after me, 'Sit back! Sit back,' as Nobby's kicks and bucks threatened to throw me over his head.

Sometimes the groom, Watts, would take me out, riding a bicycle and holding a leading rein to restrain Nobby's antics. One day we had passed Ash station, returning towards Farnborough, when Nobby shied and put his off-forefoot through the spokes of Watts's bicycle. Watts of course fell off and Nobby, for a moment of panic, felt his foot caught. Then, with a plunge he pulled his foot free and bolted up the road at full gallop. This time there were no bucks – he was really terrified.

We galloped at full speed up the Farnborough road. I had no hope of stopping him, and was fully occupied staying on his back and calling 'Help! Help!' at the top of my voice. Fortunately a man coming towards us in the opposite direction realized what was going on and planted himself in the middle of the road with his arms outstretched horizontally, and Nobby, who was already a bit winded, pulled up. The reader may think that I have over-dramatized this commonplace incident of a very small boy on a runaway pony, but it left a profound impression on my mind.

My father was C.R.E. (Commanding Royal Engineers) Lands. Aldershot was surrounded by considerable areas of land owned by the army and used for training, manoeuvres, and rifle ranges. My father was responsible for the care, supervision and maintenance of all these lands, most of which were grass, commonland, heather and pine trees. Much of his time was spent riding over and inspecting the lands, and often Nobby and I went with him. It was ideal country for riding, with no fences or obstacles. One day, however, we were riding on Farnborough Common; when we turned towards home, Nobby dashed off in a series of bucks and threw me off. Although I remounted and rode home, I did so without knowing what I was doing. I had concussion and remained unconscious for forty-eight hours.

Our house in Farnborough was only half a mile from Marlborough Lines, which were occupied by the Brigade of Guards. How clearly I remember the Guards on church parade, a fife and drum band beating retreat, and the whole atmosphere of the camps.

But the greatest military event I remember was when (I have an idea it was in 1908) King Edward VII reviewed the whole Aldershot Command on Laffans Plain. My father, being a staff officer, took us as spectators. He was wearing uniform and a cocked hat with a plume. As we approached the field on foot, the plume fell off his hat. It was impossible to wear a cocked hat without a plume; we closed together in a huddle, my mother produced a safety pin from somewhere and succeeded in fixing the plume once again, and the situation was saved.

The ensuing review was the greatest military spectacle I ever saw, and one the like of which will probably never be seen in the world again. Battalion after battalion in red tunics marching past in line, lancers with their fluttering pennants, dragoon guards in red coats and shining helmets, batteries of horse-drawn guns in full dress, companies of sappers, and the massed bands playing the regimental march of each unit as it passed the saluting base, where the King on horseback took the salute.

When we left Aldershot after three years, I had acquired two qualities – I was to be a soldier at heart for the rest of my life, and my chief passion was horses.

In those days, the War Office had an unpleasant habit. When an officer finished his time as a lieutenant-colonel and did not wish to retire, he was placed on half-pay to await his chance of being promoted to colonel. For a man with a wife and two children suddenly to have his pay halved was no slight matter, especially if, like my father, he had no private means.

Switzerland in those days was the cheapest country in Western Europe, and we moved to a small hotel in Vevey on the Lake of Geneva. I was sent as a weekly boarder to a school in Vevey called Bellerive. Switzerland then, as now, was a meeting place for all nations, and the boys at Bellerive were of many nationalities, for the most part sent there to learn French. A few were Swiss, but there were also British, Germans, Americans, Canadians, an Egyptian and others.

In order to ensure that everyone learned French, the headmaster, Monsieur Sillig, had a system of honour. Every morning after assembly and prayers, he would open a vast ledger on his desk and ask every boy the same question: 'Glubb. *Avez-vous parlé français?*' We were most conscientious and almost always could reply truthfully, '*Oui, monsieur.*' But we always admitted the slightest infraction of the rules. 'Yes, sir,' we would say, 'except that at lunch I said to Armstrong, "Don't be a silly ass".'

The great sport at Bellerive was rowing on the lake, which we did in a very professional manner, even having boats with sliding seats. The summer holidays we spent at Boenigen on the Lake of Brienz, near Interlaken. We went up to Lauterbrunnen and Mürren, from whence the dazzling view of the snow-covered Eiger, Monch and Jungfrau has remained engraved on my mind to this day. In those times it was not possible to reach the summits of the higher snowy mountains by train, as it is now.

We spent the Christmas holidays in the Bernese Oberland for skiing. In those far-off days, sports and amusements had not become so specialized as now. We used our skis as a means of getting about. We would take our lunch, put on our skis, and trek through the miracle of the pine forests, an enchanting realm where every branch and twig was covered with snow and sparkled in the midday sun.

After a year on half-pay in Switzerland, my father was made Chief Engineer, Northern Command, and we moved to York where we took a house in Mount Vale, overlooking the racecourse and the Knavesmire.

Yorkshire was a great county for horses, and my father bought me a grey Arab pony called Jumbo, who jumped like a stag. During the holidays, I rode alone every morning from breakfast till lunch-time. Riding was my passion, and I had few friends. In winter, my father took me hunting with the York and Ainsty or the Bramham Moor. It was fine country for jumping, with fly-fences and no wire. Jumbo used to jump so big that I could not stay on his back. My father accordingly arranged a contraption by which my stirrups were tied together by a strap under my horse's chest. This kept my legs in position, and enabled me to sit over the biggest fence.

On 24 January 1911, the York and Ainsty had a very fast hunt which ended in their killing their fox at Pallathorpe. Jumbo and I were up at the kill and the huntsman, in a fit of enthusiasm, blooded me on the face with some of the fox's blood. He then gave me the fox's mask, or head, and it still hangs in the entrance hall of our house.

Nowadays much is heard of the cruelty of foxhunting. The fact remains, however, that foxes are beasts of prey who kill chickens and even young lambs, and whose numbers have to be controlled. I have heard opponents of foxhunting reply that, in that case, their numbers could be kept down by killing them with poison gas in their earths. If a referendum of the foxes were to be taken, I suspect that most of them would vote to take their chance of an occasional hunt rather than extermination by poison gas.

The Puritans, according to Lord Macaulay, prohibited bear-baiting, not because it caused pain to the bear but because it gave pleasure to the people. Perhaps the opponents of foxhunting are similarly inspired, not by compassion for the foxes, but by a dislike for the ancient tradition of those country gentlemen who once engaged in it.

Personally I was never much interested in hounds or foxes, but in the excitement of a thrilling gallop across country. January 1914 was the last time I ever went out hunting, but the memory of those early hunts has remained with me all my life. As compensation for my youthful joy in hunting, I may add that, in all my life, I have never killed an animal or a bird.

Perhaps the ethos of hunting should be judged in the light of circumstances which prevailed until seventy years ago, before the use of cars became general. Horses were then the only means of transport, apart from the railways. To be a fine horseman was the supreme ambition of dashing young men. It was also an essential accomplishment for all armies.

Galloping across country, jumping fences, ditches and streams, was an unrivalled way of learning to ride, at a time when riding was an essential accomplishment. The fact that the hunt followed a wild animal made its course infinitely varied and unpredictable.

Another form of hunting was with a carted stag. The stag was a tame one, kept in a stall and transported to the meet, where it was released. When hounds overtook the stag, it was able to keep them at bay with its horns for a few minutes till the huntsman could call off the hounds. The stag was then put back in its cart and taken home. It is not possible for us to estimate how frightened the stag was, but when the process had been frequently repeated, it seems unlikely that it was much alarmed.

Another alternative was a drag. A man ran across the country dragging a bag containing a scent, which the hounds could follow. This process, however, did not produce the varied and unexpected features of following an animal.

In brief, hunting was an unrivalled way of producing horsemanship, when this was an essential quality for a man. Sport is justifiable when it has a practical object. When that condition is no longer fulfilled, it becomes merely a frivolous occupation.

I was sent as a boarder to a school called Stancliffe Hall, near Matlock in Derbyshire. My father put me down for boxing, which was an extra, and at first I did quite well; my right hook to the jaw was highly acclaimed. But later another boy came; he was much bigger and stronger than I was, and used to give me a battering. After every lesson, I would retire to the washroom, my nose pouring with blood.

Boxing used to be a highly regarded manly sport – 'the noble art of self-defence'. Actually, nowadays, judo seems to me to be a much more practical way of properly defending oneself.

At Stancliffe I had a friend, A.T.T Lindsay, who was as mad about horses as I was. We invented a racing game which we drew out on a piece of card and used to pass backwards and forwards to each other in class – at imminent risk of detection. I think Lindsay, like so many of my school contemporaries, was killed in the First World War.

My father had originally put me down for Wellington, where he had been, but later, discovering that more boys were passing into the R.M.A. from Cheltenham, he entered my name there instead. As the fees were a problem, I sat for a scholarship exam to Cheltenham College.

The headmaster of Stancliffe Hall had originally been a clergy-man, the Reverend E. Owen, but in my last year the school was taken over by two partners, Mr Harcourt-Clarke and Mr Conway.

One evening we were all in bed in the dormitory and the lights were out. I suppose it must have been about half-past nine. Suddenly there was the sound of running footsteps in the passage outside, the door opened and the light was switched on, to reveal Mrs Harcourt-Clarke running in front and waving a telegram, followed by her husband and Mr Conway. 'Glubb has won the top scholarship into Cheltenham,' she cried excitedly, and the three of them gathered round my bed, saying 'Well done'. It was the first time since they took over the school that any boy had gone up for a scholarship, and they were correspondingly elated.

I suffered a profound shock when I got to Cheltenham College. I think it was the swearing which most took me aback. I had never heard swearing before, but there seemed to be little in that line that the boys did not know. Otherwise I got through my time at college reasonably well. There was virtually no fagging or bullying as there used to be in earlier times.

I was never any good at games. I really enjoyed rugger and there was nothing I liked more than falling on the ball in front of a line of enemy forwards and fighting into the scrum amidst knocks and kicks. But I could not run fast enough to be a three-quarter, so, although small and light, I was made to play as a forward. It was always my ambition to be a scrum half, but I never succeeded in getting that place in any team.

At cricket I was hopeless, almost a laughing stock. My last summer term, I took up rowing, and rowed bow in my house second boat. Not a very distinguished position, but in bumps we bumped the boat above us on three successive occasions, and finished up top of the second boats. It so happened that, while I was there, my house, Christowe, had several fine athletes and won all the house cups, for rugger, cricket and almost everything else. Our first boat was head of the river.

The most fortunate thing that happened to me at Cheltenham was that one day I received a bash on the nose at rugger, and the partition between my nostrils was damaged. I was taken to St Thomas's Hospital in London where I was operated on. The operation did not seem to make much difference to my nose, but I was forbidden to play rugger for a year. My father arranged for a horse to be hired for me from a livery stable in Cheltenham, a lively little thoroughbred mare called Spider. Every afternoon, while the boys played rugger, I used to go out riding on Spider and together we explored the Cotswolds up to Seven Springs and Leckhampton, in long, lonely, happy rides together.

Boys can be devils, and we derived some amusement from baiting the masters. My first form master was known as Boozer Bennett. I don't suppose Mr Bennett ever touched a drop, but the alliteration was too tempting. The one thing that annoyed him was if one said, 'I don't know.' We would begin the day, for example, by his saying, 'Jones. Why were you late for Chapel this morning?'

'I don't know, Sir.'

This always produced the desired result. Rapping on his desk, he would shout, 'Great fool to be sure! What do you mean, you don't know? You *must* know!'

The form master of my next form was known as the Bun. The thing that annoyed him most was when somebody in class hummed a tune. As a result, the drill was for someone at the back of the room to start humming when we were all supposed to be writing.

The Bun would snort with rage and come striding down the form room, the boy at the back would stop and another at the front would begin. The Bun would swing round and stand glowering, at bay, like a bull in the arena surrounded by picadors. It always surprised me how masters failed to realize that their little foibles were being constantly exploited.

In 1912, my father was transferred from Chief Engineer, Northern Command, to Chief Engineer, Southern Command, and we moved from York to Salisbury.

My mother was a deeply Christian woman and I had always been brought up accordingly. My father also, though he rarely spoke of it, used to pray every morning, for I often entered his room and found him doing so. He would stand by his chest-of-drawers (which I still have), resting his elbows on the top of it, with his hands covering his face.

When I was at Stancliffe, my mother used to send me little tracts in her letters, which I would take with me into the toilet to read quietly. I remember one little paper book called *Words of Comfort and Consolation*.

At Cheltenham College I had less difficulty with religious books, as we had our own desks and, during my last year, I had a study to myself.

I was confirmed in the college chapel, and I must have found the service moving, for ever since I have remembered two of the hymns sung: 'O Jesus I have promised/To serve Thee to the end. . .' and 'Now thank we all our God'.

On one occasion, while I was at Cheltenham, I had flu and was in bed in the sick-room, when Mr Bishop the under housemaster came in to see me. He asked me what I was reading. I showed it to him. It was *Charles O'Malley* by Charles Lever. 'Hm,' said Bish. 'A little racey, I think.'

I enjoyed *Charles O'Malley* – a racey story of an Irish dragoon in the Peninsular War.

> The kings of Oudh
> Were mighty proud,
> And so were once the Caysers [Caesars].
> But old Giles Ayre
> Would make 'em stare
> If he had 'em with the Blazers.★
> To the divil I fling
> Old Ranjit Singh
> He was only a prince in a small way.
> He knew nothing at all
> Of a five-foot wall,
> O, he'd never do for Galway.
> With debts galore
> But fun far more,
> Sure that's the man for Galway.

Ranjit Singh was the great leader of the Sikhs in the early years of the nineteenth century.

Bish too was killed in the First World War. He was a very tall man, which was a danger in the trenches.

I still remember an evening in July 1914 when I was sitting in my study doing my prep, hearing a deep-voiced chorus marching down the road outside, singing 'It's a long way to Tipperary'. It was a territorial battalion returning from a route march. I had never

★The Galway Blazers were a famous pack of foxhounds.

before heard the tune which was to become almost the theme song of the Great War. It is curious how, sixty-six years later, little pictures of past events here and there remain deeply and vividly engraved on our memories. I was not interested in world affairs at that time and had no idea that war was impending.

From my earliest childhood, it had always been assumed that I would be an officer in the Royal Engineers like my father. No alternative career had ever been dreamed of – much less discussed. As a result, my name was entered for the entrance examination to the R.M.A. Woolwich, which was to be held in August 1914.

At the end of July 1914, I went into camp with the O.T.C., and was there when war was declared. The camp broke up immediately, but before we left, our instructor, an officer of the Rifle Brigade, made a little speech in which he said, 'Perhaps, before this war is over, some of you boys may have the supreme honour of commanding British troops in battle.'

It was with difficulty that I got home to Salisbury. The railways were in chaos, blocked by trains full of reservists joining their units. I arrived home at 7 a.m. one morning, having obtained a lift in a milk-cart. My father was under orders for France. The First and Second Army Corps were already embarking. My father was to be Chief Engineer, Third Corps, which was to embark four days later at Southampton.

It was generally believed that the war would be over by Christmas. Inspired by our instructor in the O.T.C. camp, I was unwilling to take the entrance examination to the R.M.A. and expressed the wish to enlist immediately in the Rifle Brigade. My father had some difficulty in deterring me.

I drove with him down to Southampton to see him off. The quays were crowded with troops embarking and I said goodbye to my father in the South-Western Hotel, overlooking the harbour, then returned disconsolately home.

My mother gave up our house in Salisbury, stored our furniture and moved into a small hotel in South Kensington. A few days later I sat for the entrance to the Royal Military Academy and passed in second. Forty years before, my father had passed in third.

On hearing that I had passed into the 'Shop' (as the R.M.A. was familiarly called), my father wrote me a letter from the front in France.

My dear old boy,

You will know well how proud I was when I heard the news of your having passed into the shop second.

You are very nearly a commissioned officer and a man now, dear old boy. See that you are also a gentleman, a simple honest English gentleman – you cannot be anything better whatever you are. Never lower your standards, old boy.

And remember that now you are a man, work is no longer 'beastly swot' but preparation for your duties as an officer.

In those days, the R.M.A. Woolwich took cadets for gunners and sappers only, the other arms going to Sandhurst, which was called the Royal Military College. The normal course at Woolwich lasted two years, but owing to the desperate need for officers we remained only six months and I was commissioned a second-lieutenant in the Royal Engineers in April 1915, and was sent to Chatham, to learn field engineering.

It appears to be an accepted principle nowadays that children must be taught about sex, and that both sexes can attend the same schools. Neither of these ideas existed when I was young. At my school and college there were only boys. All my holidays were spent riding horses. In my youthful imagination, women were beautiful, virtuous and romantic, far beyond and above me, and I rarely if ever spoke to one, except my mother or sister.

At Chatham, the barracks were crammed with extra recruits and new officers and no rooms were available. I was quartered in Brompton village, just outside the barracks, and was given a small room with a family who lived above a tobacconist's shop. One evening, returning to go to bed, I found a young woman, the daughter of the house, sitting in my bedroom. When I entered, she gave no sign of leaving. I was intensely embarrassed, and also afraid that her father might suddenly burst into the room, accuse me of improper conduct and demand that I clear his daughter's honour by marrying her! I had to face this embarrassing situation every night without ever approaching the girl, until at last a quarter became vacant and I could move into barracks.

In view of the endless stories today of boy-friends and girlfriends, it may seem incredible to some that in 1914 and 1915 we young officers never spoke of women. Any of us who was thought to be interested in girls was rather contemptuously called a poodle-faker.

We were convinced that this would be the last war in human history. If the great German empire were defeated, we believed, no nation would ever again attempt to disturb world peace. Now, sixty-six years later, we realize only too well that wars never end war, they only spawn vast numbers of new wars. Year by year, weapons become more lethal, and wars and violence increase. A hundred years of peace between the Great Powers is probably the only hope for the survival of the human race.

I well remember my mother telling me at this time that she had been married to my father, an army officer, for twenty-six years, during which there had been occasional small campaigns (my father had gone to the Boer War). But in all those twenty-six years, it had never once occurred to her, or to anyone else she knew, that there could ever again be a war between the civilized Powers of Europe.

At Chatham, we were all in anxiety lest this war – the last war in human history – be over before we could take part in it. The order in force at the time forbade the despatch of officers to the front until they were eighteen and a half years old. I was, therefore, obliged to remain fretting at Chatham and then at Aldershot until the autumn of 1915.

It may be useful here to insert a word of explanation on the anxiety soldiers sometimes express in wartime to go to the front. In my experience, the desire to take part in a war is not a sadistic lust to kill, but is a product of the innate human instinct for self-donation.

To make a comparison, let us consider some disaster, such as an earthquake or a famine in another continent. We are moved to compassion by the press reports and wish to contribute more than we can really afford. If we are nurses, doctors or are members of professions which are in demand for relief work, we may volunteer to go ourselves. We did not wish the famine to occur; we realize that the relief work may be dangerous, or we may sacrifice our careers in Britain; but nevertheless we want to go and help.

In the same way, if a war occurs, soldiers feel that ingrained human desire to give themselves, their souls and bodies, a living sacrifice, which is their reasonable service. Soldiers do not originate wars – politicians do that – nor do they desire wars. But when wars occur, they are stirred by a deeply ingrained human instinct to give themselves.

However much we may pretend to be cynical or materialistic, we realize overwhelmingly that, when the need arises, it is more blessed to give than to receive.

4

Duty and Glory

On 24 November 1915, I arrived at Southampton and embarked for France from the same quay from which my father had left in August 1914. Meanwhile the original three British army corps which had gone to the front in 1914 had grown into several armies. My father had been knighted for his part in the Battle of the Aisne. He was now a major-general, Chief Engineer of the Second Army, which held the northernmost sector of the British line, from about twelve miles from the sea at Nieuport to Armentières. Their front included the Ypres salient, where the first German poison-gas attacks had taken place in April and May 1915.

I reported to the R.E. Base Depot at Rouen, and on 27 November I received orders posting me to the 7th Field Company, Royal Engineers, with the 50th Territorial Division, which consisted almost entirely of Durham Light Infantry and Northumberland Fusiliers.

An infantry division consisted of three brigades of infantry and three engineer field companies – apart of course from the field artillery, divisional headquarters, army service corps, signals and so on. The three field companies worked with the three infantry brigades. We normally operated with a brigade of Durham Light Infantry, but were not rigidly attached to it. Any company could work with any brigade.

The 7th Field Company was a regular pre-war unit, although all the division were territorials, including the other two field companies. Regular and territorial units were sometimes inter-mixed in this way. With the 7th Company, I found H.A. Baker, who had been with me at Woolwich. In those days people were never known by their Christian names. Men knew each other by their initials – H.A. Baker, C.B.O. Symons (our company com-mander), or J.B. Glubb. Nicknames were common, but Christian names were private. It was almost indecent to know or use a Christian name, which was something personal to its owner. Baker was called Albert, but this was after Albert Baker, a much-advertised firm of, I think, tobacconists. C.B.O. Symons was my company commander, and we were to be hit by the same shell – but to this day I do not know what his initials, C.B.O., stood for.

When I joined the company, the division was in support, that is to say it was two or three miles behind the front, with no one in the trenches. An R.E. field company was divided into four sections, each of one officer and about twenty-five sappers. I was placed in command of No.1 Section.

When I joined the 7th Field Company, I began my life of living with people. At school and college, one is a member of a crowd who have only to obey orders, with no real independence or relations with outsiders. Now I was a separate person, meeting other people some of whom were above and some below me.

On 4 December 1915, I took my section to a farm called La Flanque, near Armentières; we were told to put it into a state of defence, as part of the reserve line. The process consisted in digging trenches, making machine-gun posts and putting up barbed wire. At about midday, we were lightly shelled and again in the afternoon – my baptism of fire. During this process, I found Pioneer Chilvers crouching in one of the trenches, while we went on working. When C.B.O. Symons came to see us on the work, I brought Chilvers up to him and said I wanted to charge him with cowardice in the presence of the enemy. Symons was doubtless amused at my youthful enthusiasm, but he spoke a few words of reproof to Chilvers.

After ten days in Armentières (called by the troops 'Armenteers'), we marched northwards to a farmhouse behind Ypres. It rained all day and every day, and everything was soaking wet.

I soon got to know the twenty-five men of my section. On 13

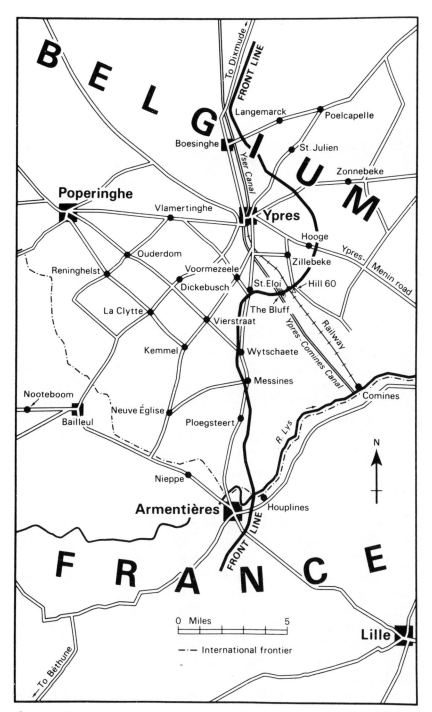

Armentières to Ypres, autumn 1915.

December, my section moved up into the line in front of Ypres, and we took over a sector of front-line trench in Sanctuary Wood. Our trenches were only twenty-five yards from the German front line.

The enemy used to shell Sanctuary Wood most of the day, for they had immensely more ammunition than our gunners had. As soon as it was dark, I would take a party of sappers up, to repair the damage done during the day. This was accomplished largely by filling sandbags with earth and building them up carefully, like laying bricks. Thus where a shell had burst in a trench, making it into an open crater, we built sandbag walls across it, making it once again a narrow trench.

My sergeant was a dear man but, to my mind, immensely old. (I was eighteen and he probably in his thirties.) I soon knew which of the boys did not worry about shells. I had what I called (to myself) my brave squad. On dark, rainy nights with the enemy artillery active, I would go up the line with my brave squad and, in between sudden tempests of enemy shells, we sandbagged up the trenches which had been demolished during the day.

We lived under the ruins of Zillebeke village, which was about two miles behind the front line. On the morning of 19 December 1915, at 5.30 a.m., we had just returned from night work in Sanctuary Wood when a shattering explosion seemed to shake the whole earth, followed by a continuous and deafening succession of 'krumps' all around us.

All the houses of Zillebeke had already been reduced to heaps of rubble and broken bricks. Under these mounds of debris, we lived in tiny cubby-holes, scooped out of the earth and supported by timber beams from the ruined houses. Baker and I lived in one such little dugout which was about the size of a double bed.

The intense and deafening bombardment lasted for about an hour. Every ten or fifteen minutes, I slipped out and ran along the line of cubby-holes in which the men were crouching, to see if they were all safe. After an hour the Germans lengthened their range and we could see the shells falling half a mile behind us. We had no idea whether there had been an infantry attack on the front line, but we later discovered that no attack had occurred on our front, though the trenches had been heavily shelled. The whole affair was a diversion, while the Germans attacked Hill 60, three miles to the south.

The next morning C.B.O. Symons came up from the rear billet

and I accompanied him in inspecting the damage to the front line. Suddenly something happened – one does not hear the shell which hits one. The infantry battalion Commander and my own O.C., Symons, were lying on the floor of the trench with three others who were already dead. I ran down the trench and fetched some stretcher-bearers, who carried Symons to a dressing station in a nearby dugout in Maple Copse.

When Symons had been carried away, I noticed blood flowing out of my own boot. The doctor cut the boot off and found that my left big toe had been broken by a shell fragment. I hobbled back to our little dugout in Zillebeke, where I stayed for five days, hopping up the line painfully every day.

My father had heard of my wound, but realized that I would never leave my men in the front line. But on 31 December we were relieved, and a cart came up to Zillebeke at night and took me back to company headquarters. My father sent a car for me, ostensibly to visit him at Second Army Headquarters for the day. But this was a trick – when I got there, I was sent to the Casualty Clearing Station at Hazebrouck, where I remained for three weeks.

A Casualty Clearing Station, as the name indicates, is a place where the wounded are collected and then sent down to the base. But I escaped clearance, and was back in my company on 26 January 1916.

Such was my first experience of war. The chief impression I had received was the lesson of comradeship. With my section, we numbered some twenty-five young men, bound together by an intense feeling of brotherhood. It is this deep feeling of comradeship which carries soldiers through all their hardships and dangers and gives them, even in the most intense moments of stress, a kind of feeling of elation.

Such was doubtless the bond which united us all, but I had in addition a background of soldiering from childhood. The motto of the Royal Engineers was *ubique quo fas et gloria ducunt* – Everywhere where duty and glory lead us – a motto which I took seriously to heart. In those days, children were made to learn the catechism by heart on Sundays. The line which I had remembered from infancy was 'to do my duty in that state of life, unto which it shall please God to call me'. Duty and service were the two words which were most constantly rammed down our throats throughout all my days as a child and at school.

These events took place sixty-five to seventy years ago, and seem almost unimaginable when we look at the world around us today. Under the present systems, children are not told that the object of life is duty and service, but, on the contrary, that they should 'develop their own personalities'. This is tantamount to preaching selfishness. Young people brought up with such ideas cannot be blamed for 'wanting to do their own thing'. Their ideal is to be free of all duties and obligations, either to their country, their community or the individuals with whom they are in close contact.

Another complete contrast with the days of my youth is that of the general attitude to money. My father had virtually no private means, and we lived on his pay. Yet I never remember the subject of money being mentioned at home or in social conversation.

I am, as a result, one of those persons – perhaps regarded with contempt in the modern world – who cannot raise any interest in money as an objective. I never used to know the amount of my salary or the allowances to which I was entitled. Sometimes, of course, we are obliged to think of money matters, but I find it an effort to do so.

Compared to sixty or seventy years ago, money seems to me today to have taken the place of duty and service, the objectives constantly held before our eyes. Work is no longer a joyfully rendered service, but a wearisome and boring necessity, the object of which is to obtain money.

I remember one of my own men at this time saying to me, 'Give me the man who is in love with his job.' To those who can attain it, this is one of the principal keys to happiness.

One of the finest tributes I ever received was on the occasion of my dismissal by the Jordan Government in 1956. The incident was reported in the press; the editor of the *Daily Express* received a letter which he forwarded to me:

Dear Sir,
A few weeks ago we seen [sic] the column in your paper concerning General Glubb of the Arab Legion and this is the remark I heard my husband pass, as he served under him in the First World War and was with him when he was wounded. He was the finest officer you could meet. He would never send any of his men where he would not go his self. Please if there is any chance of

getting a message to him, please say Corporal Moss is still alive and wishes him the best of luck.

Yours truly,
C. Moss

I received this letter forty years after I had served with Corporal Moss, but it did give voice to a principle in which I have always believed: *'Noblesse oblige'* – the top man must do more than he asks any of his subordinates to do. This is one of the first principles of leadership for all in authority, whether in or out of the army.

If enemy shells are falling, say, 'Come on, lads, let's go,' and start out in front of them. If work in the factory begins at 7.30 a.m., the boss should clock in with the boys. Whatever your subordinates have to do, do it yourself.

Perhaps the second principle is to look after their interests. I discovered a patriotic female organization in England which devoted itself to sewing shirts for soldiers. ('Sister Susie's sewing shirts for soldiers' was a popular song at the time.) I communicated with these ladies, and they sent me bales of shirts, which I issued. They looked a bit fancy for formal parades, but could be concealed under woollen jerseys when the sergeant-major was not coming around.

But perhaps the most delicate lesson to acquire was how to be intimate without being familiar. The commander must face more danger and hardship than his men; he may be united to them by a profound affection and comradeship, yet he must never be just one of them. Part of this delicate matter of leadership may depend on social behaviour. An officer should never swear, tell vulgar jokes or behave in an undignified manner.

The phrase 'an officer and a gentleman' is nowadays often the subject of mockery, but in this respect our ancestors had a better insight that we have into human nature.

Unfortunately the word 'gentleman' has, it seems, always had a double significance in English. Neville Coghill's version in modern English of Chaucer's *Canterbury Tales* has the following passage:

> Whoever loves to work for virtuous ends,
> Public and private, and who most intends
> To do what deeds of gentleness he can,
> Take him to be the greatest gentleman.

Christ wills we take our gentleness from Him,
Not from a wealth of ancestry long dim.

Canterbury Tales was written in the late fourteenth century, and it is evident that the double meaning of the word gentleman was already realized.

The greatest gentleman was the man who always worked for virtuous ends, using gentleness as a means to securing them. But already some people used the word gentleman to express the idea of descent from a distinguished family. When our forebears connected the word gentleman with that of officer, they did not mean to refer to the man's wealthy ancestors, but to his own noble character.

'Conduct unbecoming the character of an officer and a gentleman' was a court-martial offence. Obviously an officer could not be tried by court martial for not having a long pedigree, but for behaving in an immoral (or undignified) manner, in such a way as to forfeit the respect of his soldiers.

While living with one's own soldiers, one had to gain over them that moral ascendancy which ensured their respect, but without any suspicion of being superior or snobbish.

The double meaning of the word gentleman still causes misunderstanding. When we read in an old book that Smith or Jones was unfortunately not a gentleman, we are quick to exclaim, what disgusting snobs our ancestors used to be! But we should not be too hasty in passing judgement. The intention may have been that he did not work for virtuous ends, or was coarse, immoral or blasphemous.

King James I summed up the matter when he said, 'I can make a man a lord, but only God Almighty can make him a gentleman.' Indeed, history teems with kings, princes and aristocrats, who were very far from being gentlemen.

During the period of the Commonwealth under Oliver Cromwell, 1649–60, Britain was governed by major-generals, an experience which the people did not enjoy. Their hatred of military rule caused them to fear professional soldiers. A policy consequently developed, according to which regular army officers were never paid enough to live on. This ensured that only men with private means could become army officers – indeed, at one stage, they were expected to buy not only their commissions but every step in promotion.

Officers who could not afford to do so were obliged to serve in some distant or unhealthy land. Such was the West India Regiment, whose toast was said to be 'to a bloody war or a sickly season' – their only hope of ever achieving a transfer or promotion.

Yet, like so many illogical and absurd customs in Britain, the system which allowed only men with private means to become officers was remarkably successful. The principal object was that an army, commanded solely by men in comfortable circumstances, would be unlikely to stage military *coups d'état* and establish military rule. But these officers frequently became passionately dedicated to their regiments. Some spent their own money on their men, their uniforms or their horses. The greatest ambition of every officer was to command his regiment before retiring.

Regiments had each their battle honours written on their colours. They acquired their own nicknames: the Fighting Fifth, the Diehards, the Loyals, the Old Braggs. But these officers, so devoted to their units, were not professional students of the military art. The administration and staff-work were often inefficient.

They were usually extremely contemptuous of danger: there is a nice story of Sir Hugh Gough in the Sikh wars in India, riding up and down in a fancy uniform to draw the enemy's fire away from his troops! British officers all over the world exhibited the same devotion to their units, be they Gurkhas, Sikhs, Arabs or of any other race.

The results of these apparently fortuitous developments were threefold. First, since 1660 the British army has never interfered in politics, nor is it conceivable that it should do so today. Second, on the regimental level, the British army produced the finest units in the world. Third, the British army was usually behind the other armies of Europe in the art of war, command, staff-work or administration, for its officers were first of all gentlemen, not professional militarists. But as individual regiments or battalions, the British army was the finest in the world.

When, therefore, my father urged me to be, before all else, a simple, honourable English gentleman, he had in his mind a very clear picture as to what an officer and a gentleman should be.

5
Endless Desolation

Let us now return to our narrative after these lengthy digressions.

When C.B.O. Symons was wounded, Captain Atkinson, the second-in-command, took command of the company. On 8 February 1916, I took No. 1 Section up to the front line again at Zillebeke, but on the same day Atkinson was wounded. In theory I was in command of the company, but I continued happily with my section in Zillebeke.

At 11 a.m. on 15 February, we were working in a trench called Warrington Avenue, in Sanctuary Wood, when a salvo of German whizzbangs came over, killing Sapper Smith and wounding Penson and Girdler. A splinter went through my cap and drew blood from my head. Penson, Girdler and I were evacuated to Vlamertinghe as walking wounded, but from there I slipped away and rejoined the company.

On 20 February, Captain J.A. McQueen took over the company. I begged him to allow me to stay up in Zillebeke with my section, but he refused and said that I must come back to the rear billet; I must hand over my section to a new officer called Chaplin and myself become second-in-command of the company. This meant living at the rear billet near Vlamertinghe and being in charge of administration. However, I also took charge of the transport, which consisted of some hundred and twenty horses and about sixty-five men.

Almost all horses in military vehicles worked in pairs, two horses, four-horse, or six-horse teams, so every driver looked after two horses. As I was devoted from boyhood to horses, I gradually came to enjoy the work and love my drivers as I had my sappers.

In March 1916 we moved out of Sanctuary Wood and went into the trenches again a few miles further south at the Bluff. There had just been an intense local battle here, the Boche having taken our front line, after which our 3rd Division took it back. On 20 March we took over from the 3rd Division.

The Bluff was a spoil bank made by the digging of the Ypres–Comines Canal. In this flat country, a mound twenty or thirty feet high enabled one to overlook the enemy for many miles. As a result, a spoil bank like the Bluff was fought for bitterly. Our dead were still thickly strewn over the flanks of the Bluff but no one could get out of the trenches to bury them.

On 23 March, Chaplin, who was commanding No. 1 Section in the front line, went sick and, to my delight, I was sent up and retook command of my old comrades.

There was no continuous line of trenches on the Bluff sector. After a succession of to-and-fro battles the front was held by a number of isolated posts in shell-holes. Trying to visit these one night, I walked between them and found myself lost in no-man's-land. In a sudden panic, I lost my sense of direction, not knowing in which direction lay the Boche or our own chaps. After an unpleasant quarter of an hour of cautious crawling, I found one of our own posts.

The Bluff was positively saturated with corpses. During the battles, both we and the Germans had suffered very heavy losses, and neither side could get out to bury the dead. As a result, they lay rotting in the open or were just trampled into the mud in the shell-holes or the trenches.

In August 1916, we moved down to the Somme and took part in the big attack of 15 September against High Wood – the first battle in which tanks were used. We remained on the Somme front from 15 September to the end of January 1917.

The Somme battlefield was some six miles wide from the front line to the town of Albert. The whole of this area consisted of an endless sea of mud, dotted here and there with a few heaps of brick or powdered masonry where villages had been and, in one or two places, with splintered stumps of trees where formerly woods had

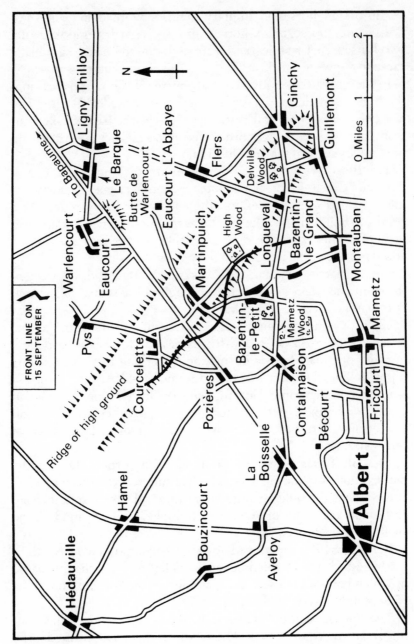

Fiftieth divisional front on the Somme. *It extended from the Albert–Bapaume road to the Albert–Mametz road and thence through Bazentin-le-Grand to Longueval exclusive. Over the whole area there was not a tree or house standing. A ridge of high ground ran Longueval–High Wood–Martinpuich to Courcelette. The highest point was High Wood. On 15 September 1916 this ridge was taken.*

been. Everything and everyone was soaking wet and caked with mud. Low grey clouds, mist and driving rain or snow completed this indescribably dreary landscape.

Once during these eighteen weeks, Baker and I took a day off and rode into Albert, a town then still only half-demolished, though there were scarcely any civilians left in it. We discovered the Café du Jeu de Paume, where we had lunch, and where there were actually two women!

My greatest delight was on one occasion when I was given two days off to visit my father, who was at Second Army headquarters in Cassel. He sent a car to fetch me, and we drove out of the area of desolation into unspoilt country and through towns with shops and busy streets and well-dressed women. Although I was absolutely indifferent to personal relations with women, four months on the Somme had taught me that life without women was life without beauty or joy.

Reporting this visit in a letter to my mother, my father wrote,

Jacko turned up on Tuesday evening. I kept him here three nights and took him to the ordnance shop for officers and made him fit himself out with underclothes and socks of which my batman told me he was in dire need. The worst thing about the place where they are is the awful boresomeness. He has not seen a civilian, a shop or even a house for 4 months. He is looking very robust and healthy.

While we were on the Somme, I once wrote in my diary: 'One gets very materially minded in this common round of endless work in dreary surroundings, without ever a Sunday or a spiritual tonic. I must try reading Brother Lawrence's *Practice of the Presence of God* more often. All the same, though I think of Him so rarely, God never refuses the joy of His presence when I ask for it.'

One day I had been in the line and was walking back in a grey, misty drizzle; I sat down for a few minutes to rest on a heap of rubble in the ruined village of Martinpuich. Suddenly I was overwhelmed by a feeling of joy so intense as to be completely beyond description; it lasted for several minutes, after which it gradually faded. At least since then, I have always known the meaning of the word ecstasy.

Reading now, in my old diaries, of how readily I felt the presence of God when I thought of Him, I can only conclude that these spiritual joys come more easily to emotional young people. Sixty-four years have passed since my ecstasy on the Somme, and life is now more steady and sober, but lacking in these snatches of spiritual emotion. The old war horse has replaced the frolicking colt.

My mother kept the letters I wrote to her from France, and here I transcribe two of them, selected at random.

21.1.17

My own dear Mum,
First of all thank you so much for the parcels which contained (1) Mars oil (2) electric batteries, soup tablets etc. (3) the wonderful tooth powder, a handkerchief, socks. Also please thank Aunty for parcel containing two excellent cakes.

I have another Commission. Can you order some tins of blanco, please? It is a kind of pipeclay for cleaning white head-ropes, rope traces etc.

I also received the patterns returned with scorn by Mr Alfred Webb Miles. I must try and fudge my measurements up to the ones he thinks I ought to be. It reminds me of Cinderella and the Venus of Milo in 'A Kiss for Cinderella'. Do you remember how we enjoyed that?

I wonder you did not go and see 'The Professor's Love Story' by J.M. Barrie, instead of H. Lauder.

We are in the grip of winter here. We had four inches of snow five days ago, and ever since a biting black frost and north wind. The snow is dry and powdery, all the pools of water and mud are solid. The north wind nips one's ears, nose and chin.

I must stop now, though this is a very poor letter. Goodbye Darling and much love.

Jack

As today I remember the dreariness of that six-mile-wide belt of utter devastation on the Somme, I read in the daily papers of the possibility of nuclear war between the United States and Soviet Russia, which would reduce the whole of North America, Europe and Russia to expanses of rubble without any form of life. The agonizing desolation of six miles of a lifeless waste of mud can now be extended to the devastation of whole continents – such is the outcome of sixty-four years of 'progress'. It is impossible to find a logical explanation for the apparent determination of mankind to commit race suicide. The world contains ample resources to supply the human race. Moveover it is the richest nations which lead the mad race to the destruction of human (and animal and vegetable) life. Different nations need have no quarrel with one another, except for mutual fear.

Having heard continually all one's life of Christ's command to love our enemies, it comes almost as a shock in our old age to realize how essential and how down-to-earth practical this order really is. There is no reason whatever why the Americans should not love the Russians – in fact when they meet as individuals they probably do.

To love everyone on earth – or, let us say, to regard them all with benevolence and affection – is the only method by which the human race can survive. If we cannot all learn universal love, the human race may be exterminated before these lines can appear in print.

To say that God – that is, the Spirit of the Universe – is love is not a poetic piece of idealism. It is a strictly practical statement of principle, without which life on earth cannot much longer exist.

Here is another of my letters, dated 13.3.17.

My own dear Mum,

Thanks so much for the parcels which were as usual very welcome, and consisted of dates, socks, camembert and tea tablets. I also received the beautiful muffler you sent and I have used it in this cold weather.

It is a good deal warmer this evening and may be a thaw at last. Fancy Aunty saying my breeches smelt of stale tobacco. I am sure they didn't, at any rate I never noticed it. No, I don't smoke now. Anyhow I wouldn't smoke with my legs and make my breeks smell of smoke!

Yes, do get the gurgly grunts stopped in the gramophone, although I am afraid your optimistic remark about my getting leave soon is rather premature.

We are living back in a civilized part of the world far from the madding crowd and are only reminded of the war by an occasional Boche plane. We are having a recherché dinner tonight to celebrate our sojourn in civilized Europe.

The weather has been warmer lately yet beautifully fine. This evening is absolutely perfect. The sun has just set and there is not a breath of wind. The sky is still quite blue overhead, then gradually paler and paler towards the horizon, then a very, very light greeny yellow, merging into the palest yellow, orange red and on the horizon misty grey. I love the pale yellow part, it gives one an idea of infinity. Everything is so perfectly still and quiet, that the perfect peace of it seems to enter into one's whole soul.

Now I have to trot round to the office. One never gets away from an office of sorts, even commanding a field company, which I am doing at present as McQ. is off doing a course of instruction.

Goodbye Darling and much love.

Jack

In March 1917, our division – the 50th – joined the XVIII Army Corps, which began training as a Corps of Pursuit. A new battle was to be launched at Arras. When we had broken through the German trench lines, the XVIII Corps was to burst through the battle and pursue the enemy to Berlin!

On 11 April 1917, in a snowstorm, we marched all night and entered Arras at dawn. In fact the British attack drove the Germans back about six miles, but failed to break through. Instead of pursuing the fleeing enemy, we occupied the trenches in front of Wancourt, and resumed the old routine of trench warfare.

On 6 August 1917, I wrote to my mother:

My own darling Mum,
Leave is going 'a treat' just now and I'd not be surprised if I might be dropping in on you about the end of this month. Have you got my plain clothes suit, my black shoes, my stick and my bowler hat? By George, I am looking forward to leave . . . Goodbye, darling. I do hope you are better lately. Much love.

Jack

Alas this leave never happened, as I was wounded first.

On 21 August 1917, at Heninel, east of Arras, I was hit by a fragment of a German shell which completely shattered my lower jaw, and I was not expected to live. I was evacuated to England, and for three months I lay in the Third London General Hospital in

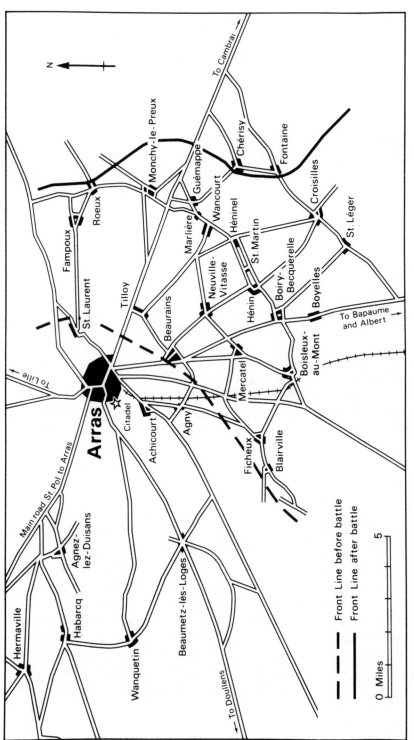

The Battle of Arras, April–May 1917.

Wandsworth and received no treatment at all, my wound remaining septic and emitting a foul odour. Then I was transferred to a special hospital at Frognal, Sidcup, Kent, especially established for the treatment of face-wounds.

Frognal had been a large private country house which still contained the owner's library. Here, for the first time, I read a book denying the existence of God and attributing the world about us to an automatic process of evolution. I had always accepted the rule of God over the world and had been able to withstand all the trials and sufferings of life, in the quiet belief that God was in charge. Suddenly, with the suggestion that perhaps there was no God, the bottom fell out of my world.

The face-wounds hospital soon cleaned up my wound and removed the bits of dead bone and dead teeth. They then cemented my upper and lower jaws together. Not until March 1918 did the bones of my lower jaw begin to grow together again.

I was intensely depressed at my enforced inaction. My whole heart and soul were with the boys in France. My mother was living in a large bed-sitting-room at 37 Alfred Place, overlooking South Kensington station. The house was owned by two Belgian women who were war-refugees from their home in Belgium. They gave me a small bedroom at the back of the house.

Something had gone wrong on the occasion of my birth and my mother had suffered continual pain ever since, especially if she were tired. She spent many hours, or even days, in bed with this old pain which she referred to as the O.P. I remember kneeling at her bedside and saying, 'I can't stay here in England doing nothing, while the boys are going through so much suffering in France.'

The surgeons had cemented the broken parts of my lower jaw to my upper jaw, which thus acted as a splint to keep the fractured portions of my lower jaw together and enable them to reunite. Thus I could not open my mouth. However, as I had lost nearly all my teeth, I was able to push pieces of bread and butter into my mouth between my gums. I could talk only with difficulty – as anyone will realize who tries to speak while keeping his jaws closed.

We had an old wind-up gramophone in my mother's room, and used to play the short ten-inch records of those days. I remember Handel's 'Largo', Boccherini's 'Minuet', 'Les Millions d'Harlequin' and 'Nights of Gladness'. Once when we were playing Edward German's Nell Gwyn dances, the Belgian housemaid put her head

in at the door and exclaimed, *'Ah! C'est joli ça.'* We also used to play
the songs of the Irish tenor, John McCormack.

For several months while my jaws were cemented up, I was able
to walk about, but felt idle and useless. I consequently volunteered
to work in Kensington Town Hall, where ration cards were issued.
I sat at a small table just inside the door, beneath a notice which said
'ENQUIRIES'. People crowded in at the door to obtain new ration
cards or to ask why the shops had refused to sell them any more
bacon, butter or sugar.

The experience impressed me with the unreasonableness of many
people. They were, of course, all women, mostly housewives
whose husbands were away at the war. Some would grow angry
with me over their allegedly inadequate rations, although I was only
there to explain the system to them. It was not my fault if they had
used up a month's bacon or sugar coupons in the first fortnight.

To keep my spirits up, my mother used to take me to the
matinées of musical comedies or plays. I remember we went to *Chu
Chin Chow, Tonight's the Night, Tales of Hoffman* and, I think, *The
Chocolate Soldier.* We also saw *Sweet Nell of Old Drury,* with Oscar
Asche and Lily Brayton.

At last the bones of my lower jaw grew together and I persuaded
a medical board that I was fit to return to the front line. In my
absence, however, the 50th Division had taken the full force of the
German offensive on the Somme in April 1918. The remnants of the
division were moved to a quiet sector near Soissons, whereupon the
Germans delivered their next attack precisely in that area. As a
result, the 50th Division ceased to exist.

When at last I succeeded in getting back to France, on 11 July
1918, my father at my request arranged for me to be posted back to
the 7th Field Company. This was a disappointment to him, as he
wanted me to accept a posting as Staff Captain, in an infantry
brigade headquarters. With an eye to my future career, it would be
most advantageous for me to gain some experience on the staff
before the war ended.

But I insisted on returning to my old company, because I knew
and loved the men. I was not interested in my future career. Indeed
my whole life has been a repetition of this attitude. My motivation
has always been supplied by love of people, not money or
advancement.

I found the 50th Division resting at Martin Eglise, near Dieppe

. . . But it was not the division I knew. The Northumberland Fusilier and Durham Light Infantry battalions had been exterminated and the division had been re-formed with battalions brought back from Salonika, riddled with malaria.

The 7th Field Company likewise had been exterminated. No officers and very few sappers had survived, though some of the old transport drivers were still there.

At last, on 16 September, the reconstituted 50th Division returned to the front. We marched back across the devastated Somme battlefield. Even the town of Albert, half-ruined in our time, had ceased to exist.

The Germans were retiring all along the line. We came into action at Vendhuile on the Cambrai–St Quentin canal, on 3 October. The whole front was on the move. Every second or third day, we would attack and advance a distance of four or five miles. Passing Le Cateau, we reached the edge of the Forêt de Mormal, south-west of Maubeuge.

I was in command of the 7th Field Company when we delivered our last attack on 4 November. The country here was undamaged by war and was cut up by thick hedgerows and orchards and the village of Fontaine-au-Bois. The infantry were scattered in small posts in ditches or under hedges.

The attack was fixed for 4 November and was to be carried out on a very broad front. The problem was to get the infantry lined up during the previous night, so that the whole attack could go forward together. For this purpose, the sappers were ordered to peg out a long line of white tapes under cover of darkness in front of our most advanced posts. At the same time, we had to cut and signpost lanes of approach, hacking through the hedges and orchards to enable each infantry battalion to find its way forward to its position on the jumping-off tape. All this had to be done in the dark during the night before the big attack, to prevent the enemy from seeing and hearing what was happening.

All went well as a result of our strenuous efforts. The infantry advanced at dawn from the taped line. For a short time there was some shelling and machine-gun fire. Then the enemy vanished. From 11 a.m. onwards, we were advancing everywhere, unopposed. We never saw the German army again. On 11 November we were told to stand fast where we were, as the war was over.

Being a regular officer, I was recalled to Chatham in February 1919, for a year's course of engineering. Our work in France had been simple, carried out with spades, sandbags, pickets, wire, pontoon bridges and slabs of gun-cotton.

At Chatham, we were taught building work, the stresses and strains in steel structures and girders, and mechanical engineering, such as it was in those days. In between lectures we drilled on the barrack square.

My father had ridden into Cologne on horseback with army headquarters, as Chief Engineer of the army of occupation; but a few weeks later he retired from the army, and he and my mother rented a house for a year at Buxted in Sussex.

My father was in his sixties and had spent his life with horses. England had changed, however, and he could no longer keep a horse, but bought an old second-hand car.

One day he drove me up to London in this precarious vehicle. Just as we reached the busiest intersection of traffic streams at Hyde Park Corner, the engine stopped. In 1919, cars did not have self-starters. It was necessary to crank up the engine by hand with a starting handle. I took the latter, jumped off the car and stood in front of it, trying to turn the engine over to start it. Nothing happened.

'Give her a good swing,' shouted my father.

I did my best but the engine refused to fire.

The traffic was held up. A crowd collected. A kind policeman (they were kind and helpful in those days) offered words of encouragement. I swung the engine till my arm ached, but without result. At last the crowd pushed us across the road, under the colonnade and into the park, whereupon she started with a bang and a loud roar!

My supplementary course at Chatham ended in June 1919. My father and mother were staying on the Italian lakes and wanted me to join them. (As a child I had been through the Mediterranean to Mauritius, but in 1919 I had been for four years in the mud of the trenches and then nine months in Brompton Barracks, Chatham.)

Arriving in Italy by the Simplon Express, I was suddenly over-whelmed by the beauty of that country. From Milan to Como and then by lake steamer, I seemed to be in a dream of beauty, warmth and colour. My parents were staying in a small village called San

Mamette on the Lake of Lugano. The little hotel was on the lake shore, and we had our meals on a terrace beneath a trellised vine with the lake lapping at the terraced wall beside us. The colour, the warm sun, the lake and the mountains were to me a vision of earthly paradise of which I had never before had any conception.

6
East of Suez

My supplementary course at Chatham had ended and I was due for posting. What was I to do? A year at Chatham had sickened me of life in barracks. There was nothing to do in England; I was not a ladies' man and had no social life.

My lack of social gifts gave me some discomfort in the matter of 'calling'. Young officers were expected to call on the families of senior officers and leave visiting cards which might result in an invitation to dinner. Calls were paid at teatime, when the husband was probably still at work, and only the women of the house would be in. How often did I stroll past a house and back again, trying to locate any signs of movement. If I saw anyone through the windows, I walked on and postponed my call for another day – when I might have the good fortune to find everyone out.

I remember one occasion when another young officer and I set out to call on the family of (let us say) Colonel Jenkins, who lived a mile or so away at Gillingham. But when we reached the street we could not remember whether the house was Number 17 or 27. We decided to ring the bell at Number 17 and, when the maid opened the door, to ask if Mrs Jenkins lived there.

To our acute embarrassment, however, the door was opened by the lady herself, who greeted us cordially, asked us in and gave us tea. We had to make halting conversation for half an hour, without knowing if we were talking to Mrs Jenkins or not . . . or even if the lady's husband were an army officer. Our ignorance considerably restricted our conversation, as we did not wish to reveal the fact that we did not know who she was.

But while these formal social calls were a nightmare to me at twenty-three, I can appreciate the system now, sixty years later, when formal calls and visiting cards have been abandoned. In the old days, if one arrived to live in a new area, the neighbours would all call within a few days, leaving cards with their names and addresses. Probably within a week or two, one would return their calls and find some of them at home. Within a month, the new arrival would know everyone in the vicinity.

Today it is possible to live for months in a new area without knowing anyone, or anyone else knowing you. How many old formal institutions, now regarded with contempt, had in reality a very practical purpose!

When God closes one door, He opens another. In the course of operations against the Turks, during the First World War, Britain had occupied the valleys of the Euphrates and the Tigris, now known as Iraq. The armies had since been demobilized, and only skeleton forces had been left to keep order.

The endless negotiations to settle the peace of the world dragged on at Versailles, principally concerned with the Great Powers – France, Germany, revolutionary Russia – and President Woodrow Wilson's plans for mandates and a League of Nations. The future of a distant fragment of the Ottoman Empire came low on the agenda. The Iraqis grew restless as their future continued undecided.

In the spring of 1920 disorders broke out. Most of the officers in the denuded British forces were due for release from the army. As a result, the War Office appealed for three hundred regular officers to volunteer to go out to Iraq. I put down my name and was accepted.

With the fickle and unthinking swings of popular opinion, empires are nowadays regarded as immoral in Britain. In 1920 this was not the case. My father believed that it was the duty of Britain to protect, help and encourage the many peoples of the empire. The duty was often onerous and involved the long separation of members of many families. This was in those days a white man's real and painful burden . . . a phrase treated with ridicule in these cynical days.

I left England gaily, full of hope and inspired by the same joy of service as I had felt on the Somme. My mother was deeply distressed. Young people rarely realize how much old people need them. Children are weak and perplexed, and are obliged to rely on the strong support of their grown-ups. As they become older and acquire self-confidence, they are pleased to break away from parental control, which is as it should be. But as the young become strong and mature, they forget that their parents are becoming weaker. Soon their relative positions are reversed, and it is the old who become feeble and anxious and desperately need the cheerfulness, the support and the help of the young. The latter rarely appreciate this reversal of the roles, nor that it is their duty to protect their parents, as their parents once protected them.

And yet the opposite can also produce its tragedies: daughters, and sometimes sons, devote themselves selflessly to the care of their parents. When eventually the old people die, they leave behind them a middle-aged spinster or bachelor, too old to marry, and destined to spend the rest of their life in loneliness. (The ideal solution is geographical. The young people should leave their homes and marry, but live near enough to their old people to be able often to visit, help and cheer them.)

This problem in an exacerbated form was part of the burden of empire, and a heavy one at that. While the parents were serving in some remote part of the empire, their children were at school in England. When the young generation grew up, family tradition drove them to serve in some far imperial province – probably the one in which their parents had themselves passed most of their service. But at the same time, the parents had grown old and returned to England to die, just when their sons and daughters left home for service beyond the seas.

The ship touched at Malta, where I received an anguished telegram of farewell from my mother. We disembarked at Bombay where, after a week's wait, we boarded a ship which took us up to Basra, whence we travelled slowly, frequently sticking on mudbanks, on a steam-boat to Baghdad. The journey took more weeks then than it now takes hours.

The situation in Iraq in 1920 was complicated: two years had passed since the First World War had ended, but the various peace conferences had failed to produce any decision on the future of Iraq. On the one hand, Britain had encouraged Arab nationalism under the Shareef of Mecca, in order to assist in the campaign against the Ottoman army in Palestine and Syria. In fulfilment of the pledges she had given, she set up the Ameer Faisal, a son of the Shareef, as King of Syria in Damascus. The French, our allies, then attacked and captured Damascus and drove out Faisal, whose officers took refuge in Iraq, bitterly denouncing Britain for her betrayal of Faisal. In fact, Britain had not betrayed Faisal; she resented the high-handed action of France in Syria, but could not declare war on her ally while the peace negotiations were still going on at Versailles. As a result, many educated Iraqis in Baghdad turned against the British, whose army (much reduced) was still in Iraq.

Meanwhile, an Occupied Enemy Territory Administration was endeavouring to administer the country, a process including the collection of taxes. The Turkish authorities had never succeeded in collecting regular taxes from the tribes, particularly in the turbulent lower Euphrates area. O.E.T.A., however, was more methodical, possessed the power and could not be bribed.

At the same time, however, the cultivators in Iraq were aware of what had happened in Egypt in Lord Cromer's time. Whereas Egypt had been bankrupt under the Khedive Ismail in 1879, she had become prosperous and wealthy under the influence of Lord Cromer, the British Consul General. In Iraq, many cultivators realized this, but the city intelligentsia were more nationalistic.

Nationalism was a curse imported from Europe. The old Ottoman Empire had ruled for centuries over a multitude of racial stocks without partiality. The Euphrates tribes had no nationalist sentiments – Turks, British or Arabs were all the same to them – but they did not want to pay taxes to anyone. When the British army became weak, owing to general demobilization, the tribes rebelled and refused to pay taxes.

Meanwhile there was much popular opposition in Britain to the continued presence of British forces in Iraq. However, there was in Baghdad a group of people – consisting of both Iraqis and British lovers of the country, such as Gertrude Bell – who realized that an immediate British withdrawal would lead to chaos and who advocated the continuance of a British presence, not out of 'imperialism' but out of genuine love of Iraq.

Their view may or may not have been wrong. If Britain had

withdrawn, chaos and bloodshed would indeed have resulted, lasting for many years, but Britain could not have been charged with imperialistic greed. In practice, however, Iraq would doubtless not have survived, for the Turks were claiming the provinces of Mosul and Kurdistan. Their claim was pressed for several years and it was only Britain who defended Iraq's ownership of Mosul. So tense, indeed, did the Mosul dispute become that for a considerable time war between Britain and Turkey seemed imminent.

Arriving in Baghdad in October 1920, I was given a small room in the Old Serai to live in, until I was posted. One Sunday afternoon, looking out over the broad waters of the Tigris, I sat down to consider the object of my life, and committed my meditations to paper. This is what I wrote:

Of the Object of My Life

I am actually writing these notes because of the seriousness which I feel myself tempted to give to such questions as whether I should play bridge or tennis, and to the thought that I am not the same as other people in my pursuits and pleasures, questions which, if I can formulate sharply in my mind the essential objects of my life, I expect to find of no importance whatever. But though everyone, or nearly everyone, is prepared to admit such things to be in the abstract quite unimportant, yet it is necessary for a distinct and constant view of the vital points to be always in front of us, before we can actually regard the small everyday questions with indifference.

I will first divide my life into two, (1) the concrete earthly accomplishments (2) the spiritual perfection of my own character; these being thus in the reverse order of importance, because they are easier to discuss in this order.

Firstly, my earthly career. I was very much struck on reading a passage of Alfred de Vigny, in which he is regretting his life spent in the army, and where he says, 'I found that I had forced into a purely active life, a purely contemplative disposition.' I find both the active and contemplative to be strongly present in my own character, so that when I am on quiet holidays or alone in the evenings, I feel the same disgust with the army as did de Vigny; whereas in my everyday work, I become so interested in even the smallest practical details that I forget everything else in the restless energy of working, pushing on, and 'getting things done'.

These two sides have led me at various times on two separate ambitions, firstly that of the soldier for distinction, and secondly that which desires quiet and retirement, to study and read, so as one day to produce a great book, the means of bringing light and virtue to thousands of lives. As these two ambitions are essentially at variance, I am sitting down now for the first time, to weigh the advantages of the one against the other, and to assign to each its relative place.

In favour of the literary project is:

(a) that I have been worried to some extent by conscientious scruples as to the rightness of the view that a soldier is bound to obey orders, and though my mind is even yet not fully clear, I am inclined to believe that in the event of my being ordered to do anything which was against my idea of right, my duty would be to resign.

(b) that I do not believe my character to be suitable to the employment of a high command, though if I set myself to it in peacetime, I might with my brain attain to it.

(c) that if the righteousness of war be admitted, it must also be admitted that the soldiers are of benefit to the human race. As men can only be good soldiers by practice, so the whole of a soldier's life spent in practising war must be admitted to be of benefit to the human race, provided he does not lend himself to an unrighteous cause. Yet an author has more power of appeal to other people, and that directly, by speaking out his own soul.

Contrary to the literary project:

(a) that I have no idea if I possess literary capacity nor if I shall ever be read, which somewhat counteracts consideration (c) above.

Balancing the above I conclude:

I. that, for the moment, being far from prepared as yet to write anything and having no means of living, I must remain a soldier, unless some very strong dictate of conscience compels me at some time or other to resign;

II. that while I remain a soldier, I must be perfectly efficient and devoted to my duty in a profession than which none except the service of the Church can be more honourable;

III. that now and for many years I must devote all the time which I can spare from II. to the furnishing of my mind, with broad and general ideas, which will be necessary to any form of authorship.

IV. that nothing can be admitted into my life which does not conduce to II. or III., or to that spiritual advancement mentioned in the beginning, which is the first duty of every man's life.

The Serai, Baghdad
Sunday, October 24th, 1920

This solemn document was thrust into one of the many boxes of papers which I have dragged around all my life, and I only discovered it again in 1979, fifty-nine years later. Perhaps it may appear a little sanctimonious – young people are apt to take themselves rather seriously – but it was of course written for my own eyes alone.

A few days later I was posted for duty, and the ensuing thirty-six years were to be spent in intensely active duties, mostly out of doors. During these years, I entirely forgot my early thoughts of authorship. When, at the end of the Second World War, John Attenborough, the director of Hodder and Stoughton, suggested to me that I write a book, the proposal came to me as a complete novelty.

When I arrived in Baghdad, the tribal rebellion had already been suppressed, but various military columns were moving about the country to show the flag and to collect fines of rifles.

The Diyala river emerges from the Zagros Mountains of Iran through a gorge in the Jebel Hamrin. At the point of emergence, a number of irrigation canals were drawn off from the river to water the crops on the wide plain stretching down to the Tigris. The regulators on the canal heads had been smashed and were being rebuilt by the Department of Irrigation. An Indian army battalion, the 99th Infantry, was covering the repair work.

I was sent up, a solitary engineer officer, to construct and operate a ferry across the Diyala, as the work lay on both sides of the river. First I erected an aerial cable, anchored into the cliffs on either side of the gorge through which the river emerged from the mountains. On this was swung a box like the basket under a balloon, in which passengers hauled themselves across. As, however, a number of labourers had to cross every morning and evening, a more rapid means of transport was required. I accordingly fixed a steel cable across at water level; to this a boat was attached on a pulley and hauled across. This device seemed to be perfectly adequate.

One night we were woken in the small hours by an increasing roar of waters. Peering out of our tent, we saw that the river had suddenly been transformed into a boiling torrent but, as our camp was on high ground, we went back to bed. The river came from the Zagros Mountains, less than a hundred miles away, and a violent storm on the mountains could cause it suddenly to rise and come roaring down in spate. We had no knowledge of these local conditions, however.

Next morning, my boat ferry set out as usual, but the ferryman, alarmed by the roaring torrent, lost his nerve and pulled back to shore. In the confusion of the moment, an Indian coolie fell overboard. I was sitting in our tent when suddenly I heard a chorus of shouts and screams. Running out, I was told that an Indian had fallen off the ferry boat and was being carried downstream.

Without pausing to think, I jumped into the river, though I could not see the drowning man. I was immediately swept away, mostly under water. Swimming was impossible; I could see the bank racing past, but succeeded in getting my head above water, now and again, just enough to take breath. As the river emerged from the gorge into the plain, however, it flowed more smoothly and I was able to keep my head above water.

Far ahead, I saw an island covered with shrubs in midstream, and was able to swim towards it and catch hold of a branch as I swept by. I dragged myself on to it, and lay, exhausted. Fortunately an Arab had seen me and came to my rescue, swimming on an inflated goatskin. With his help, and using the goatskin as waterwings, I succeeded in reaching the shore, after drifting some distance downstream. The Indian coolie was never heard of again.

As soon as he saw that I was safe the Arab disappeared, and I was never able to thank him.

Early in 1921, I was transferred to Ramadi, on the Euphrates, where it was my duty to maintain a rickety floating bridge over the river, carried on boats made of reeds daubed with bitumen. Here there were no British or Indian troops. My bridge gang were local Arabs from the Dulaim tribe.

Always principally motivated by human relationships, I soon

became friends with the members of my bridge gang; and they, like all Arab tribesmen, immediately invited me to meals in their homes. The Dulaim were mostly cultivators along the banks of the Euphrates, watering their wheat, barley and date palms by *kerids*, or water lifts worked by horses. Yet they had but recently settled, and still lived in black goat-hair tents.

Working alone among Arab tribesmen, I soon became intimate with them and picked up a smattering of Arabic. My friendship was exclusively with the families of labourers. The Dulaim were a large tribe but I never met any of the shaikhs. Nor, of course, did I ever see or speak to a woman. Although the men and women mix fairly freely among their relatives, when a stranger was a guest the women remained behind a curtain which divided the tent in half.

In 1921, Winston Churchill called a conference in Cairo on Middle Eastern policy; there the bold decision was taken to replace the army by the Royal Air Force to maintain security in Iraq. As a result, I was moved to Baghdad and put in charge of the building of huts and hangars for an R.A.F. base just outside Baghdad at a place called Hinaidi – a word which, curiously enough, means 'the little Indian'.

The clerks and artisans of my workforce were all Indians, including a large proportion of Sikhs. My head clerk was a Goanese, with a long, aristocratic, Portuguese name. But my labourers were Arabs. The majority were from the Dulaim with whom I had become familiar near Ramadi, many of whom had followed me from there. But it was also impossible to avoid engaging labourers from the Tigris, below Baghdad. These were Shiahs, whereas the Dulaim were Sunnis; and there was always a certain latent hostility between the two groups.

As usual, I fell in love both with my Indian artisans and with my Arab labourers. One day, a party of gypsies pitched their tents by our labour camp, and the gypsy girls danced before the workmen. Some of the latter had no hesitation in kissing and indulging in physical familiarities with the girls, who were doubtless accustomed to such treatment and, indeed, earned their living by it.

But my innocent and chivalrous attitude to women filled me with disgust at such conduct. I collected all my labourers and made them all remove their *agals*, the little circles of rope by which they kept their kerchiefs on their heads. The *agal* was the mark of manhood – women did not wear it. I then had all their *agals* burned. My gesture was intended to express my opinion they they were not men. The labourers, who saw no harm in their handling the gypsy girls, were mystified by my action and merely thought me a little mad.

In spite of this slight misunderstanding, I identified myself completely with my labourers. The Baghdad police suspected that a large labour camp might contain thieves or criminals, and sent a spy to the tents. The men reported his presence to me. Highly indignant, I mounted my pony and chased him from my camp in a somewhat undignified manner.

Meanwhile the R.A.F. had assumed responsibility for public security in Iraq, and several squadrons moved into my new camp in Hinaidi. The tribes in Iraq were still largely uncontrolled. The theory was that when tribal disorders broke out in any district – possibly hundreds of miles away – aircraft would take off from Hinaidi and bomb the offenders . . . and the disorders would be ended between breakfast and lunch.

In the event, however, it turned out that the aircraft would arrive over the troubled area quickly enough, but, when they had done so, the pilots were unable to identify the target. On several occasions they erroneously bombed the government's most loyal adherents! This problem of the difficulty experienced by R.A.F. pilots in identifying their targets threatened to demolish the whole theory of 'air control'. (It should perhaps be mentioned here that the bombs dropped in 1920 were tiny affairs called Coopers which, I think, weighed only five or six pounds. The overall effect of bombing a village was normally to injure one person and perhaps kill a cow, or something of the kind.)

The solution adopted by Air Headquarters was to post officers in rural areas, whose duty it was thoroughly to familiarize themselves with all the tribes and villages. In the event of disturbances, this officer would go to Hinaidi and lead the aircraft sent to attack and suppress the rebels. As I had already acquired the reputation of knowing Arabic, Air Headquarters offered me one of these positions. The British army was already leaving Iraq and, as a soldier, I should have been obliged to go with it. Having already fallen in love with the country, I readily accepted.

I bade a fond farewell to my Indian staff, who wrote me a joint letter of good wishes and congratulations. They were charming people with whom I was learning to converse in halting Hindustani.

When one is in action, one does not pause to analyse one's motives. It is only since my retirement in England that I have thought over the psychological factors which have shaped my life. It seems to me now that I had an irresistible impulse to identify myself with the community among which I worked. This impulse had drawn me close to my sappers or drivers in France, to my bridge gang in Ramadi, and to my Indian artisans and Arab labourers in Hinaidi.

We can only help people by being one with them, sharing their miseries, their poverty, their joys and sorrow. Christ did this. You cannot help people from outside of them. Mother Teresa saw Christ in everyone she met. When she greeted them with a smile, she was smiling to God.

Perhaps nowadays, when I am old, I summarize this tendency as the duty to love everybody, but in those days I did not analyse it. It just so happened that when I met a new lot of people, I soon grew fond of them. But it is everlastingly true that with what measure we mete, it is measured to us again. When I loved the community with which I was working, they automatically returned my affection.

Thus my career as an engineer came to an end with the construction of the Air Force camp and hangars at Hinaidi, when I was twenty-four years old. To use one of my mother's Irishisms, my engineering life had been 'short and sweet, like a donkey's gallop'.

It may perhaps be relevant to note at this point that the system of mandates was not, as has sometimes been suggested, a disguised way of acquiring more colonies, or of 'exploiting' other countries. The system was originated by Woodrow Wilson, President of the United States at the end of the First World War and was intended to be purely idealistic. To assist undeveloped countries to form modern, that is to say, Western administrations, was said to be a sacred duty laid upon the greater nations.

In point of fact, all my services in the Middle East were rendered in countries the governments of which were established under mandates, but which have all long since become independent. In my experience, such British officers as served in Iraq and Jordan were devoted to those countries and did everything in their power to set up incorruptible and efficient administrations there.

Britain did not exploit either country; on the contrary, Jordan received a substantial grant-in-aid from the British Treasury as long as she was a mandate. In my opinion, insofar as these countries were concerned, sneers about imperialism were mistaken.

Self-depreciation may be a British quality, but it is at least preferable to misplaced arrogance.

7

Down to the Grass Roots

Thus it came about that I was appointed an intelligence officer under the R.A.F., with the title of Special Service Officer, and was given the Euphrates as my parish.

There were scarcely any office duties, though I submitted a monthly report to Air Headquarters; otherwise my duties were merely to know every tribe and village in my area so that, in the event of operations, I could lead aircraft to their target. The aircraft of those days flew slowly at about two thousand feet, and the fuselage was open. Targets could therefore be selected by leaning over the side.

To me an additional pleasure in the work was that nearly all my tours were accomplished on horseback though, in the marshes of the lower Euphrates, travel was by canoe. There was no nationalism among the tribes and, being a person of no importance, I was everywhere treated by the Arabs as one of themselves. Thus I really got down to the grass roots.

In the winter of 1922–3, I was moved for a short time to Mosul, when the danger of war with Turkey seemed to be imminent. I was obliged to fly long hours in a Bristol fighter over the jagged mountains of Kurdistan. When the engine, as often occurred, began to pop and splutter, one could not help looking over the side in some trepidation, wondering where it would be possible to force-land, an everyday occurrence in the aircraft of the 1920s.

In the summer of 1923, however, the danger of war with Turkey seemed to recede, and I was moved back to Nasiriya on the lower Euphrates. Sixty miles above Nasiriya, and also on the Euphrates, was the small market town of Samawa, the surrounding country being occupied by a tribal group known as Beni Huchaim, which was out of control.

Here an anomalous situation existed, for the railway from Basra to Baghdad ran for fifteen miles through Beni Huchaim tribal territory, where the government exercised no authority. A kind of tacit live-and-let-live situation existed between the government and the tribes. The government abstained from interference with the tribes or from collecting taxes. The tribes, in return, did not interfere with the railway.

No self-respecting administration, however, could permanently accept such a situation. It was therefore decided that Beni Huchaim must be brought under control. The area was too large to be all bombed simultaneously, so it was decided to make an example of two tribes, the Barkat and the Sufran. There were, however, no maps to show where these tribes lived, so I was ordered to prepare one.

Arriving on horseback at Samawa, I was told by the *qaimaqam*, or district commissioner, that it was impossible for any government representative to visit the tribes, who were in revolt. Relying on Arab hospitality, and wrapped in an Arab cloak over my uniform, I rode out with two Arabs to the village of the Shaikh of the Barkat. We dismounted outside the guest house, walked in and gave the greeting of peace. Those present returned our greeting and we knew that we were safe. I therefore slipped off my Arab cloak and the tribesmen were surprised to see a British officer in uniform. Once in the guest house, however, we were safe and enjoyed a long and friendly talk with the tribesmen.

This led to amicable relations, allowing me to visit all the camps and the villages of the Barkat and Sufran, where I was everywhere hospitably entertained. Meanwhile I was making the map which was to enable the R.A.F. to bomb them, and, in view of their friendliness, I felt obliged to tell them so.

The government plan was to summon the shaikhs of the two tribes to report to Samawa and, if they failed to do so, to bomb their tribes. I explained all this to the tribesmen. This was not to betray my duty. The object was to persuade the chiefs to come in and work with the government. If I could persuade the shaikhs to come in without bombing, so much the better. When I had finished my map, I explained to the tribesmen that I was going to Baghdad and that the shaikhs would be summoned to report. If they did not do so, they would be bombed and I would lead the bombers. They said that they quite understood.

When summoned, the shaikhs did not report, and I duly led the bombers, each of the pilots of which had a copy of my map. As soon as the tribes heard the sound of the aircraft – knowing already from me what was going to happen – they all ran out of their villages and lay in the many irrigation ditches. Only one old woman was killed. As a result of the bombing, however, *all* the shaikhs of the Beni Huchaim confederation (not only the Barkat and Sufran) reported to the government, and the whole area was brought under control without bloodshed.

Unfortunately, to my mind, the government thereupon made the same mistake as the Allied Powers did at Versailles. Having defeated their enemy, they tried to impose terms which would prevent their ever rising again. They accordingly ordered the Barkat and Sufran to hand in a fine of several hundred rifles.

Two days later, both tribes had completely vanished, having scattered among the neighbouring tribes. The fine was never collected, and this brilliantly successful operation ended on an unsatisfactory note. The moral seemed to me to be, 'Fight and win if you must. But as soon as you have won, forgive and forget, and make your late enemies into your closest friends.' I wished the government to give a banquet to the Barkat and Sufran, thereby proving that it was their truest friend, but the authorities thought differently.

The tribes had been suppressed and never rebelled against the government again. But in my opinion, the opportunity to make them the government's most devoted subjects had been missed. In fact such an idea had never entered into anyone's head.

The R.A.F. recommended me for a decoration, but the British government, afraid of questions in parliament, did not want it to be known that there had been operations in Iraq. As a result, I was awarded the King's Police Medal, usually given to a police officer for arresting a dangerous criminal!

The area for which I was responsible extended some five hundred miles down the Euphrates from the Syrian frontier to near Basra (exclusive) and perhaps for thirty or forty miles on each side. To the south-west, however, the desert extended for about two hundred miles to the frontier of what we then called Nejed – now Saudi Arabia. I was not the only Special Service Officer on the Euphrates. At various times, others were posted there, when the area was too large for one man.

My duty to know everyone and go everywhere was made easy by the fantastically hospitable customs of the rural Arabs. Every tent or hut in the 100,000-odd square miles of my area was open to any stranger who walked in and sat down. In most of the area, the people lived in black tents of goats' hair, but in the marsh areas of the lower Euphrates, they used *sarifas*. These were split reeds from the marshes, woven into large reed mats and then bent over to form tubular-shaped huts, the ends being closed by other reed mats. Some *sarifas* constituted quite sizeable buildings, decorated with ornamental designs in reeds.

Whether their homes consisted of black tents or reed *sarifas*, they were normally divided down the middle by curtains, on one side of which lived the family. The other side was reserved for male guests. Any man, even a complete stranger, could walk in here and sit down, and thereby become a guest. Good manners in theory forbade the host to ask his guest any questions until he had been there for three days.

Thus the greater part of my time was spent riding with one Arab attendant from camp to camp or, in the marshes, travelling by canoe from one group of reed huts to another, and sitting up half the night talking to my hosts on every aspect of life.

Throughout the winter of 1923–4, I was based on Nasiriya, which was the headquarters of the Muntifik division – a province which included not only the arable plains and the marshes, but also an area of desert extending down to the border of Nejed.

The local market towns covering the whole area were mostly built of mud bricks dried in the sun, though the better buildings were sometimes of burnt brick. In these small towns lived the local administrative officials. The governor of a province was called a *mutassarrif*, and of a sub-district, a *qaimaqam*. All without exception were friendly and hospitable.

Central Arabia, or Nejed, had from time immemorial been largely inhabited by nomadic bedouin tribes which bred camels, sheep and goats and, in small numbers, horses. The camels, sheep and goats found a precarious livelihood from the small bushes and dry blades of desert grass, but the horses (though some of the most beautiful in the world) could only be bred in small numbers because they required additional food.

There were also oases in central Arabia, which grew date palms. The men of the oases were mostly merchants, generally known as *aqail*, who bought animals from the nomads and, in winter and spring, drove them to Syria, Trans-Jordan or Egypt for sale.

In or about 1700, a boy was born in Arabia in the tribe of Beni Temeem; his name was Muhammad ibn Abdul Wahhab. Dedicated to religion, he studied in Mecca, Medina, Basra and Damascus. In 1742, he returned to Nejed and preached a religious puritan revival, on the basis of return to the Quran and no innovations.

Nobody seemed to be much interested until he met a minor shaikh, of the tribe of Anaiza, called Ibn Saud who became a convert. The preaching of the reformer, supported by the sword of the chief, swept over central Arabia in a sudden wave of enthusiasm. In 1803, the Wahhabis captured the Holy Cities of Mecca and Medina, which were nominally under the suzerainty of the Sultan of Turkey. This first period of Wahhabi power lasted from 1803 to 1813, when Mecca was recaptured by an army of Albanians and others, sent by Muhammed Ali Pasha, who had made himself ruler of Egypt. After six years of desultory warfare, the Wahhabi power was shattered.

For nearly a hundred years, central Arabia remained in a confusion of warring tribes and chiefs until, in 1902, a young scion of the Saud family called Abdul Aziz seized Riyadh, the former capital of his family. To rouse the enthusiasm of his supporters, he raised a fanatical revival of the old Wahhabi puritanism. By 1920, he had established his rule all over Nejed and had become the neighbour of Iraq, now under a British mandate. The fanaticism of the Wahhabis having been fanned to white heat, they saw no reason to stop at political frontiers.

In March 1924, I obtained two months' local leave and rode a camel across the Syrian desert from Iraq to Amman in Trans-Jordan. While I was away, a Wahhabi chief, Faisal al Duweesh, of the Mutair tribe, delivered a shattering raid on the Iraqi tribes in the desert.

There was not enough water in the desert for large raids in summer, but as the autumn aproached the Iraqi tribes became increasingly anxious.

The Wahhabis – then known as the Ikhwan or Brethren – were all camel tribes who lived in the great deserts. But in Iraq there were large numbers of semi-nomadic tribes which bred only sheep and used donkeys to carry their tents. These people summered on the Euphrates, but moved out into the desert, where there was fresh grazing and water, from November to March. These sheep tribes were completely at the mercy of the Ikhwan camel riders. The Ikhwan killed all males. It was this practice of massacre which struck so much terror.

Sometimes I have seen the desert referred to as a dead land without life, a barren waste, or a landscape of the moon. Nothing could be further from the truth, for the desert is in reality indescribably beautiful, with its pure air, its distant blue horizons and its rolling hills and valleys covered with shrubs. There is a magical fascination about the desert which fills one with a wild elation.

In the old days, bedouins who visited towns or villages used to stop up their nostrils with plugs of material to protect them from pollution. Then, when they rode out of the villages and the cultivation, into the intoxicating purity of the desert air, they would pull the plugs out of their nostrils, burst into song and tap their camels into a trot.

When a halt was made for a meal, the soil was clean and fresh, as if no human being had ever before passed that way. In a few minutes a fire would be lit from desert shrubs, many of them as fragrant as incense.

Most of the northern deserts of Arabia are on limestone, and sand dunes are rare and far between. But sand dunes, where there are any, are pleasant in many ways. They produce tall feathery bushes as well as grasses, and the sand supplies a soft mattress on which to lie at night, rolled up in one's cloak.

Nor is the desert without life; beetles, flies, lizards, jerboa (the little desert rat), foxes, gazelle, wolves and hyenas all survive, some apparently almost without water. But perhaps the chief beauties of the desert are the purity of the air and the distant blue horizons.

Killing raids, December 1924.

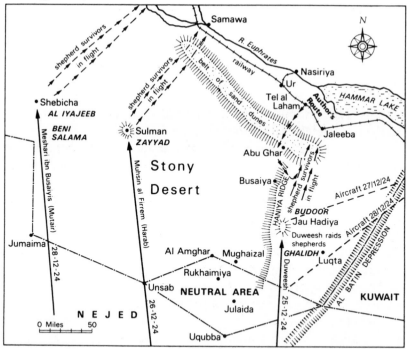

Shortly before Christmas, 1924, I received reports that Faisal al Duweesh was about to raid. The Iraqi shepherds were already scattered in the desert, the leading camps being at Jau Hadiya, seventy miles from the Euphrates. The Iraqi government took no interest in the desert, as the Turks had not. Air Headquarters (when informed) asked for further confirmation. I hired camelmen to go to the shepherds and tell them to come back, but they delayed.

Accordingly I decided to go myself and hired a camel for me to ride and three bedouins to go with me. On the day appointed, the camels were not ready and I was delayed for twenty-four hours. Finally setting out, we arrived some twenty miles from the shepherd camps at about ten o'clock in the morning, when suddenly, topping a low ridge, we saw before us a wide valley filled with panic-stricken people, flocks of sheep, donkeys and a few horsemen, fleeing in a wild rout to the north.

A mile to the south we could see the Ikhwan camelmen with their war-banners, overtaking the fugitives, killing them and rounding up the sheep. The fugitives running past us, wide-eyed with terror, called out, 'The Ikhwan! The Ikhwan! A battle! A battle! Where is the government?' The sight of the terrified women carrying babies and dragging small children, crying and sobbing, was pathetic in the extreme. They cried in anguish, 'Oh God! Oh Ali! Oh God, save us and have pity on us.'

Already the three bedouin with me had caught the infection. 'Let us flee,' they cried. 'It is the Ikhwan. They are on us!' I couched my camel and dismounted to steady my companions and my own nerves. There was nothing much I could do. It was nearly fifty miles to the nearest telegraph office at Jaliba station.

On our camels, we could have fled faster than the shepherds on foot, but I could not make up my mind to abandon the terrified fugitives, so we rode along quietly in the midst of the anguished pandemonium. We could see the pursuing camelmen and hear the crackle of rifle fire close behind but gradually, as the evening approached, the pursuers slackened. They had doubtless marched all the previous night to surprise the camps, were themselves exhausted and had already rounded up many thousands of sheep.

At sunset, I borrowed a horse from a camp and galloped for Jaliba station. Suddenly I realized it was Christmas Day!

I reached Jaliba at dawn and sent off a series of clear-the-line telegrams to Air Headquarters and 84 Squadron R.A.F. at Shaiba, begging for all aircraft to take off and giving the map location. It was blowing a gale and pouring with rain, and I was drenched to the skin. The squadron replied that the weather was unfit for flying, but in the afternoon they sent an aircraft to pick me up and fly me in to Shaiba. On the morning of 27 December, I flew out (but with only three aircraft). There, sure enough, an area of desert perhaps three miles by two was covered with thousands of camelmen moving south, driving the flocks of plundered sheep. We attacked them that day and again the following day, but it was doubtful whether we caused many casualties.

But of one thing I was vividly conscious: I had been delayed for twenty-four hours because the camels I had hired were not ready on the day I had ordered them. If I had started when I had intended, I would have been sleeping in those shepherd camps at dawn on Christmas Day and could not have survived. God works in His own mysterious ways.

Having personally witnessed one of these desert massacres and panic-stricken flights, I thereafter had a new cause to which to devote myself – to save the Iraqi shepherds from destruction. There were perhaps thirty thousand of these people in the southern area, who moved out into the desert in winter, using donkeys to carry their tents.

It was a cause, however, which met with little outside sympathy. The last years of the Ottoman Empire, before its collapse in 1918, had been spent in endeavouring to imitate Europe. In 1924, all but the most junior Iraqi officials had grown up in this Turkish atmosphere of mimicking Europe. They wanted nothing to do with tribes, and were not interested in their sufferings.

The British government held a mandate for Iraq, the object of which was to assist the Iraqis to form a 'modern', that is to say a Western, administration. To imitate the West was likewise the desire of the Iraqis. It was also the duty of the British government to defend the borders of Iraq from attack until Iraq could produce her own army. As, however, the Iraqi government did not ask for its desert tribes to be defended, the British were not particularly anxious to do so.

Moreover, the British government in London wished also to maintain amicable relations with Ibn Saud. Naturally, in these high circles, an enthusiastic young man with a quixotic sense of obligation to defend poor shepherds was thought to be slightly unbalanced – not to say conceited – and often lacking in proper respect for his seniors.

I had become so passionately engrossed in Iraq that I allowed five years to pass without returning on leave to England. The world is full of excitement to young people.

In the summer of 1925, I at last came on leave and met my mother in a hotel in Naples. I still remember her passionate embrace and her joyful cry, 'It's five years, my treasure, but you are still the same.'

Together we travelled northwards through Rome, Florence and Milan, meeting my father and going on to Sirmione on Lake Garda.

Italy had been my dream paradise ever since my first brief visit to San Mamette in 1919, after the trenches in Flanders. But now, to the warm sun, the blue skies, the mountains and the lakes was added the romance of history and architecture. I threw myself enthusiastically into the study of the medieval Italian cities.

In Rome, we saw the Forum, the Coliseum, the Vatican with its Swiss guards and the Sistine Chapel. But my enthusiasm was roused even more passionately by the beauty of Florence, Siena and the cities of the north. At the end of my leave, we returned to England for a fortnight. I then returned to Iraq by the Orient Express from Paris to Istanbul, in itself a memorable experience.

Back in Nasiriya, I was confronted by a critical situation on the Saudi border, where the raiding season was about to begin. In summer the desert was almost empty, but in October or November the first rains begin to fall and the tribes move out.

The only way the sheep breeders could graze their flocks in winter was by moving into the desert. The Air Officer Commanding regarded the shepherd tribes as civilians and, when raids were threatened, ordered me to clear them out of the desert. I objected that if this were done their sheep would die, and that it was the duty of the government to protect them in their normal habitat. The A.O.C. regarded me as disrespectful, if not insubordinate.

The following winter, 1925–6, Ibn Saud and the Ikhwan tribes invaded the Hijaz, the ruler of which was King Husain, formerly Shareef Husain of Mecca, and the father of King Faisal of Iraq. When the first rains began to fall in October and November the Iraqi tribes were afraid to move out, fearing a repetition of the Jau Hadiya raid of the year before. Meanwhile their animals began to die for lack of grazing.

The Dhafeer were the only camel tribe in the southern desert of Iraq, all the rest being sheep and donkey tribes. I consulted Ajaimi ibn Suwait, the Dhafeer shaikh, as to the best course. The Ikhwan were away in the Hijaz, and raids on Iraq appeared unlikely. Ajaimi replied that the tribes would not move out unless I went with them.

I accordingly pitched a white tent for myself (all the Arab tents were black). Ajaimi and his followers thereupon moved out into the desert, accompanied by myself in the white tent. The shepherd tribes were still cautious and sent scouts to Ajaimi's camp, where they saw the white tent. 'What is that white tent?' they asked. 'Oh, that is the government,' Ajaimi would answer in a casual tone. Emboldened by the presence of 'the government', the shepherds moved out to join him. Soon we moved boldly forward to the Neutral Area where the grazing was luxuriant. (The Neutral Area contained a number of deep wells, which were needed by both the Iraqi and Nejed tribes, and which had thus been made neutral to the subjects of Iraq and Nejed alike.)

72

I could not remain all the winter in my white tent in the desert, as Air Headquarters required me to answer letters and write reports, but I left the white tent with Ajaimi's camp to symbolize the presence of the government, visiting it myself from time to time. The Year of the Tent passed without raids. The Ikhwan were fighting in the Hijaz.

Meanwhile, in 1926, I received a letter from the War Office informing me that I had been five years away from the army and would shortly be posted back to Britain. I had, however, become so devoted to Iraq and the Iraqis that I replied to the War Office by resigning my commission. Fortunately, the Adviser to the Ministry of the Interior, Mr (later Sir Kinahan) Cornwallis, came to my rescue by offering me a ten-year contract as a civilian administrator with the Iraqi government, which I joyfully accepted.

In fact, the contract was of doubtful value, as the British mandate for Iraq was due to end in 1928, when the latter would become completely independent and would be free to dismiss her British officials; but as usual my personal emotions and my affection for the Iraqis completely outweighed any considerations for my own security or future career.

It may be worthwhile here to emphasize how completely the internal situation in the Middle East has been transformed since the 1920s. At that time, many Arab countries contained armed tribes, whose turbulence was a constant threat to law and order. As a result, town-dwellers were always loyal to the government, from whom they expected protection against the tribes. This situation continued as long as government forces were armed with rifles, which tribesmen could also obtain.

But as soon as Arab governments were able to arm their forces with modern weapons such as aircraft and armoured vehicles, the tribesmen became helpless. Then the city-dwellers (no longer loyal for fear of the tribes) became the rebels, the tribes remaining loyal.

City resistance to the government took two forms. The first of these was the seduction of the army, which then supported the dissident politicians to effect a *coup d'état* to overthrow the government. Many Middle East governments introduced conscription, hoping thereby to obtain a large army on the cheap. The result was that ill-paid conscript armies were often disloyal.

They would have been better advised to form well-paid, voluntarily enlisted armies, on whose loyalty they could count.

Later, a second form of city opposition to develop was assassination, terrorism or the time-bomb.

The wheel has now turned full circle. The tribes are loyal in general, though indifferent to party politics. But the governments are constantly threatened by rival city politicians, often resorting to terrorism or assassination, or to *coups d'état* carried out by disloyal elements in the army.

8

Iraq and Britain

Iraq was divided into *liwahs* or provinces, each governed by a *mutassarrif* who was head of all the departments in his province. With him was a British Administrative Inspector whose duty it was to advise and to help him. In reality, I was probably too young for such an appointment, for though reasonably intelligent and passionately devoted to the work, I was younger than the *mutassarrif* whom I was supposed to advise.

I spent the year from the spring of 1926 to that of 1927 in the civil administration of the provinces of Hilla and Diwaniya on the Middle Euphrates. This year gave me an intimate knowledge of administration, taxation, and especially of tribal land disputes.

In Turkish times, all agricultural land belonged, in theory, to the government although, in practice, the cultivators bought and sold land to one another. These transactions, however, were not recorded in any official register, as the government claimed to be the owner of all agricultural land.

About the beginning of the twentieth century, however, the Ottoman authorities, desirous as usual to imitate Europe, decided to encourage the private ownership of land. Instructions were therefore issued to facilitate the transference of government land to private ownership.

Like everything else, however, during the last decadent years of Ottoman rule, these measures were corrupted by the venality of the

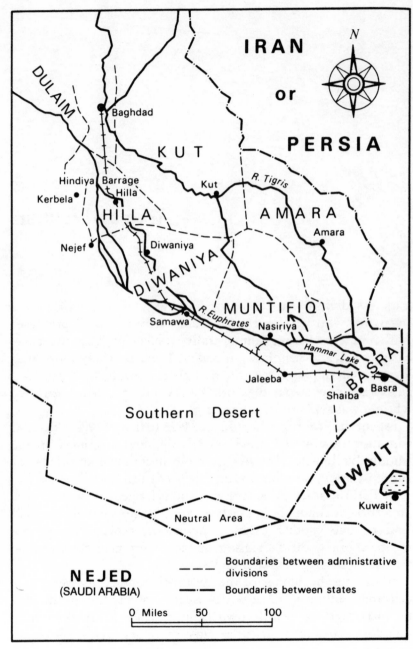

Administrative districts of Southern Iraq.

officials of the Lands Department. Wealthy or influential men could go to the Lands Department and, in return for a bribe, obtain deeds of ownership to any area of land which they coveted.

Quite probably the land in question had been farmed for generations by the local tribe who were quite unaware that some rich man had meanwhile obtained deeds of ownership to it. Often the rich man acquired these deeds as a speculation and did not attempt to enforce them, as the tribe would have resisted. An opportunity would occur some time, when a Turkish military column happened to be in the area, and the speculator would produce his title deeds which were legally valid, even though they had in fact been obtained by bribery.

The tribe which had farmed the land for generations would violently resist the speculator's claim and clashes with the troops sometimes resulted. In some cases, a compromise was arranged. It was impossible to evict the tribe, who alone could cultivate the land but who eventually were forced under protest to pay rent to the speculator.

Another difficulty was the fact that the land had never been surveyed. When, therefore, a rich man – probably after paying a bribe to the Lands Department – obtained a deed of ownership to a piece of land, the lands clerk would ask what boundaries to show on the deed. Often the boundaries would be defined in such terms as 'on the east, Hajji Muhammad's garden, on the west the desert'. I remember a deed of ownership, dating from Turkish times, produced by a claimant, which defined the boundaries of the area involved as 'on the north the marsh, on the east the marsh, on the south the marsh, and on the west the desert'.

I mention some of these problems in order to show the administrative confusion left behind by the Turks, and the immense amount of work involved in sorting out these tangled situations on a reasonable legal basis. Unfortunately, politics and nationalism are the two subjects which receive the most publicity. Nobody was interested in the immense amount of administrative spadework which had been needed to reduce this Ottoman chaos to a modern state.

In Turkish times, taxes were collected, based on the amount of grain, rice or dates actually harvested each year. This principle was unsound, because a farmer who allowed all his land to lie fallow paid no taxes at all. If a fixed tax had been payable on the land, the farmer would have been encouraged to produce as much as he could.

The procedure for taxation was that the farmers at harvest time were supposed to collect their grain on the threshing floor. A government estimating committee then inspected the heaps of wheat or barley and 'estimated' the amount of grain and its value, and the government share in tax. Stacking the grain in different heaps was the time-honoured method of sharing the crop between the farmer and the agricultural labourers working for him.

The method of estimation was, of course, open to the disadvantage of the possible bribery of the estimating committee, though this was difficult to conceal where committees consisted partly of government officials and partly of local notables.

More serious was the possibility that the committees would underestimate the crops of a local magnate, but would overestimate those of a poor man, who could not possibly go to Baghdad and complain.

I am personally convinced that, during the eight years of the British mandate for Iraq, an immense amount of work was accomplished in all these fields, with the assistance of the devoted labours of a small band of dedicated British officials.

Similar work was, of course, being carried out in other departments. The Iraq army was being raised and trained with the assistance of a British military mission. In the same manner, the Public Works, the Irrigation, the Railways and the ministries in Baghdad had double staffs in the higher ranks.

While I believe that Iraq by this means was enabled to become a modern independent state within the period of the eight years of the British mandate, the system was resented by the politically minded classes in the cities. In the rural areas, where alone I worked, this was not normally the case. The country people and the administrative officials were almost invariably friendly and helpful.

Yet dyarchy, or double rule, was a difficult system on which to work. In the administration, all executive authority was vested in the Iraqi official, his British colleague being only an adviser. Yet inevitably people with an axe to grind attempted to sow dissension between them. In general, however, they normally worked happily together. The friction, when it occurred, was usually limited to Baghdad. Yet, on the whole, the net result among politically minded Iraqis was one of resentment.

The whole system of mandates, as already stated, originated with the American President, Woodrow Wilson, an academic idealist. The United States, a nation then not yet 150 years old and largely isolated beyond the Atlantic, perhaps too readily assumed its own superiority and failed to make sufficient allowance for cultures many thousands of years old in other parts of the world. Thus, unwittingly, the mandatory system contained an element of assumed superiority and condescension.

The mandates were distributed by the League of Nations and were imposed on the countries subjected to them, without the latter being consulted. These tactless errors started the mandates off on a note which provoked resentment. There can be no doubt that the countries which had formerly belonged to the Ottoman Empire needed advisers and technologists from the West but, if left to themselves, they would probably have selected them from different nations, thereby avoiding the humiliation of being subjected to one dominant power.

Although mandates were an American idea, the United States almost immediately withdrew, leaving the other Allies to sort out the situation. If all the Allies had been able to establish a pool of advisers from the West European countries and allowed the mandated countries to choose their advisers, resentment would have been avoided. Each country would have selected a mixture of British, French, American, Italian or Scandinavian advisers, and would thus have avoided the humiliating suspicion that they were a subject race under a particular Western country.

Each of the Western nations who received mandates treated them differently. Some did indeed treat them virtually as colonies and retained all the senior executive posts for their own officials. I do not think that Britain did this in Iraq, for all British officials were advisory.

In Iraq particularly, two other factors were involved. The Turks had agreed during the peace negotiations to surrender all their dependencies which were inhabited by an Arab majority. But they claimed that Mosul and Kurdistan did not have an Arab majority, and should thus have remained under Turkey. The Iraqis had no armed forces as yet, and the Turks could easily have seized Mosul and Kurdistan, had not Britain defended them for Iraq.

Had the Turks marched in, they might well have gone on to Baghdad; and Iraq, if she had survived at all, would have ended up as a small state like Trans-Jordan, which had been severed from Syria by the French invasion of the latter.

Thus there can be no doubt that, had not Britain defended her in the 1920s, Iraq as she is today could never have come into existence. Yet the resentment against the mandate, which had been imposed on her without her being consulted, could not be overcome. The whole period of dyarchy, which had enabled Iraq to emerge as a modern state from the chaos of Turkish rule, was resented by Iraqi politicians.

In 1928, when the mandate ended, Britain sponsored Iraq's entry into the League of Nations as an independent state. Thus theoretically, the services rendered to Iraq by Britain were immense. Nevertheless the memory of the eight years of dyarchy continued to cause resentment among Iraqi politicians.

In the 1920s, when I was still in my twenties, I at first felt a certain inferiority complex *vis-à-vis* the French. Britain, I thought, was still a monarchy, whereas France was a republic. Doubtless the French would be more egalitarian. But when I had met French people in various conferences on the Syrian frontier, the superficiality of my views became apparent to me.

When Arab shaikhs or officials were present, I could not help noticing that French officers treated them with much less comradeship and friendliness than the British showed to the Iraqis.

I do not think that the accusations of imperialism so freely directed against Britain by her own citizens can be justified in the case of the Arab countries. The mandatory system was tactlessly worded and the legitimate pride of small nations was hurt. The presence of British forces may have been resented, but after the First World War there was no alternative as the new Iraqi nation had no forces of its own.

Perhaps the charges of imperialism were based on suspicion of British intentions. When Britain punctually surrendered the mandate on the date of its termination, the Iraqi nationalists claimed that she had not originally intended to withdraw, but that the strength of their opposition had compelled her to do so. In actual fact, there was much opposition in Britain, not on the grounds of the wickedness of 'imperialism', but, on the contrary, because it was claimed that we were not under any obligation to spend so much money on so remote a country.

It was often distressing to me to be told by a younger generation in Britain that they were so ashamed of the wickedness of British imperialism after the First World War. To me, my service in Iraq had always been a labour of love.

My year as a civil administrator in Iraq was instructive and enjoyable. Everybody, whether Iraqi officials or tribal shaikhs, was friendly and helpful. It was, however, rendered unhappy by the politicians in Baghdad, who constantly applied pressure on the *mutassarrif* to assist the adherents of their parties by administrative favouritism, such as reducing their taxes or settling land disputes in their favour. This experience made me hate and shun party politics for the rest of my life.

Indeed if Britain is open to any blame in her relations with Iraq, it is probably due to the fact that she used her influence to install a system of democracy and party politics in that country. But this was due to a mistaken philanthropy, not to wicked imperialism. I have not the slightest doubt in my own mind that different races, owing to their differing temperaments and to thousands of years of varying culture and tradition, need different systems of government. To think that any one form of government is the ideal for the whole human race is a dangerous illusion.

In the 1920s, Britain was no longer in an expansionist mood. She was already commencing to reduce her control of India – why at such a moment should she desire to acquire more territory in the Middle East?

In view of her still surviving interests in India, the Far East and Australia, her only fear was that some other Great Power such as Russia or Germany, would establish itself in the Arab countries and cut British communications with the Indian Ocean. She had been happy to see Turkey in control, because the weakening Ottoman Empire was not a danger to her. But the fortune of war had caused the Ottoman Empire to disappear and had left Britain in control of Iraq.

Britain must also be credited, I think, with a certain sense of responsibility. Finding herself, willy-nilly, in Iraq, was she not right to remain there until the country could become an independent self-supporting state, and *then* to withdraw? At the same time, the suggestion of inferiority, which was thought to be implied in a mandate, unnecessarily embittered a system intended to be a fruitful co-operation between friends.

By hindsight we can see how misunderstandings occurred, but there is no excuse for violent denunciations one way or another. There was no villain in this story.

9

The Tables Are Turned

The years 1925 and 1926 had passed peacefully on the Saudi frontier, because Ibn Saud was away in the Hijaz, capturing Mecca, Medina and Jidda, and driving out old King Husain, the father of King Faisal of Iraq. In the autumn of 1926, however, Ibn Saud returned. His fanatical followers, the Ikhwan or Brethren, had realized that *they* had conquered the Hijaz, not Ibn Saud who had no regular army. Believing that the power lay in their hands, the tribes were ready to reject his authority.

Abdul Aziz ibn Saud found himself in a quandary. He had fanned the fanaticism of the Ikhwan in order to defeat his Arab rivals. Now he could not restrain them, though he did not wish to antagonize Great Britain by raiding Iraq. In the winter of 1926–7, accordingly, the Ikhwan carried out massive raids on the Iraqi shepherds. One of these raids reached a point only twenty-five miles from the R.A.F. station at Shaiba, outside Basra. Indeed if they had gone on, they could have destroyed the whole station. The R.A.F. completely failed to deal with the problem. I was still engaged on the civil administration of the Middle Euphrates.

On 2 March 1928, I suddenly received a telegram that I had been transferred to the Southern Desert, and I found myself back once more, though now as a civilian 'inspector', an appointment regarded with little respect by Air Headquarters.

Ever since I came to Iraq, from the days of my Ramadi bridge gang, I had been nicknamed 'Abu Hunaik'. Arabic makes great use of diminutives which are formed by inserting the syllable 'ai' in the middle of the word. Thus *hanak* means the lower jaw, but *hanaik* means a little jaw. In calling me 'Little Jaw', the Arabs were of course referring to the war wound I had received near Arras in 1917.

In 1928, I received a new name of honour – limited, however, to the bedouin world. Among camel tribes, warriors often take their names from their herds and call themselves 'Lord of the Aliya', or 'Lord of the Dhabta', Aliya and Dhabta being camels. One day in our guest tent (in my absence) some bedouins were discussing the possibility of my protecting their flocks from the Ikhwan, when one exclaimed, 'By Allah! he is the Lord of the little white one', (his camel). I became known thereafter as 'Rai al Buwaidha' – 'Lord of the Little White One'.

Anyone who camps in the desert must needs provide for guests, who cannot be prevented from walking in and sitting down. Consequently, beside all our posts or camps, we always pitched a guest tent – which was also useful as a means of collecting information. It was from one of our guest tents at this time that I received a compliment which I have always remembered. A bedouin traveller from another area asked a local tribesman what sort of a fellow the Englishman was who was with them. He replied in two words – *daimen yadhhak* – he is always laughing.

I have always liked the remark made by Robert Louis Stevenson: 'There is no duty we so much underrate as the duty of being happy.'

In March 1928, the grazing season was nearly over and the tribes were returning to the banks of the Euphrates. I had six months to prepare for the next raiding season, which would probably be a heavy one.

I conceived the idea of teaching the Iraqi tribes to defend themselves. Air Headquarters thought exactly the opposite. Regarding the Iraqi tribes as civilians, they demanded that they be swept out of the desert to allow the R.A.F. to engage the raiders – whom, however, they could never locate. 'Air control' was perhaps still too much on trial, and Air Headquarters were anxious to prove that everything could be done from the air alone. Since then, we have learned that the air and the ground are essential partners, but in 1927 the R.A.F. would not consider ground forces.

The Iraqi government, however, was extremely co-operative. At my request, they sent me four commercial one-ton trucks and four vanettes which they had bought in the bazaars in Baghdad. They also authorized me to enlist a hundred desert bedouin as police. Meanwhile our own tribes were intensely resentful against the Iraqi government which made them pay taxes but did nothing to protect them. The next task was therefore to win the confidence and co-operation of our own tribes, which I did by frequent visits and discussions with them.

My plan was to secure the wholehearted co-operation of our own tribes and also to arrange ground patrols of desert police in trucks to scout well in advance of our tribes, thereby saving the R.A.F. from endless hours of vague patrolling over the empty desert, and at the same time making sure that we could locate advancing raiders.

I knew that, in Turkish times, before Ibn Saud had resuscitated religious fanaticism in Arabia, the Iraqi tribes, shepherds and bedouin alike, had been in the habit of offering battle to the tribes of Nejed, including Mutair. I saw no reason why the Iraqi tribes, with suitable leadership, should not defend themselves against the Ikhwan. They had become demoralized by being treated by the R.A.F. as civilians and ordered to run away whenever warnings of Ikhwan raids were received.

In April 1928 I accompanied an Iraqi diplomatic mission to Ibn Saud, who was to receive us in Jidda. Sir Gilbert Clayton, who already knew him, was to act as the British arbitrator.

On arrival in Cairo, however, we were told that it was the season of the annual pilgrimage to Mecca. By international agreement nobody was allowed to land in Jidda during the pilgrim season unless he had been inoculated against a long list of oriental epidemic diseases; I was therefore told that I could not go. The doctors told me that eight weeks would be required to enable me to receive all the inoculations, with suitable intervals between them. I asked if I could not have them all at once, but the doctor said that he had never heard of such a procedure. However, I persuaded him to give me all the inoculations in half an hour, and I experienced no reaction at all. I think there were seven, including bubonic plague, cholera, yellow fever and others.

On 7 May 1928, we met Abdul Aziz ibn Saud in Jidda. As a man, he was immensely impressive. Head and shoulders taller than any of his entourage, he possessed that indefinable power of personality which compelled everyone to do what he ordered. At the same time his manner was charmingly frank, patriarchal and benevolent.

Unfortunately we were not able to negotiate with him directly. He was represented by a group of Lebanese, Palestinian and Egyptian lawyers who, as my mother would have said, could have 'argued the hind leg off a jackass'.

Ibn Saud was faced by two dilemmas. The first – and the more important to him – was that his most fanatical tribes, Mutair and Ataiba, were defying his authority. He was, however, unwilling to admit the fact. Secondly, for several years past, he had endeavoured to justify their raids on Iraq by complaining loudy that bedouins from Iraq were raiding him. These complaints had been supported by strongly worded notes from the British government. At first these minor raids from Iraq had indeed been secretly encouraged by King Faisal of Iraq, whose family had been driven from the Hijaz by Ibn Saud.

On 5 October 1925, a large Shammar raid from northern Iraq had looted camels from Kuwait, a friendly neighbouring state. I was still with the R.A.F. at the time, and we had overtaken and bombed the raiders who had watered at the two main groups of wells in the southern desert, Busaiya and Sulman.

As a result of this raid, I recommended the construction of police forts on the wells of Busaiya and Sulman, as being the easiest way to end desert raiding. Moreover, if such desert posts were equipped with wireless, they could report all raids and tribal movements to the authorities.

My recommendation, which had been made to Air Head-quarters, was passed to the Iraqi government who sanctioned the erection of a police post on the wells of Busaiya. By this time (1926), however, I had left the desert and become an administrative inspector in Diwaniya.

The Ikhwan immediately appreciated that my plan for forts on desert wells would put an end to desert raiding. In September 1927, a party of twelve workmen was sent out to Busaiya to build the post, accompanied by an escort of seven policemen. On the night of 5/6 November 1927, a party of some fifty men of the Ikhwan Mutair tribe rushed the camp, killing all the workmen and police except for one man, whom they left for dead but who actually survived. Other workmen were sent back to Busaiya, but with an escort of R.A.F. armoured cars this time, and the fort was completed.

To placate his own rebellious tribes, Ibn Saud at Jidda demanded the destruction of the Busaiya fort. We replied that the post had been built to enable us to prevent our tribes from raiding him, which was true.

No solution to the impasse was possible because Ibn Saud could not control his own followers. Personally, I greatly sympathized with Ibn Saud. It seemed to me desirable to assist him to restore his authority, failing which Arabia would simply fall into chaos. I was therefore in favour of making more concessions than either the British or Iraqi governments would accept. We returned to Baghdad at the end of May 1928 without having reached an agreement. I had five months to prepare for the next raiding season.

I had already submitted my proposals to the Iraqi government in March. I asked for the formation of a Southern Desert Camel Corps, consisting of:

70 camelmen
30 machine-gunners in trucks
 8 miscellaneous vehicles, 2 of them with Vickers guns
 4 new Ford trucks with Vickers guns
 2 wireless vans

These proposals were resisted by the A.O.C. who said that he did not wish the police to fight; the R.A.F. would do the fighting. In fact, the real answer to raids by thousands of camel riders was armoured cars, which the R.A.F. possessed but would not commit to action.

The British government had failed to grasp that Ibn Saud had lost control of his own tribes, and consequently obstructed our defensive plans which they regarded as directed against Ibn Saud. It seemed utterly hopeless to conduct operations in the desert, controlled in every detail by numerous officials sitting in offices in Baghdad and London. I accordingly decided to use my new desert force as a mobile strong-point, round which the Iraqi tribes would rally.

Although Air Headquarters were difficult to persuade, we depended largely on aircraft, of which the Ikhwan were afraid. I also enjoyed the close and enthusiastic help of 84 Squadron R.A.F. at Shaiba, which was the unit actually involved.

As soon as our tribes moved out, in November 1928, they poured down to the frontier. We were obliged to go with them, and camped at Mughaizal, at the northern apex of the Neutral Area. In addition to organizing the Iraqi tribes to operate under our orders, I had greatly improved my intelligence system in Ikhwan territory. My spies now brought me regular reports from the Ikhwan camps.

From enquiries which I had made regarding the old desert tribal wars, I had discovered that a recognized system of defence had once existed. It consisted in pitching all the tents in a straight line so close to one another that the tent ropes overlapped. All the camels and sheep were then hobbled behind the tents. If the camp was a large one, a second line of tents could be similarly drawn up behind the first. These lines of tents with inter-crossing tent ropes formed an impenetrable obstacle to charging horses or camelmen.

In fact, camels as mounts are too unwieldy to be used as chargers. When faced with a serious battle, the people of Nejed would couch and hobble their camels and advance on foot. But if the defenders' tents were already lined up, they could have scooped out a rifle pit each in front of his tent, from which he could fire on the enemy advancing on foot.

Such were the old bedouin defensive tactics. But we had improved on these old methods by digging a redoubt slightly in advance of our line. We then unshipped the machine-guns from our trucks and dug them into this redoubt. This gave us both frontal and enfilade fire against an advancing enemy.

The one great drawback to this system, however, was that the flocks and herds could not graze. Consequently the tight defensive line could not be maintained for more than twenty-four, or at most forty-eight, hours. Secondly, so dense a concentration of tents required a very large water supply, preferably a large pool of rainwater.

The fact that the defensive position could only be held for so short a time meant that the tribal camps must be left widely dispersed for grazing, until about twenty-four hours before the enemy attack. This necessitated extremely accurate information regarding the enemy's probable date of attack. It also necessitated instant obedience on the part of the tribes who, when they received the summons to concentrate, would have to march day and night to arrive in time to take up the defensive line.

All this I had explained in great detail to all our tribes. In view of the impossibility of carrying on operations through officials sitting in offices in Baghdad or Whitehall, the only course was to use tribal methods to defend ourselves, abandoning hope of government support. Fortunately the Ikhwan did not know that the R.A.F. would not support us in battle.

On 17 February 1929, one of my most reliable spies came in with detailed information. Faisal al Duweesh of the Mutair tribe was advancing against us with many thousands of camelmen. He would attack us at dawn on 20 February. I sent off a wireless message to Air Headquarters, begging them to send their armoured cars. I then sent vehicles out to all the Iraqi tribes to rally round our police camp at Al Abtiyya.

We had carefully planned this operation with them and all complied immediately. By 19 February, all the Iraqi tribes were concentrated in a solid line, with the desert police in a redoubt in the centre. A signal came from Air Headquarters, refusing to send armoured cars and suggesting that we withdraw before the Ikhwan raiders came.

On 19 February, we held war dances to warm up our courage. These dances offered an interesting contrast between different cultures. The shepherds performed what was called a *hosa*, an active and energetic dance, in which rifles were brandished in the air. The camel bedouins were as usual more dignified. They stood in a long line, swaying slightly to the sound of their chant. It was remarkable how the culture of central Arabia emphasized quietness and dignity, in contrast to the boisterous dances of the Iraqis.

At dawn on 20 February, we awaited the onslaught of many thousands of charging camelmen, but nothing happened. It was three days before we heard that Faisal al Duweesh had indeed come on the night of 19/20 February. At midnight he had arrived at Julaida, in the Neutral Area, some thirty-five miles from our position, which, as we had calculated, he proposed to attack at dawn.

He had taken the precaution of placing a spy in our camp, who was to meet him at midnight at Julaida. This spy informed him that all the Iraq tribes were drawn up, ready for battle. The Duweesh did not, of course, know that the R.A.F. had refused to support us. On his spy's report, he decided that to attack would be too risky, and hastily withdrew to the south.

It is impossible to realize (fifty years later) what a shattering event this was in the desert. For ten years, the Ikhwan had carried plunder and slaughter all over the southern deserts of Iraq. Now, all of a sudden, they had ignominiously retreated. Such an event seemed nothing less than a miracle. With the Iraqi tribes we passed the last two months of the grazing season in magnificent green grass and indescribable exhilaration of spirit. Was the end of the ten long years of terror really in sight?

Incidentally we had also saved Ibn Saud. If the rebel Ikhwan tribes had returned laden with loot, they would have turned on the king and central Arabia would have relapsed into a chaos of warring tribes. The fact that the Ikhwan raiders had returned empty-handed caused the remainder of Nejed to rally to Ibn Saud.

On 29 March 1929, Ibn Saud fought a pitched battle with the rebel tribes of Mutair and Ataiba at Sibilla and defeated them. Thereafter major operations in the desert were impossible due to lack of water. Throughout the summer of 1929, Nejed was in chaos, the rebel tribes and the loyalists raiding one another. Two rebel Ikhwan raids which entered Iraq were caught and defeated by our armed desert trucks, without air support.

During the summer, Ataiba surrendered to Ibn Saud, leaving only Mutair and the Ajman, who were now hopelessly out-numbered. On 30 November 1929, we camped at Julaida in the Neutral Area, with my mobile desert police camp and surrounded by the Iraqi tribes, now full of fighting spirit. On 13 December 1929, a deputation from the Mutair tribe, who for the past ten years had endlessly plundered and slaughtered Iraqis, arrived to beg asylum in Iraq. Shammar and other Nejed tribes, loyal to Ibn Saud, hastily joined the Iraqi tribes with us, out of fear of Mutair. During all the past ten years of terror in the desert, we had never dreamed of so dramatic a reversal of fortune – a complete turning of the tables.

No words which I can now find can describe the dramatic effect of this incredible change of fortune. For ten years, the Iraq tribes had lived in continual fear of massacre, cautiously venturing out into the desert to seek the new grass and then fleeing pell-mell in panic at some rumour of danger. Almost every year two or three shepherd encampments had been caught and exterminated.

For six years, I myself had lived in constant fear of Ikhwan raids, venturing out into the desert with two Arab companions on camels or in my Ford van, or living alone in my little white tent, seventy miles out in the desert, to encourage the Iraqi shepherds to move out.

It was not as if I could feel that I was risking my life in the service of Iraq, supported by the approval and the enthusiasm of the Iraqi or British governments. On the contrary, the Iraqi government was intent only on modernization and regarded all tribes with dislike and indifference. The British government was anxious to be on good terms with Ibn Saud and saw no need to annoy him when the Iraqi government had not asked for help. In this situation, the R.A.F. had, understandably, in periods of alarm, merely told the Iraqi tribes to run away.

Now, after so many years skulking in fear, we suddenly found ourselves surrounded by our own tribes, with Ibn Saud's loyal tribes sheltering behind us and the dreaded Ikhwan begging us to allow them to shelter in Iraq. I rubbed my eyes, scarcely believing that it could be true.

On 21 December, in this precarious situation, with the rebels on the frontier and the Iraqi tribes and Nejed loyalists camped around us, we suddenly received a peremptory order to 'withdraw'. The next day, however, the Chief Air Staff Officer, Air Commodore Burnett, landed at my camp. After nearly ten years of operations, for the first time the Air Staff sent a senior officer to the front. Thereafter all went well. On the ground, the facts of the situation were obvious.

On 5 January 1930, Ibn Saud with all his forces suddenly appeared at Al Riqai, only three miles from my camp; a car arrived from the king carrying Yusuf al Yaseen, one of Ibn Saud's Syrian lawyers. Meanwhile the rebel tribes panicked and fled into Kuwait territory, where they were outside our jurisdiction. On 20 January 1930, a meeting took place between Ibn Saud and representatives of Britain and Kuwait, at which it was agreed that the rebel tribes would be evicted from Kuwait and returned to Nejed, which was duly carried out.

The British government, anxious as always for peace, desired to seize the opportunity to effect a reconciliation between King Faisal of Iraq and Abdul Aziz ibn Saud. As neither monarch was willing to visit the other, a meeting was arranged on a sloop, H.M.S. *Lupin,* in the Persian Gulf, out of sight of land.

On the evening of 21 February 1930, three ships arrived at the rendezvous. One of these conveyed the Iraqi delegation, consisting of King Faisal, the Prime Minister of Iraq, the Adviser to the Ministry of the Interior, Mr Cornwallis, the British High

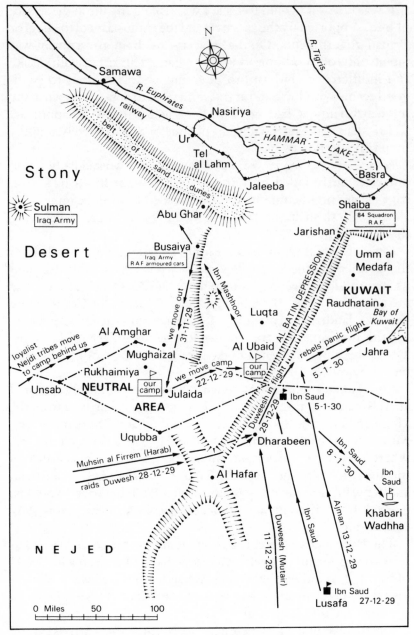

The dénouement, December 1929–January 1930. *At the end of November 1929, we camped at Julaida, surrounded by the Iraq tribes. A few days later, the rebel Mutair arrived and begged for sanctuary in Iraq. On 27 December Ibn Saud arrived with his army and the Nejed rebels fled into Kuwait.*

Commissioner for Iraq, and myself, in the humble capacity of tribal expert. A British ship had been sent to bring the Saudi deputation. Meetings were to take place on H.M.S. *Lupin*.

The same evening we went on board *Lupin* to arrange the details. The captain was asked to lower two gangways, one on the port and one on the starboard side, to allow the two rulers to board the ship simultaneously and meet in the middle of the deck. The captain, however, announced with regret that he had only one gangway. This fact almost caused a crisis, but the captain himself produced the solution.

'In the navy,' he said, 'the senior man always comes on board last. Why not explain this to King Faisal and ask him accordingly to come on board last? Then you could invite Ibn Saud, who is unlikely to know naval custom, to come on board first.' This suggestion was adopted with success, each monarch believing that he had gained precedence.

It cannot be said that the two kings loved one another at first sight, but the fact that they had met and had eaten and drunk together was of far-reaching significance. Most important of all, the *Lupin* meeting led to permanent peace. More than fifty years have elapsed since then, and raiding has never been resumed on the frontier of Iraq and Saudi Arabia.

It is true that the Iraqi government had not been greatly concerned at the massacre of its shepherd tribes by the Ikhwan, being much more preoccupied with the modernization of its own administration. My dedication to the defence of the shepherd tribes had been because of my personal affectionate attachment to them.

Nevertheless, in the 1920s, the Ikhwan were a serious menace to Iraq. In the previous period of Wahhabi power at the beginning of the nineteenth century, they had terrorized all the towns on the lower Euphrates and had even sacked the city of Kerbela, a place sacred to the Shiah division of Islam. It was surely better to meet and repulse the Ikhwan far out in the desert, rather than allow them to reach and to terrorize the towns and villages along the Euphrates.

I had been more afraid in the desert than I had been in France during the First World War. The likelihood of being killed in France had been greater, but one was supported by the comradeship of one's brother officers and men. The fact that so many comrades had been killed seemed to make death less alarming. But in the desert I was completely alone with no compatriots to sustain me. My operations had not received the support or approval of the British or Iraqi governments. If we had met with disaster, the responsibility would have rested on me alone.

10
A Band of Brothers

While our tribal war, the Ikhwan rebellion and the *Lupin* meeting had been taking place, the League of Nations' Mandate for Iraq had come to an end in 1928, and Britain had pressed for her admission to the League of Nations as an independent state. I was personally devoted to the country, but my future as a member of the administration seemed to be dubious.

Meanwhile the government of Trans-Jordan, which was still a mandate, had as yet taken no steps to enforce its authority in its deserts. Hearing of the establishment of law and order in the deserts of Iraq, the Trans-Jordan government was emboldened to follow its example, and offered me employment for this purpose. In view of my uncertain future in Iraq, I readily accepted.

I was called to the palace in Baghdad to take my official farewell of King Faisal and to receive from him the order of the Rafidain. The king was familiar with Trans-Jordan for, as the Ameer Faisal, he had led the Arab forces which had fought their way from Aqaba to Damascus in the First World War as an ally of Britain.

This was, of course, the campaign in which T.E. Lawrence had acquired fame and in which he had achieved notoriety for his generous expenditure of money (all in gold) to the nomadic tribes. King Faisal gave me a parting word of advice. 'Never,' he said, 'give money to bedouins. They will do everything for honour, but to give them money is to destroy all their moral qualities.'

The ameerate of Trans-Jordan extended some two hundred and fifty miles from north to south and one hundred and thirty from west to east – almost the same area as England, without Scotland or Wales. But the cultivable area, the rainfall of which was sufficient for grain crops and trees, constituted only a little over one-sixth of the country. The remainder was desert.

This desert area consisted principally of undulating limestone hills, liberally strewn with flints. In the north, it was covered with lava from extinct volcanoes. In the south it included a range of mountains called Jabal Tubaiq. The western boundary of Trans-Jordan was the Jordan River, the Dead Sea and the great rift valley – the Wadi Araba – down to the Gulf of Aqaba.

Government administration and authority was established only in the cultivated area and included the areas known as Moab and Gilead in the Old Testament. The Ameer Abdulla, the ruler, was a brother of King Faisal of Iraq, and son of Shareef Husain, who had been driven from Mecca by Ibn Saud.

The two principal nomadic camel tribes in the desert were Beni Sakhr and the Huwaitat, although minor camel tribes existed, for instance the Sirhan, Isa, Serdiya, and Ahl al Jebel – the mountain people – from the northern lava hills.

As the Ameer Abdulla was a son of Shareef Husain, there was no love between Trans-Jordan and what was soon to be called Saudi Arabia. But the Trans-Jordan border was much further from the areas occupied by the fanatical Ikhwan tribes, and consequently raiding into Trans-Jordan had been much less severe than into Iraq.

In 1924, moreover, a full-scale Ikhwan force, many thousands strong, had burst into Trans-Jordan and reached a place called Ziza, only some ten miles from Amman which it would shortly have captured and virtually exterminated. There was an R.A.F. landing ground at Ziza and, by a pure coincidence, an R.A.F. lorry carrying petrol to the landing ground arrived at the critical moment. The driver saw that some kind of a battle was in progress, and hastily returned to the R.A.F. camp at Amman to report.

Aircraft took off and checked the raiders by dropping small bombs, and then the R.A.F. armoured cars arrived. Many thousands of camelmen advancing across open country were helpless before armoured vehicles, and the Ikhwan suffered a crushing defeat which preserved Trans-Jordan in the ensuing years from further major raids of massacre.

As a result, from 1924 to 1930, relations between Trans-Jordan and Ibn Saud subsided into a war of diplomacy. Minor raids by both sides continued – raids for looted animals, not raids of massacre. Ibn Saud, however, maintained in London a shrill stream of complaints.

Britain held a mandate for Trans-Jordan and was responsible for the defence of her frontiers, but wished also to maintain friendly relations with Ibn Saud; thus the latter's complaints were passed on to Trans-Jordan with added virulence.

In this diplomatic fencing, the Trans-Jordan government was at a disadvantage, because it had no control over its own deserts and no knowledge of what went on there. It could not refute the accusations of Ibn Saud or reply with counter-charges of Saudi raids (which were just as frequent), because it had no idea of what was happening.

When Trans-Jordan had come into existence in 1921, as a result of the dismemberment of the Ottoman Empire, it inherited most of the army with which the Ameer Faisal had taken Damascus in 1918. This force, though only some fifteen hundred strong, included small units of artillery and signals. As the only Arab army to fight in the First World War, it was called the Arab Army. When the French drove Faisal from Damascus, the remnants of this army rallied round his brother, the Ameer Abdulla. However, the British government, not always conspicuous for its sense of humour, declared that 1,500 men could not be called an army, and dubbed it the Arab Legion.

Colonel F.G. Peake, who had been with Faisal and Lawrence, was given command. Unfortunately for the Arab Legion, Lord Plumer was made High Commissioner for Palestine and Trans-Jordan. (He was a field marshal and had commanded the Second British Army in France and Belgium in the First World War, my father being the Chief Engineer on his staff.)

Peake with his little army had been engaged in a series of operations in Trans-Jordan against rebellious tribes whom the Turks had never been able to control, and was successfully establishing law and order. At this point, however, Lord Plumer, the new High Commissioner, came to pay a formal call on the Ameer Abdulla. The Arab Legion was told to supply a guard of honour, and a number of men were hastily shown how to present arms.

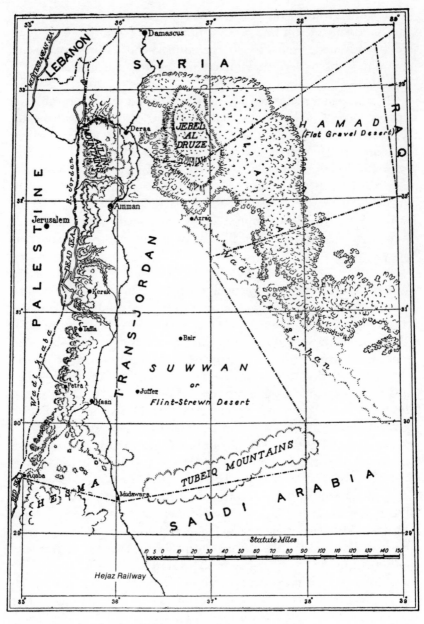

Trans-Jordan in the 1930s. *The railway marked the approximate boundary between cultivation and the desert.*

This they duly did when Lord Plumer arrived. He inspected the guard but, instead of entering the palace as he was expected to do, he remained standing and said, 'March off the guard, please.' This was a manoeuvre for which they had not been prepared, and it threw them into no little confusion.

Plumer reported adversely to London on the Arab Legion as a result and suggested that it be reduced to half its strength, and that a new force be raised, commanded by British officers to defend the frontiers of Jordan for which Britain was responsible under the mandate. It was to be called the Trans-Jordan Frontier Force. The reduced Arab Legion was deprived of its artillery, signals and ancillary units, and was made responsible only for internal security.

Meanwhile, however, Ibn Saud continued his one-sided charges that the Trans-Jordan tribes were raiding his subjects, and the British government ordered that the new Trans-Jordan Frontier Force be sent to the desert with stringent orders to prevent the Trans-Jordan tribes from raiding Saudi Arabia. No mention was made of preventing raids from Saudi Arabia into Jordan, although these had in fact been as numerous as those in the opposite direction.

In the spring of 1930, two Ikhwan raids, one commanded by a cousin of Ibn Saud, had inflicted staggering losses on the Trans-Jordan tribes. Just at this moment, the Trans-Jordan Frontier Force arrived in the desert with orders totally biased against the Jordan tribes. The latter found themselves bullied by their own side and ruined by raids from the other side.

It was to try and introduce some order into this chaos that I had been invited by the Trans-Jordan government to take over control of their desert. I was given the rank of brigadier in the Arab Legion and told to establish law and order in the desert area. I applied for authority to enlist a hundred men, seventy camelmen and thirty machine-gunners in trucks, an exact replica of the desert police which I had raised in Iraq. This of course required money and, while financial sanction was being obtained (for Britain would have to pay), I set out for the desert.

The Huwaitat were in despair, constantly harassed, threatened and pushed around by the Trans-Jordan Frontier Force on the charge that they were raiding Ibn Saud, but regularly raided from the Saudi side – for the Trans-Jordan Frontier Force had no orders to guard against raids from Saudi Arabia.

In November and December 1930, I simply drove round all the camps of the Huwaitat, talking to them. Nomad hospitality had the immense advantage that one could stop at any tent and be immediately invited to dine and spend the night. In almost any other community, contact can only be obtained between the people and their government administration, if the former call at a government office or, in Britain, by letter.

Amongst tented Arabs, it was possible to arrive as an uninvited guest in any family, to dine and sit up half the night talking in a relaxed atmosphere. People sitting together on the ground around a fire, passing round endless cups of coffee, are more genial and open than one man sitting at a desk, while another man stands before him.

The situation was ideal for the application of my motto, *Love and trust and you will be loved and trusted*. The Huwaitat could not but agree with my suggestion that they were on the way to extermination. They could not fight at the same time their own government and the Saudi government with its tribes. But they could see no way out of the dilemma.

They were dubious about the feasibility of my suggestion of supporting their own government, in return for which their own government would protect them. 'Would it?' they asked incredulously. 'It has never done anything but tax, bully and imprison us.' But they had, of course, heard of what had happened in Iraq, for in those days the desert was one world. A bedouin would know all that occurred in the desert five hundred miles away, though he might know nothing of events fifty miles from his camp in an agricultural area.

My first success was due to the arrival of some of my desert police from Iraq who had resigned from there and followed me to Trans-Jordan. These were bedouin among bedouin, and thus could confirm all that I had said about events in Iraq. When my budget was sanctioned, these veterans from Iraq were the first men I enlisted.

The Huwaitat were starving and in rags, but inspired with the bitterest hatred of their government and of the troops. They were convinced that the British were the allies of Ibn Saud in destroying them. In spite of these deeply embedded hatreds and prejudices, I was slowly gaining their friendship and confidence.

Two months had passed in this manner and it was January 1931. I had collected seven or eight bedouin soldiers from here and there, but no Huwaitat. The alienation between them and the Trans-Jordan government and the troops was so intense that I asked the authorities to remove all the armed forces.

After some argument, the government agreed to withdraw the Frontier Force on 1 February 1931 as an experiment, fully antici-pating that chaos would result and the troops would have to return in a hurry.

This gave me the opportunity to invite the Huwaitat to save themselves. We sent out pickets of horse and camelmen to watch the frontier for Saudi raiders. The trucks which I had ordered arrived, and instruction began in Lewis and Vickers guns. Gradually relations became more trustful. By the end of February, I had twenty men, including some Huwaitat.

News came in of the advance of a Saudi force of several thousand men, under one Ibrahim al Neshmi, a retainer of Ibn Saud. I succeeded in persuading the Huwaitat to concentrate and prepare to fight. Their response was half-hearted, for they had not learned entirely to trust me as had the tribes in Iraq. Fortunately Neshmi did not come.

In March 1931, I received information that a raiding party of forty Huwaitat had left for Saudi Arabia. I never employed spies in our own tribes, but already I had so many friends among the Huwaitat that I always knew what was happening.

This question of spies was one of some interest, for everyone in the Arab countries believed that the government had thousands of spies. At first, men would say to me, by way of flattery, 'We know that you have hundreds of spies.' I do not think that I ever employed a spy in Trans-Jordan. In Iraq, I had sent spies to watch the Ikhwan for raids, but I never spied on our own tribes in Iraq, for they always told me everything.

Upon hearing that a raiding party of Huwaitat had set out, I loaded some fifteen of my newly enlisted men in trucks. We went to the camp from which the raiders had left, and took all their camels. There was no resistance. Three weeks later, when the raiders returned, they found that all their own herds had gone.

There was nothing they could do but come to me. We had a good talk and they promised not to do it again, whereupon I gave them back their herds, and the incident was closed. If the regular govern-ment had received news of raiders, they would have posted the

names of the offenders as wanted by the police, who would rarely –
if ever – find them. But if one of them did happen to be arrested, he
would be sentenced to a long term of imprisonment. As often as
not, such a man whose whole life had been spent in the open air
would die in prison, probably of turberculosis against which
bedouins seemed to possess no resistance.

There followed one or two more incidents of small raids setting
out, one of them against the tribes south of Beersheba in Palestine.
In each case I received information. I would then at dawn surprise
the camp from which the raiders had set out. The advantage of
arriving at dawn was that the herds of camels would still be couched
in front of the tents. I would post my four machine-gun trucks
overlooking the camp. The elders of the camp would come out and
I would give them the names of the men who had gone out raiding,
and ask for their camels.

There was never any argument, and the camels would be handed
over. When the raiders returned, they would come to see me rather
shamefacedly, would be given back their camels and told not to be
stupid again. Sometimes I retained one or two camels as a fine. This
system put an end not only to raiding but even to stealing between
the Trans-Jordanians themselves.

Raiding ceased within three or four months. During this period,
no shots were ever fired and no tribesmen were ever sent to prison.
The last raid ever to occur on the Trans-Jordan–Saudi frontier was
in July 1932, and came from Saudi Arabia.

I had won over the Huwaitat by pointing out to them that they
could not fight the Saudi and the Trans-Jordan governments simultaneously. The second proposal I made to them was that, instead of
having government troops driving around, it would be better for
them to join my hundred-man Desert Patrol and police their own
deserts. This suggestion took a little longer to sink in but, within a
few weeks, I had recruited the necessary number.

They came from all the tribes; a necessary condition of enlistment
was the renunciation of all tribal prejudice and devotion to the
government service alone. It is impossible to enlist and train any
force in which tribal sentiment is permitted, such, for example, as a
company of Huwaitat, a company of Shammar and a company of
Beni Sakhr.

We dressed our Desert Patrol in their own natural clothing: white cotton trousers and a long white 'nightgown' or *thob*. Above this was a long khaki gown, a wide, red, woollen belt, a mass of ammunition belts and bandoliers, a revolver with a red lanyard and a silver dagger. The headgear was a red-and-white-checkered head-cloth, which has since then (and from us) become a kind of Arab nationalist symbol. Previously, only white headcloths had been worn in Trans-Jordan or Palestine.

A hundred men is the ideal military command. As soon as the number becomes larger, intimate personal touch is lost. We in the Desert Patrol were a real and truly devoted band of brothers. The spirit which bound us together was one of genuine devotion. More-over, we were not all bedouins, for we had truck drivers who were townsmen and two or three wireless operators who were Arab Christians. But no differences of original background were felt in the overpowering sense of comradeship. Of them, I could truly say, like Henry V, 'we few, we happy few, we band of brothers'.

Soon there was an ever-lengthening list of young men waiting to join us. Discipline was well-nigh perfect because it was self-imposed. Punishments were almost unknown. The most dreaded penalty was dismissal. The only offence which I punished heavily by a fine from the man's pay was sleeping when on sentry duty. Constantly bivouacking for the night while patrolling in the desert, the lives of his comrades depended on the vigilance of the sentry. Soon the immense prestige and popularity of the Desert Patrol enabled us to select only the highest possible standard of recruits.

By April 1932, raiding along the Saudi frontier was a thing of the past, and we turned our attention to the north, where some 5,000 square miles of desert were so thickly strewn with lava rocks as to be passable on foot only with difficulty.

The lava fields had been produced, perhaps thousands of years before, by a chain of volcanoes stretching south-eastward from the Jebel al Druze. The lava-strewn hills were inhabited by special nomadic tribes known as Ahl al Jebel, the mountain people. The lava country had been arbitrarily cut in half by the peace-makers after the First World War, doubtless with a blue pencil on a small-scale map.

The mountain tribes spent the summer in the Jebel al Druze in Syria, but the winter on the lava fields in Trans-Jordan. They never camped outside the lava whence, however, they made sudden petty raids on the tribes camped in the open desert. Normally these sorties occurred just before sunset when two or three horsemen would emerge from the lava, dash at a nearby flock of grazing camels, round up three or four, and dash back at full speed to the lava, just as the sun was setting.

One day, I drove across the rolling limestone desert hills up to the edge of the lava, a few miles west of Azraq. I was in my own car, followed by three machine-gun trucks. Stopping on the edge of the lava, I got out of the car, walked round to the front and began rolling away boulders of lava. The men jumped out of their trucks and, without any word of command, began beside me to move the lava rocks. That day we advanced several hundred yards into the sea of lava.

In the next few days we developed a technique. First a look-out was posted on the nearest hillock. Then we all set to work clearing lava rocks, except for one man on each truck, who would remain sitting behind his loaded machine-gun.

We worked for many months all through the summer, penetrating several miles into the lava along our track which was some nine feet wide. During the summer, the tribes moved northwards into French-mandated Syrian territory. They would return in October or November, when they would find us directly in the line of their migration. There may have been 8,000–10,000 of them. I normally had some twenty-five men on patrol with me.

In November it poured with rain. One day, we saw three camel-men approaching. All our men had been carefully instructed what to do. Calling out loudly, 'God give them life! A blessed hour it is to see you!' they unrolled a very damp carpet on the ground, lit a fire of local shrubs and pushed the kettle and the coffeepots into the embers. Soon everyone was chatting happily.

A few days later, one of the shaikhs came to call and was given a cordial reception. Soon the whole situation was transformed. Again no shots were fired and no men sent to prison. In a few months we were on the most cordial terms with the Jebel tribes, many of whom begged to enlist in the Desert Patrol.

Having made firm friends of all the nomadic tribes of Trans-Jordan, one step remained in order to make government control permanent. This was to build a fort on every permanent well. In winter, it is true, rain pools often formed in valleys here and there on which tribes could camp. But normally all were dependent on the permanent wells – thus, if a fort were built on every well, the government would have a complete grip on the whole area.

Four such forts were erected, at Azraq, Bair, Juffer and Rum. At Mudawara, we occupied an old fort built by the Turks. (Mudawara, where there was a good spring of water, had been a staging post on the old pilgrim route from Damascus to Mecca.)

Our forts were not made to resist artillery, but might conceivably be attacked by a force of several thousand Ikhwan raiders from central Arabia. These men were often fearless and might try and climb the wall on one another's shoulders. We accordingly designed our forts to enclose an open space some twenty yards square, surrounded by walls twelve feet high. At two diagonally opposite corners we built towers two storeys high, with loopholes to shoot in enfilade down the walls.

The basis of our desert control was not force but persuasion and love. In the office of every desert fort, a notice was fixed on the wall: 'Example is stronger than precept, so guide the people by your noble deeds.' I visited all the desert posts at frequent intervals and often collected the men and spoke to them of our duty to the people. These were rough men, brought up to raiding and robbery, but they were simple. I have often seen the tears run down their faces as I spoke to them of our duty to the nation.

Such methods might not have been so successful in a more sophisticated society. How right was the author of the first psalm when he wrote: 'Blessed is the man . . . that sitteth not in the seat of the scornful.' Sarcasm and mockery are always the weapons used against those who try to give service to others. These men were not sufficiently intellectual to have learned to sneer.

Having thus established a firm but affectionate control over all our tribes, I accompanied a Jordan delegation to negotiate a Bon Voisinage Treaty with Ibn Saud in Jidda. As already described, I had previously been to Jidda on deputation from Iraq. On both occasions Sir Gilbert Clayton represented the British government.

The first time, Ibn Saud accommodated us at a house called Kandara outside the town. In the evenings, he would come out to visit us, sit cross-legged on the sofa, and chat away amicably on many subjects. But when I returned with the Trans-Jordan delegation three years later, everything was changed. Ibn Saud no longer dropped in on us for an informal chat. We received an official notification that His Majesty would receive us at a certain hour. We were escorted into his presence by officers in European uniforms, and were merely permitted to shake hands and then escorted out again.

This attempt to imitate the protocol of Western nations seemed to me regrettable. Abdul Aziz ibn Saud was a man of tremendous personality who would have dominated every gathering in any nation in the world. He was a frank and simple-minded bedouin, who spoke the truth without fear or favour. But his Egyptian and Syrian advisers had persuaded him that this was not the way to deal with Europeans. As a result, Ibn Saud became inaccessible and the discussions dragged on endlessly with the lawyers, who were completely ignorant of raiding and of desert life.

Ibn Saud claimed, not without justification, to be the natural ruler of all the bedouins in Arabia, but his representatives had no experience of them at all. More than once I found myself obliged to explain bedouin customs and expressions to them. However, in the end a treaty was signed. But the cessation of raiding was not due to the lawyers' treaty, but to the fact that the desert was now under control.

It was my pride and joy that this new peace and security had been established without the firing of a single shot or the arrest or imprisonment of a single man.

'Win hearts,' said Blaise Pascal, 'for men are more important than affairs.' His epigram exactly represented the method we employed in the deserts of both Iraq and Trans-Jordan.

A few years ago, an experiment was tried in France, under which a number of priests were sent to work in various industrial factories in order to establish a closer relationship between the workers and the church. 'Do not try to convert them,' the priest-workers were told. 'Just love them.' This was sound advice. Conversion as an intellectual process often breeds resentment. 'What you believe is wrong, what I believe is right,' only rouses resentment; but love is the solvent of all dislikes. One thousand and seven hundred years ago, Tertullian was able to write, 'See how these Christians love one another' – and everyone else too.

Prior to the formation of the Desert Patrol, a cousin of the Ameer Abdulla, the Ameer Shakir, had been chairman of the so-called Bedouin Control Board. However, as the Board had no forces in the desert, it was unable to control anyone. From the date of the formation of the Desert Patrol, the Ameer Shakir became one of my closest friends and supporters. He was a true embodiment of the phrase, 'Nature's gentleman', always frank, friendly, cheerful and courteous. His son, the Ameer Zeid ibn Shakir, is today the Commander of the Jordan Armed Forces.

11
A Confusion of Courtships

When I was a boy, children were not 'taught' about sex. The only incident I can remember occurred when I was about sixteen, when my father once said to me, 'Don't chase after women, old boy. If you do so, you will regret it bitterly when you ultimately meet the woman you want to marry. Some men can think of nothing else, but I have not been greatly tempted in that way, and I hope you will not be.' That was all the 'sex education' I ever received.

When I was at school, horses were my ruling passion. On my school holidays, I spent nearly all my time riding. At first I did so on my own pony, but later my father allowed me to exercise his horse also. This occupied me practically all day long and also gave me a passionate devotion to the countryside.

Boys and girls in those days were, of course, educated at different schools, and I never even met, much less became friendly with, a girl.

In 1914, when I left Cheltenham for the Royal Military Academy at Woolwich, and subsequently at the Royal Engineers Depot at Chatham, we were all dedicated, body and soul, to the great adventure of 'the war that was to end war'. Even a year at Chatham after the war (when my father and mother rented a house for a year at Buxted in Sussex) failed to inspire in me any interest in women.

In June 1920, I volunteered for service in Iraq and spent ten years in that country, living entirely in tribal areas. Throughout this whole period of intense out-of-doors activity, women never entered into my head.

In 1925, I rode across the Syrian desert on a camel from Ramadi on the Euphrates to Amman in Trans-Jordan, where I sold the camel and went on by taxi to Jerusalem. I called on the High Commissioner, Sir John Chancellor, who knew my father. In government house, I came across a beautiful lady, clad in diaphanous clothing, lounging gracefully on a sofa.

When the conversation turned to my journey across the desert on a camel, she exclaimed to my horror, 'Oh, I'd love to come with you across the desert.' It was Rosita Forbes, then a famous traveller and authoress. I stammered my excuses and shortly afterwards took my leave.

I was thirty-three years old when I left Iraq and was charged with the pacification of the deserts of Trans-Jordan. It was within the next two years that I first remember feeling a longing for a home and a companion.

I remember one evening sitting by the embers of a camp fire in the southern deserts of Jordan, talking to Annad ibn Jazi, the brother of the principal shaikh of the Huwaitat. He was congratulating me on my success in winning over the loyalty of the tribe, when suddenly I burst out with the complaint: 'All this is nothing. What I really want is a wife, and children and a home such as you have.'

During my first five years in Iraq, I never took leave to England. But after my move to Jordan, I began to take leave home every two years. My parents were growing old and, perhaps for the first time, I began to feel an obligation to them.

My father wrote to me:

. . . poor little Mum is worrying badly over her eyes. Who could blame her? It's just heartbreaking, there's darkness ahead. There must be something to be done, but no one will tell one. I am trying to read aloud to her now, but I am very bad at it . . . My letters seem to be becoming one long grouse. I hope they don't sound to you like that. Ever your loving

Dad

Since then, having become a parent and a grandparent, I have often thought of this youthful indifference as one of life's little tragedies. The young grow strong and self-reliant and are engrossed in their own world. The old remember what it was like to be young, but it is impossible for the young to realize what it is like to be old.

From Trans-Jordan I was entitled to two months' home leave every two years. But my mother loved to spend the early summer in Europe, principally in Italy and Austria, and always wanted me to share her joy there. This indeed I did, revelling in both the history and the scenery. But the result was that on every leave I only had one month in England, and I was now beginning to yearn for a life companion and a home.

It so happened that the best friends and neighbours of my parents had a marriageable daughter, a few years younger than myself. The parents of both families would have been delighted if we had made a match. I hired a car for my month in England and we drove together for hours through the countryside. We were blissfully happy together, talking endlessly of every subject under the sun. If, for any reason, one day we could not go out, we had to exchange letters.

The few days of leave soon came to an end, and I asked her to marry me, but she replied that she could not. No sooner had I returned to Trans-Jordan than I received from her a letter: 'Oh Jack! I am so sorry! And now you have gone away, what shall I do?'

When, two years later, I again came to England, she had married someone else. But, only a few hundred yards from my parents' house, there lived a retired colonel and his wife, who also had a daughter of the right age. Once again I had only a month in England, but I hired a car and soon made friends with this girl. The whole family were deeply religious, including their daughter. Once again we went for long drives in my car and were blissfully happy. Once again, shortly before the end of my leave, I asked her to marry me but was refused.

I returned to Trans-Jordan in perplexity and despair. I could not understand what was wrong. In both cases, we had gone out driving in the car for hours on end and had been infinitely happy. Neither girl was frivolous or flirtatious.

Looking back now on these frustrations and heartaches, I can only conclude that my failures were due to my inability to perform any physical endearments. This was partly due to my innocence and my lack of experience. But not entirely so – I also felt that physical familiarities before marriage were sinful.

In 1936, I again spent my biennial month in England. I have already explained that my mother was devoted to European travel, and spoke and read several languages. It so happened that, in 1936, she advertised in a local paper for someone to come and talk German to her. My future wife, who had learned German at home from a *fräulein*, answered the advertisement.

As usual, I hired a car for my month in England and took out my mother and Rosemary Forbes, her new German conversationalist. Soon my mother decided to stay at home, and the two of us became more intimate. One new factor on these occasions, as I remember, was that I used to sing. Of course I had no voice and did not know one note from another – when I was at school, boys were not taught music, which was regarded as a purely female accomplishment.

My raucous voice, however, did not deter me and I would often go through my repertoire for the benefit of my new friend. A popular song of the time was 'My Little Grey Home in the West'. I did not hesitate to embark on Italian opera, such as *'A che la morte . . .'*, 'Ah me, how death delays, For one who longs to die'. Or 'Home to Our Mountains' from *Il Trovatore*.

But perhaps my favourite performance was 'My Old Shako'.

> I mind the time, my old shako,
> When first you graced my head,
> What time I wore a sabretache,
> My spurs and jacket red.
> I mind a dainty little maid,
> Whose cheeks were all aglow,
> When first I stole a kiss from her,
> Beneath my old shako.
> Hey ho! Many a year ago,
> We roamed the world together
> You and I, my old shako.
> And we didn't care a button if the odds were on the foe,
> Ten, twenty, thirty, forty, fifty years ago!

Once again, my brief stay in England was too short, but we promised to write to each other.

Early in 1938, my father had a heart attack. I flew to England and we had a specialist down from London. I accompanied my father in the ambulance which took him to a nursing home in London, but then I was obliged to fly back to Jordan.

A few weeks later, he suffered a stroke and died in the nursing home. I flew home again in time for his funeral. He was buried beside his mother in the churchyard of the parish church at Cowfold in Sussex where he had lived with his mother as a boy, when they returned from India following the death of his father just after the Indian Mutiny.

I gave here an extract from the obituary published on the occasion of his death in the Royal Engineers *Journal*.

MAJOR-GENERAL SIR FREDERIC GLUBB, K.C.M.G., C.B., D.S.O., who died in London on 31st July last, meant more to his generation than his career, distinguished though it was, is apt at first sight to suggest; much more than is realised, nineteen years after his retirement, by the Corps of to-day. It is no disparagement of his contemporaries to say that in the latter stages of the Great War, and particularly after Messines, his reputation as a military engineer stood second to none in the Army, and it was on account only of his age, as he was informed by the Commander-in-Chief, that he was not chosen to succeed General Rice as Engineer-in-Chief on the Western Front.

It was, however, the man himself, even more than his experience and ability, that gave him the implicit trust of his superiors, the affection and admiration of all who came in contact with him and a position something akin to that of the 'elder statesman' in the Corps in France. With a great heart in a small body and the dignity of complete simplicity, he combined high principles with a mellow sympathy and a quiet humour which endeared him to the younger generation, whilst exacting from them the last ounce that they were able to give. He had that great gift for a commander that he could inspire wholesome respect together with affection. He was not a man with whom either chances or liberties were taken and it is not possible to improve on what his liaison officer in Italy, Don Giulio Caetani [afterwards Italian Minister in Washington] said of him, after a comparatively short acquaintance – 'I shall be sorry to leave the General – he is a man.'

It is a difficult task to show a man to those who have not known him, and those who have not known Tony Glubb have missed a refreshing memory of quiet charm and intense under-lying virility. Those who have known him, know how much they owe to contact with the strength, wisdom and straight-forwardness of his personality. In his simple, self-effacing way he was a great man.

The many private letters of condolence received by my mother all bore witness to the writers' opinions that he had been the embodiment of an English gentleman.

Young people rarely appreciate the public careers of their fathers. To them his task in life is just to be dad. It was only the flood of glowing testimonials received after his death which made me realize how great a man he was.

My sister undertook to sell up our house in Pembury and I prepared to take my widowed mother back with me to Trans-Jordan. But I was then faced with the crisis in my relationship with Rosemary Forbes. As our home in England was being sold, it was doubtful whether I should ever return.

We had been corresponding for two years and obviously a decision was necessary. I could not arrange a formal wedding and reception two days after my father's funeral. We went round to the Registry Office in Tunbridge Wells, and were married on 20 August 1938. The next day I took my mother and we returned by sea from Marseilles to Beirut and thence up to Amman.

Three months later, my wife and her mother flew out to Beirut, and we were married again in All Saints, the little Anglican church on the seashore. The only congregation consisted of our two mothers. We spent a two-day honeymoon in a hotel in Beirut, accompanied by both our mothers, and then returned to Amman.

Thus at last I found my life's companion. In many ways, I was not worthy of her, and I often neglected her, because I worked so hard. We have suffered many vicissitudes together, but she has supported me through them all. We have now been married for forty-four years and have never had a quarrel. I can only thank God for His guidance, which has led me through endless dangers to a peaceful old age, surrounded by children and grandchildren. So many dangers and anxieties shared in common have drawn us closer and closer together, far more so than did the first enthusiasms of youth.

A few years ago, I heard a young man on television express the opinion that the greatest step forward achieved in recent times was the liberation of teenage girls from parental authority.

The proof of the pudding is in the eating. Until I returned to England in 1956, after thirty-six years in the Middle East, I had never known any person who had been divorced. Today, a large proportion of the marriages which take place in England result in divorce. The worst of this situation is that the two or three years of sexual thrills which follow young marriages are sufficient to produce two children. Then the excitement subsides and the young couple decide to obtain a divorce. The family breaks up and the children are deprived of the happiness and the security of a home.

I have devoted a great deal of time to the study of the rise and fall of past civilizations, and was intensely interested to discover that most national periods of decadence have been marked by increasing ease of divorce and sexual laxity.

The collapse of the Roman republic in civil war and murder was accompanied by increasing ease of divorce and the break-up of the Roman family. When Augustus set himself to restore the greatness of Rome, he decided that one of the first steps necessary was the restoration of the discipline and the security of the Roman family, in pursuance of which object he even passed a law making adultery a criminal offence.

I love young people, and am sorry to express views which may arouse their resentment, but I have not the slightest doubt that young girls do need protection. They constitute the greatest treasures of our race and it is on them that the whole future of our people depends, for it is mothers who form the characters of their children.

Unfortunately, in the last twenty-five years, thanks to the public media and the general decline in the morals of the nation, 'love' has come to be regarded more and more as a physical attraction, rather than as a spiritual and mental sympathy between kindred souls. If 'falling in love' means experiencing only a physical attraction, then within a few years' time the physical attraction will fade, and the couple will separate.

The ideal and unalloyed success of our marriage was largely due to

Rosemary's sweetness and patience, for in Amman I tried her profoundly. My negligence of her and of my family was due entirely to my work.

We woke at 5 a.m., and at about 6.30 a.m. I set off for the office. Sometimes I had a horse brought to the house and enjoyed a brief canter round the hills before dismounting at Arab Legion Headquarters. From then until 1 p.m., I was occupied with correspondence, discussions, visitors, and possible visits to the palace or to members of the cabinet.

Office hours ended at 1 p.m., but by this time a crowd of visitors and petitioners had collected. These were the poor, the illiterate, the tribesmen, who had never gained admittance to other government offices in the capital.

Under the traditional forms of Arab rule, every post of authority is occupied by one man (never by a committee, a chamber or a parliament) . . . but that man is accessible to everybody without exception.

The imitation of Europe, first by the Turks before the First World War, then after the War by the mandatory powers, destroyed this system. Cabinet ministers and officials shut themselves up in offices and were no longer accessible to the public, especially to the poor. The old forms of one-man authority and accessibility were, however, still in use in Saudi Arabia, a few miles away.

Appreciating the fact that these changes had deprived the poor and illiterate of the traditional forms of justice which they understood, I tried to make myself accessible after office hours to the poor and the ignorant.

From 1 p.m. until 4 p.m., I received visits from these humble folk, after official hours. Perhaps between 4 p.m. and 5 p.m. I went home to lunch. But thereupon those petitioners who had still not gained admission would follow me home, where they sat down on a bare piece of the hillside behind my house.

After snatching a hasty lunch, at about 4.30 p.m. I began to deal with these cases. I did not admit them to the house, but an orderly went backwards and forwards between us. At about 8 p.m., Rosemary would call from the next room, 'Couldn't we have supper soon?' and I would tell the orderly that that was enough. He would call to the remaining visitors: 'Tomorrow! Tomorrow, if God wills!' and we would at last be able to eat our supper together.

I did not intend by these actions to establish a system of my own or, even tacitly, to criticize others. It had all just happened that way. The Trans-Jordan government had entrusted me with the task of establishing law and order in the desert. This I accomplished by living with the tribes and persuading them to stop raiding.

But the tribes had never before known personally any senior official. They thus regarded me as a friend at court and would come to consult me on all their problems.

Anybody who went shopping in the streets of Amman, would find him- or herself surrounded by a clamouring group of small boys, each carrying a basket. The shopper would engage one of these who would trot round the shops with him, carrying his purchases, and would finally accompany him home with his shopping in his basket. Many of these little boys came from distant villages, and would sleep out at night in the streets or alleyways.

Rosemary was moved with compassion for these children and decided to take action. She rented a tiny house close to our own and engaged an old man to teach them to read and write. She issued them with pencils and paper, clothing and occasional meals, paid them an allowance instead of what they had earned with their baskets and generally acted the fairy godmother.

At first, the boys were highly suspicious and gave false names and fictitious locations of their homes so that, if they found it necessary, they could vanish without trace. Gradually, however, they came to trust her and began to tell her their real names. One or two of them came now and again and worked in our house.

Occasionally we were reminded that boys will be boys. One of them, named Mifleh, got into my car which was standing in front of the house, and took off the handbrake. As the house was on the side of a hill, the car charged down the road and crashed into a wall.

The most successful of the basket boy school pupils was a boy called Ata, who came from a distant country village. He was so intelligent that we gave him a full education, and he eventually went to Sandhurst and became an officer in the Jordan army.

Another, called Abdul Aziz, was a cripple from polio. He proved to be remarkably intelligent and rapidly learned to read and write. Rosemary then gave him enough money to open a shop in his home town of Kerak, where he became self-supporting.

116

In the uniform of the Arab Legion

My father, Major General Sir F.M. Glubb

My mother, Lady F.L. Glubb

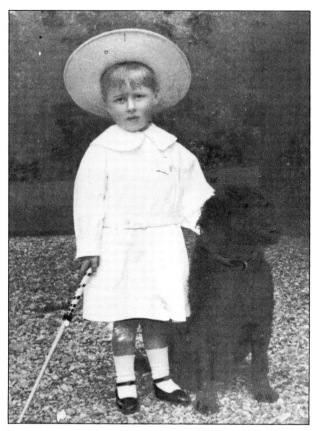

Myself aged three with sword and charger

With my pony Jumbo in Salisbury, 1913

My wife Rosemary (née Forbes) with
our eldest son in Amman, 1953

In the main square of Amman on the
occasion of the Muslim Feast Day

With King Abdulla of Jordan, 1946

In Arab Legion uniform in London, 1946

Outside the desert fort at Rum in Jordan

Saturday Review

FEBRUARY 22, 1958 / 25¢

RECORDINGS

Sir John Bagot Glubb ("Glubb Pasha"), author of "Soldier with the Arabs."
(See page 17)

Presenting the prizes at an English school sports day

Rosemary

In retirement at Mayfield, Sussex, 1980

12
War and Peace

Before embarking on the story of my courtship and marriage, I gave an account of the cessation of desert raiding in Trans-Jordan in 1932.

During our meetings in Jidda it had been agreed that the Saudi and Trans-Jordan governments would appoint frontier inspectors, who could deal with one another directly and dispose of any minor incidents which might arise. I was appointed by the Trans-Jordan government as their frontier inspector, while the Saudis nominated Abdul Aziz ibn Zaid, a professional government servant, but not a man in high social standing. The choice was apparently made because Ibn Saud was in doubt as to what kind of reception his representative would receive.

The British government, always anxious to promote peace in the Middle East, had attempted to mediate between Ibn Saud and Trans-Jordan to settle their mutual claims for loot taken in raids, but had failed to persuade them to agree. The lists were then referred to Ibn Zaid and myself.

At our first meeting, the Saudi representative produced his list of claims. Happily, I was inspired to say, 'I do not know how we can ever judge all these demands, but as I know Your Excellency to be a man of honour, I will accept any claims which you decide are just.' His manner changed instantly, and he replied that he could not make unilateral decisions, but that he would accept whatever I decided. In a few minutes, we were both urging each other to make a unilateral settlement. The ice was broken, we both agreed to abandon all claims, and parted warm friends.

Ibn Saud was presumably reassured by my reception of Ibn Zaid, as he later nominated the Ameer Abdulla al Sudairi, a cousin of his on his mother's side. We became close personal friends, and held many frontier meetings, until he was promoted to be governor of Medina, when he was succeeded by the Ameer Abdul Aziz, another Sudairi. Seeing the representatives of the two governments so friendly and cordial, the tribes mingled peacefully and even thefts became out of the question.

The years 1932 to 1936 passed peacefully, but not idly. One of the matters which distressed me was tribal indebtedness. Every farmer or stock-breeder sometimes had a bad year, as the rainfall was precarious. In former times, the tribesmen would go to the town merchants and borrow money, to be repaid in kind when times were better. Tribesmen and merchants trusted one another and no written documents were exchanged. The system worked perfectly.

Then law-courts and laws were introduced, in accordance with the universal passion to imitate the West. The merchants soon realized the potentialities of the law. In future when a farmer or sheep-breeder sought a loan, the merchant drew up a legal contract, on which the tribesman put his thumb-impression, for none of them could write.

Next year, the sheep-owner or farmer received a summons to court. A lawyer then produced a document with his thumb-impression, in which it appeared that he had unwittingly mortgaged his farm to the money-lender, who had now decided to foreclose on the mortgage and to take over the farm, or to seize the shepherd's flock of sheep. I was deeply distressed that the establishment of a Ministry of Justice should have resulted only in so much injustice and oppression.

The only cure, it seemed to me, was to teach the tribes to read and write, and I tried to open schools in the desert. No government funds were available, and it was difficult to set up schools for nomadic children whose parents were constantly on the move.

I succeeded also in obtaining a British doctor to visit nomadic tribes, who had previously had no medical attention.

In 1933, I was thirty-six, and began to think I was growing old. For the first time in my life I commenced to consider money and a pension for my old age. I had not even asked the Jordan government for a contract when I entered their service, or for a pension or gratuity on retirement.

I accordingly wrote to the British government and asked if there was any way by which I could earn a pension. They replied that there were no pensionable British appointments in Trans-Jordan. The best they could do would be to appoint me as an Assistant District Commissioner in the Palestine Government on Grade G. I had no idea what were the duties of an Assistant District Commissioner Grade G, but it seemed rather a long way down the alphabet. The salary was £300 a year, rising by annual increments of £25 to £800 a year – a process which would require twenty years. In addition there was a cost-of-living allowance of £30 a year.

The salary, however, was unimportant because, no sooner was I gazetted to the Palestine government, than I was immediately seconded for duty in Trans-Jordan. The last paragraph of my letter of appointment specified that my services would be pensionable in accordance with the Palestine Pensions Ordinance, 1925. This of course was the object of the whole manoeuvre. The letter was signed by the Chief Secretary to the Government of Palestine, under date of 28 April 1934.

By this means, although I had nothing to do with Palestine, I would gradually qualify for pension as an Assistant District Commissioner Grade G. I accepted this kind offer with pleasure.

To anticipate events, I continued to earn this pension until 1948 when the Palestine government ceased to exist. By that time I had qualified for a pension as an Assistant District Commissioner Grade G, with fourteen years' service. I still enjoy this pension, the only pension I have ever received from the British or any other government.

In 1936, the Arabs of Palestine tried to stage a rebellion against the immigration of European Jews, who took over their land. Before the First World War, Palestine and Lebanon were both in the Ottoman Empire, and many rich families owned land in Palestine but lived in their town houses in Beirut. After the war, Palestine and Lebanon became different countries, and the Beirut landowners found it difficult to deal with both the Lebanese and the Palestine governments. They therefore became largely absentee landlords and were pleased to sell their lands in Palestine to the Zionists, who then evicted the Arab cultivators and replaced them by Jews.

The Palestinians were without organization and, by 1938, their attempts at rebellion were petering out. Their leaders, and those evicted from their lands, took refuge in Syria. From Damascus, they planned to raise a rebellion in Trans-Jordan, in the hope that the British troops in Palestine would then be sent to suppress it, enabling rebellion to be revived west of the Jordan. Gangs of Palestinians from Syria attempted to enter Trans-Jordan to raise revolt.

In view of this threat, the Arab Legion was increased by two squadrons of horsed cavalry and by 350 bedouin soldiers in trucks mounting machine-guns. This unit received the title of the Desert Mechanized Force. In March 1939, guerrilla gangs from Syria moved into the mountains of Ajlun – the biblical Gilead.

The success of guerrillas depends largely on the sympathy and the help which they receive from the civil population. The Trans-Jordanians, while they sympathized with the evicted Palestinians, were eminently satisfied with their own government, and refused to rebel. We fought a number of skirmishes with Palestine guerrillas, but by April 1939 the Palestine gangs had been driven out and their attempts to raise rebellion in Trans-Jordan were abandoned.

The Arab Legion discovered that the way to deal with guerrilla gangs was to keep them on the move, day and night. The guerrillas were prepared to skirmish during the day, to cut telephone wires or block roads, but at night they liked to descend on a village, where they demanded food and hospitality. By following them by day and night and never allowing them to sleep or rest, the Arab Legion wore them out.

By contrast, British troops in Palestine would engage a gang by day, but at sunset they would return to their camps to eat and sleep while the gang did the same in an Arab village. It is true, however, that the principal difference was that in Palestine the villagers supported the gangs, whereas in Trans-Jordan the villagers were on the side of the government.

While these troubles were going on, Colonel F.G. Peake, the commander of the Arab Legion, retired from government service and left for England. On 21 March 1939, I replaced him as the commander of the Trans-Jordan armed forces, which included the police. He had originally raised the Arab Legion in 1921 and had commanded it for seventeen years. When I took over, Hitler was already threatening Poland. In Amman, we practised air-raid precautions.

When the Second World War commenced in August 1939, Britain and France agreed on their strategy in the Middle East. Britain was to maintain a garrison in Egypt, while France retained a large army in Syria. The Ameer Abdulla cabled the British government, placing all the resources of his country at the disposal of the Allies. The British authorities, however, thanked His Highness, but replied that his help would not be needed, as the war would be fought out in Europe . . . a remarkable example of government prescience. Not to be deterred, however, Trans-Jordan declared war on Germany!

It was impossible to obtain additional vehicles or weapons from Britain, but I cabled direct to the Ford Company in Detroit to ship 300 Ford trucks, which arrived safely. A few of these we made into improvised armoured cars. No armour-plate steel was available, but we used two sheets of mild steel with an intervening sheet of plywood.

On 19 October 1939, our first son was born to Rosemary and me in Amman.

Then came the disasters of the spring of 1940: the fall of Norway, Holland, Belgium and France. Precisely at the height of all these disasters, Rosemary was lying desperately ill in the Italian mission hospital in Amman – a time indeed of intense anxiety and heartache in both personal and public affairs.

With the fall of France, an Italo–German Commission arrived to take over the government of Syria and Lebanon. The large French army in Syria was transformed overnight into an enemy. Then one morning, Mr (later Sir) Anthony Eden and General Wavell, Commander-in-Chief in the Middle East, landed in Amman and saw the Ameer Abdulla. They told us that the Italians were advancing on Egypt from the west, and that the enemy controlled the large French army in Syria. In this situation, the British army was totally outnumbered. Could we raise any more men?

I paraded the 350 men of the Desert Mechanized Force for them to see. They immediately asked for its numbers to be doubled and formed into a Desert Mechanized Regiment. They also asked for an Arab Legion static infantry company to guard an important aerodrome in Palestine. Britain seemed very far away, with Italy, Vichy France and Germany lying between her and us.

Then in April 1941, a *coup d'état* took place in Baghdad. Four Iraqi generals seized power, declared war on Britain and besieged the R.A.F. cantonment at Habbaniya on the Euphrates. The young King Faisal II of Iraq and the Regent, the Ameer Abdulillah, arrived as fugitives in Amman.

Rasheed Ali, a politician whom I had known as Minister of the Interior when I was in Iraq, became Prime Minister in Baghdad. The Germans were expected in Iraq at any moment. I was asked to see the G.O.C. in Jerusalem, General Sir Henry Wilson, commonly called Jumbo. 'More trouble, I am afraid,' said Jumbo, smiling from ear to ear as I entered his office. A column was being scraped together in Palestine to cross the desert to Baghdad. An Indian division was landing at Basra under General Slim.

I was the commander of all the armed forces of Jordan, whether police or military, and thus my place was perhaps at my headquarters in Amman, but when any part of the legion was on active service I could not resist the temptation to accompany it and leave my second-in-command in the office.

Our column was to consist of the Arab Legion Mechanized Regiment, the Household Cavalry transported in improvised trucks (leaving their black horses in Palestine), a battalion of the Essex Regiment, a battery of field artillery and an R.A.S.C. company of 200 three-ton trucks, laden with water, petrol and rations, not only for our column but for the besieged garrison of Habbaniya.

The column, called Habforce, was commanded by Major-General George Clark. From Rutbah a flying column was sent ahead commanded by Brigadier Kingstone, consisting of the Household Cavalry Regiment, two companies of the Essex Regiment, one battery of field artillery, and the Arab Legion Mechanized Regiment.

Brigadier Kingstone regarded these queer-looking Arab soldiers with some suspicion and welcomed my suggestion that we go on well ahead of his column.

On the evening of 13 May 1941, the brigadier called a conference. We were only a few miles from Habbaniya, which the British proposed to relieve the next day. He suggested that the Arab Legion go scouting somewhere else – he obviously did not want us to obstruct his operations. We accordingly moved to some waterholes to the south to get out of his way. At about three o'clock in the afternoon we returned, imagining that the force must by now have entered Habbaniya; but we discovered the whole column back in the bivouac of the night before, in a state of consternation. All their trucks had stuck in the sand, and there were ominous murmurs that their water supply was running out.

The surface of the desert varies enormously in texture and it is fatal to try and travel in a straight line on a compass bearing, as regular soldiers are apt to do. We offered to guide the column into Habbaniya, which we successfully did the next day, no vehicles at all sticking in the sand. During the day we were attacked by three German Messerschmitt fighters from Syria. Two men of the Arab Legion were killed and their truck destroyed.

Habbaniya having been relieved, the British moved to Fellujah to advance on Baghdad, but the Iraqis cut the banks of the Euphrates and flooded the whole area. German Messerschmitt fighters and Heinkel bombers were operating from Mosul. The Germans in Syria were sending trainloads of munitions from Aleppo to Mosul and down to Baghdad. There was also a brigade of Iraqi infantry in Mosul. The first essential seemed to be to cut the road and the railway between Mosul and Baghdad.

We accordingly ferried the Arab Legion across the Euphrates and drove across the desert to the Tigris, south of Samarra, followed by some of the Household Cavalry, who then turned south and attacked Kadhimain, a northern suburb of Baghdad.

We seized the railway station at Meshahida after a little fighting and thus cut off the reinforcements and munitions from Mosul. But German aircraft in Mosul were increasing in numbers and in activity.

At Meshahida we accidentally captured the Governor of Baghdad, Jallal Beg Khalid, who had been on a visit to Samarra. I could not think of these troubles as a war. I had spent ten happy years in Iraq, and loved it. These were just political *coups d'état,* I felt. I found a boat in the palm gardens by the Tigris, and sent Jallal Beg down the river to return to his Baghdad office.

In war, allowance must always be made for the enemy's fears and anxieties. The cutting of the Mosul railway had unnerved the

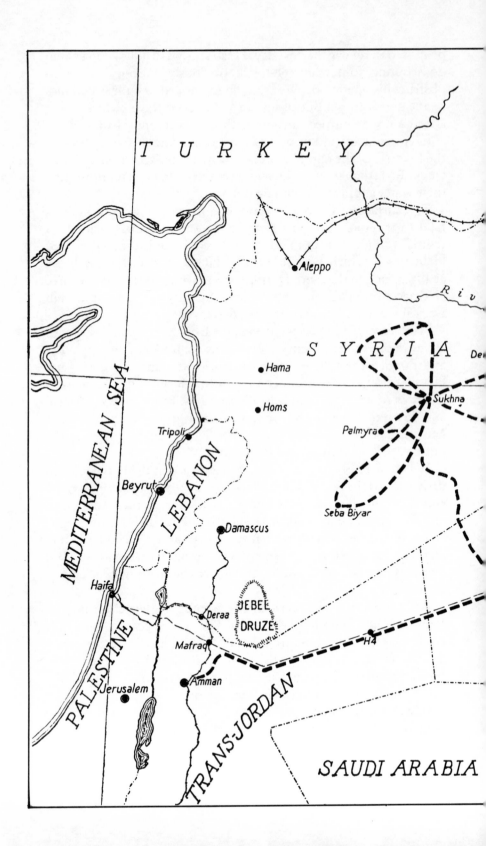

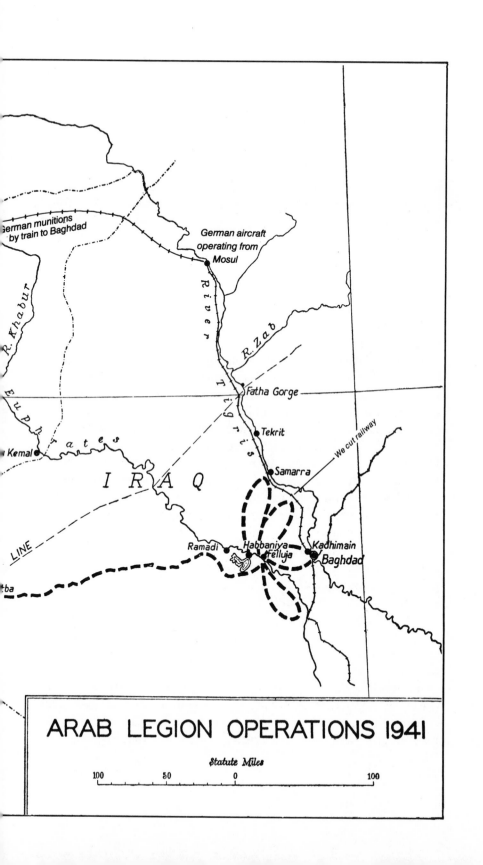

German munitions
by train to Baghdad

German aircraft
operating from
Mosul

R. Khabur

R. Zab

River Tigris

Euphrates

Fatha Gorge

Tekrit

We cut railway

Kemal

Samarra

I R A Q

LINE

Ramadi

Habbaniya
Felluja

Kadhimain

Baghdad

tba

ARAB LEGION OPERATIONS 1941

Statute Miles

100   50   0   100

Rasheed Ali government. The division from India had occupied Basra. Rasheed Ali lost his nerve and escaped to Iran. An Iraqi flag of truce approached the British front line, west of Baghdad, and asked for a cease-fire. I accompanied Major-General Clark and Air Vice-Marshal D'Albiac to meet the Iraqi flag of truce in the grey dawn of 31 March 1941.

The next morning I took my orderly, Saffah, in the uniform of the now almost mythical Desert Force and entered the British Embassy, where 360 British subjects had been confined for a month, cut off from all communication with the outside world. They looked drawn and pale, but crowded round us joyfully. The next morning the Arab Legion took leave of Habforce and drove back across the desert to Amman and home.

Iraq had been saved for the moment but the Germans were expected to fly an airborne division into Syria. General Wavell decided that it would be wiser to occupy Syria before German troops arrived.

British, Australian and Indian troops moved up from Palestine towards Beirut and Damascus. Habforce, our British comrades who had captured Baghdad, were still in Habbaniya. Then orders came for an attack across the desert on Palmyra. From there we were to advance to Homs and cut the communications of the Vichy French who were still holding Damascus. Habforce returned from Habbaniya and we met them in mid-desert with our Desert Mechanized Regiment, and led the column northwards to Palmyra.

This ancient and historical oasis city lies in a flat open plain. The French had strengthened it with concrete pill-boxes, which the field guns in our column were unable to demolish. It was actively defended by the French Foreign Legion who, in fact, proved to be nearly all Germans. The British column settled down to attack the pill-boxes, but meanwhile was attacked by wave upon wave of aircraft. No British fighters were available, and the Vichy French and the German aircraft had things all their own way. To be continually attacked from the air, with no aircraft of your own and no anti-aircraft defence, was an unpleasant experience even in those days.

Meanwhile the Vichy French were still holding the Euphrates north of Albu Kemal and had a garrison at Deir az Zor. Our communications extended for a hundred miles back to H3 on the pipeline and thence for two hundred miles west to Trans-Jordan and two hundred miles east to Habbaniya. Unidentified vehicles were frequently shooting at our supply columns over this area. Some Arabs reported that a force of armoured cars was coming from Aleppo.

On 29 June, therefore, the Arab Legion occupied Sukhna, to cover the flank of Habforce against the French from Aleppo to Deir az Zor. We carried out a reconnaissance sweep northwards towards Aleppo, but saw nothing.

At about half-past seven on the morning of 1 July 1941, a column of vehicles was seen approaching from the east. I was standing in our position on a gravelly ridge with some thirty men and our three (home-made) armoured cars. The rest of our men had moved into a little valley behind our right, where there was firewood, to make tea and breakfast.

About 500 yards from us, the column halted and the enemy infantry dismounted from their vehicles and lay down. This was a fatal mistake. We always fought from our vehicles. A man on foot with a rifle in open desert is helpless. I told our armoured cars and our thirty infantry to hold the ridge and dashed off myself to collect our machine-gun trucks, proposing to bring them round the enemy's flank and surround them.

Our thirty infantry and three armoured cars were, however, too impatient to wait and, dashing forward, overran the enemy's infantry. When I appeared with the trucks behind the enemy's flank, their vehicles were already in full flight. In a sixty-miles-an-hour charge, we overtook and rounded up all their vehicles. The unit was the 2nd Light Desert Company from Deir az Zor. We captured three French officers, eighty Syrian other ranks, six armoured cars and twelve machine-guns. Thereafter there were no more raids on our communications.

Two days later, Palmyra surrendered. On 11 July 1941, the Vichy French government in Syria surrendered, and the Germans flew back to Europe.

While the Vichy French had been fighting against us, a force of Gaullist French had been fighting up to Damascus with the British. When the Vichy French surrendered, the Gaullist French took over control of Syria. Most of the Vichy French joined the Gaullists, but a few returned to France.

During the course of these operations, an extraordinary spirit of comradeship had grown up between the men of the British army and the Arab Legion. In the early stages of the attack on Palmyra, a small patrol of the Arab Legion, consisting of some six men, had been taken prisoner by the French and were sent to the rear as prisoners of war.

The French had two prisoner-of-war cages, one for Europeans and the other for Arab prisoners. When, however, the British other ranks discovered that some men of the Arab Legion were confined in a different cage, they went on strike in protest and refused to eat until their Arab Legion comrades were moved into the same cage as the British prisoners.

Throughout the whole war, other ranks of the Arab Legion were always welcome in British canteens and cafeterias where they sat at the same tables as the British soldiers, though they never drank alcohol.

Meanwhile the Nazis had invaded Russia. The Russians were poorly armed, and it became essential to assist them with arms and ammunition. The main route for this assistance was from Haifa to Baghdad and thence up through Persia to the Russian border. The Arab Legion was made responsible for the safety of the line of communications from Haifa to the Persian (Irani) frontier, a distance of some 700 miles – approximately the distance from London to Warsaw.

A few months earlier, the British army had never heard of the Arab Legion. Now the commander-in-chief, General Wavell, asked if the Desert Mechanized Regiment could be expanded to six regiments. At the same time he asked for as many static infantry companies as possible. These were to guard the port of Haifa, allied depots of weapons and ammunition in Palestine and Iraq, and a number of posts on the desert road between Haifa and Baghdad.

This frenzied expansion in wartime, when scarcely any weapons or vehicles were obtainable, kept us all intensely occupied. We offered a desert regiment to operate in the Sahara and turn Rommel's flank in the Western Desert, and sent an advanced party there, which went into action and suffered one officer and two other ranks killed. Then General Montgomery won the battle of Alamein, the front advanced to Tunis and then crossed to Italy.

We were warned that we might be asked to send a mechanized brigade to Greece, but then the Germans evacuated that country.

I flew to G.H.Q. in Cairo to offer the Arab Legion to fight in Italy, but was told that the greater part of British and American aid to Russia was going through the Haifa–Baghdad route. The safety of the Iraq Petroleum Company's pipeline to Haifa was also vital. It was therefore essential to keep enough troops in the Middle East. If the Arab Legion went to Europe, British troops would have to take over from them. It was better to send the British troops to Europe and for the Arab Legion to remain in the Arab countries. This was obviously true and I sadly acquiesced in the fact that the Arab Legion would not gain further laurels in Europe.

Meanwhile Arab Legion infantry companies were scattered far and wide, guarding the main line of communications to Russia and also innumerable depots and dumps, holding many millions of pounds' worth of warlike stores. The task was no sinecure. All over the Middle East, gangs of thieves or terrorists were avid to steal weapons. Most of the men were on guard at night for seven nights a week. Yet by day they were always spotlessly turned out, belts and buckles shining and drilling like the Grenadier Guards.

Throughout the whole war, with Arab Legion units scattered all over the Middle East, not one serious case of misconduct came to light. No other army I have heard of was entirely innocent of cases of drunkenness, rape, robbery or misconduct. Throughout the whole war, not one such incident was reported against a man of the Arab Legion.

During the five hundred years before the birth of Christ, when Judaism spread far and wide over Europe, a class of persons appeared whom the Jews called 'God-Fearers'. These were people captivated by the personal and spiritual aspects of Judaism, but who were unable or unwilling to conform with the complicated dietary rules of the Jews. This attitude interested me.

Religions, like nations, are inclined automatically to regard one another with jealousy and suspicion; but to a great extent, the reasons for their mutual hostility are intellectual, connected with belief in certain alleged facts. I had had some experience of Muslim saints and religious men, and had observed in them many of the qualities which we associated with Christian saints. I had never been tempted to become a Muslim – Christianity laid more emphasis on love – but I found it easy to co-operate with Muslims in our common capacity of God-Fearers.

By this means, the Arab Legion was transformed into an army of God-Fearers, irrespective of creeds or sects. I always referred to our duty towards God, in all my addresses to recruits or to units. This method was far more successful than any appeal to regimental spirit or *esprit de corps* – at any rate with such simple men as the villagers or the nomads of Jordan.

It does not seem to me that any religion, much less any sect, can claim to hold a monopoly of God's favour. Such claims can only owe their origin to the pathetic narrow-mindedness of men.

Judaism owed its origin to Moses, who died some 1,300 years before Christ, who Himself lived less than 2,000 years ago. But the world was not only populated but civilized, living in towns and villages, for many thousands of years before Moses. Are we to imagine that God had no sympathy or affection for His creation before the time of Moses? On the contrary, we are told that God's loving kindness was over all His works.

But perhaps the most astounding proof of man's universal tendency towards God is the fact that, in all ages and countries, his invariable instinct in a crisis is to pray. Man, we are sometimes told, invented God to comfort himself in his worldly troubles. But this explanation is not adequate. Many men, who refuse intellectually to believe in God, instinctively cry out to Him in moments of danger or crisis.

This universal human instinct, common alike to intellectuals and to savages, in all ages and in all countries, can only be explained by the existence of a God towards whom men feel an automatic affinity, and to whom they instinctively call in moments of desperate danger, fear or despair.

On 8 June 1946, a contingent of the Arab Legion took part in the victory march through London. As it swung down the Mall past the royal saluting base, a crescendo of cheers ran through the watching crowds and voices called out, 'Good old Arab Legion,' 'Well done, Arab Legion,' – some old soldiers doubtless who had served beside them on the glaring dusty plains of the Middle East. Few British people remember today that Jordan was the only independent non-Commonwealth country which provided soldiers who fought beside the British army from the beginning to the end of the Second World War.

In February 1946, His Highness the Ameer Abdulla visited England and negotiated a new treaty with Britain, whereby the mandate was ended, and Trans-Jordan became an independent nation. On 25 May 1946, the Legislative Assembly passed a motion changing the constitution from an ameerate to a kingdom. At noon, His Majesty King Abdulla reviewed a ceremonial parade of the Arab Legion on the Amman airfield.

It was a day of immense enthusiasm and happiness. Little did we know what lay ahead of us.

Meanwhile, however, Rosemary and I narrowly escaped a tragedy. She was in bed with an attack of influenza when, at 11 a.m. a time-bomb exploded under the window of our bedroom, which was on the ground floor. The blast blew the glass from the window across the room and covered the wall opposite with fragments. Fortunately she was lying with her back to the window, and her hair was full of splinters of glass. If she had been lying on her other side, she would have received the splinters in her face and might well have been blinded.

The police reported that the time-bomb had been planted during the night by a young man from Damascus who objected to the new Anglo-Jordan Treaty. By the time the bomb exploded he had re-crossed the frontier into Syria.

Although we had no official connection with the Palestine government, we often visited Jerusalem during the years of the mandate. There was something delightful and inspiring about the Holy City. Under the control of an outside Power, all religions mingled there peacefully, all places of worship were respected and each enjoyed the spiritual atmosphere which pervaded the whole area.

With the end of the mandate, the Holy City was once more to be torn apart by fanaticism and bloodshed. Yet the years of peace in Jerusalem still remain in my mind a fragrant memory.

> 'If I forget thee, O Jerusalem,
> Let my right hand forget her cunning.'

13

Judaism – an Historical Digression

About 1250 B.C., a nomadic tribe known as Beni Israil, or the Children of Israel, invaded Canaan, the modern Palestine. Canaan had been a civilized and settled country for many thousands of years, whereas the Israelites were simple, ignorant tribesmen who had been living as shepherds on the eastern side of the Nile Delta.

Where, however, there was no regular imperial army, towns and villages were at a hopeless disadvantage. A nomadic tribe moved as a single unit, with its tents and flocks, and could capture towns and villages one by one, massacring the inhabitants, a process constantly repeated in areas bordering on the desert, in Palestine, Syria or Iraq.

Having thus killed all the people of Jericho and other towns, the Israelites received the submission of the towns and villages along the range of mountains from Hebron to Galilee. At the same time, the Philistines, a people from the Aegean, landed on and conquered the coastal plain, confining the Israelites to the mountains.

As tented nomads, the Israelites did not become villagers or farmers, but merely landlords who collected tribute from the people of the land. To imagine that the people of Canaan after the time of Joshua were all Israelites is erroneous. The latter were nomad warriors who imposed themselves on a comparatively cultured people and obliged them to pay tribute. They divided the country between their tribes, not as landowners but as landlords.

The number of the invading Israelites was about 15,000. They all watered at the well of Bair or Beer. I know this place well and built a fort on it. Some 15,000 souls was an outside estimate of the numbers who could water there (*Numbers* XXI, 16).

I was very familiar with an exactly similar phenomenon in Iraq, where, about the beginning of the seventeenth century A.D., a nomadic tribe from the desert, the Muntifik, conquered a whole province of lower Iraq. For four hundred years the nomads lived in their great tents, taking no part in the life or work of the towns or the cultivators. They constituted a class of warrior overlords who lived on the tribute paid to them by the natives, and were still doing so when I arrived in the area in 1923.

In a similar manner, the Israelites lived in Canaan as warrior landlords, while the people of the land continued their normal avocations as they had been doing for seven thousand years. I do not believe that the Children of Israel were ever the sole inhabitants of Palestine, as is sometimes supposed, or even that they ever constituted a majority.

In 2 *Samuel* VII, 5, there is a delightful passage embodying the proud spirit of nomadism. 'Yahweh speaks. Are you the man to build me a house to live in? I have never stayed in a house from the day I brought the Israelites out of Egypt until today, but have always led a wanderer's life in a tent. In all my journeyings with the people of Israel did I say to anyone, "Why have you not built me a house." ' (Jerusalem Bible). Yahweh, the god of Israel, was proud to have always lived in a tent, the hallmark of nomad aristocracy.

The translators of the Authorized Version were mistaken when they translated Yahweh as the Lord God, thereby giving the impression that he was the Creator of the Universe. During the early books of the Old Testament, Yahweh was the god of Israel, and the Israelites believed that every other tribe and nation similarly had its own god. (Astarte was the god of the Sidonians, Chemosh the god of the Moabites and Milcom the god of the Ammonites.) Thus it seems to me that Yahweh chose the Israelites to be his people, just as Chemosh chose the Moabites. It was not the Creator of the Universe who chose Israel. The early savagery of the Israelites and their primitive morals – massacre, rape, incest, murder, blood feuds – even in the time of David, cannot be associated with the God of the Universe, who is known to us as a God of Love.

After the death of Solomon in 927 B.C., ten of the twelve tribes revolted against his son, Rehoboam. The slogan of the rebels was 'To your tents, oh Israel', showing that they were still nomad landlords and had not integrated into the life of the people of the land. As a result of the rebellion, ten tribes formed the kingdom of Israel, while Judah and Benjamin formed the kingdom of Judah.

In 724 B.C., Israel was conquered by Assyria and the ten tribes were carried away captive and resettled in northern Mesopotamia, whence they never returned. Canaan was not thereby depopulated. A ruling caste of nomadic landlords was removed.

In 587 B.C., the kingdom of Judah was conquered by Babylon and the nomad ruling class was removed to Babylonia. These ancient empires did not thus remove populations to make them slaves. They merely moved them in order to prevent the formation of local patriotisms. Naturally they removed the warrior class, not the ordinary people of the land. The Judaeans settled in lower Mesopotamia, and were soon prosperous and contented.

The Judaeans had been 700 years in Canaan and had become partly mingled with the local people who worshipped their local *baals*. The word *baal* merely means 'lord'. To this day, in Jordan and Syria, cereal crops watered by rain (that is, by God as opposed to irrigation) are called *baal* crops.

Forty years after the Babylonian conquest, Cyrus the Persian took Babylon and authorized the return of the Judaeans to their homes. Only a minority did so, the others remaining in Babylonia until our own times. The people of the land were by no means gratified by the return of their former landlords and complained loudly to the kings of Persia.

Meanwhile, seven hundred years had passed since the invasion of Joshua, a period as long as that from Richard *Coeur-de-Lion* to our own times. Naturally the situation in Judah bore little resemblance to that of seven centuries before. To read through the books of the prophets, and of *Ecclesiastes, Ecclesiasticus* and *Wisdom,* is to realize that Judaism, the religion of Judah, had developed into a personal and spiritual religion.

The Babylonian conquest had caused a dispersion of the people of Judah over the neighbouring lands such as Egypt and Asia Minor. Compared with the crude polytheisms of Greece and Rome, Judaism could not fail to make a wide appeal to serious persons.

In the 580 years from the Babylonian conquest to the coming of

Christ, Judaism made vast numbers of converts in Egypt, North Africa, Asia Minor and Europe. The Graeco-Roman geographer, Strabo (born 63 B.C.) wrote that by 87 B.C. 'it would be difficult to find a place in the whole world which did not have a large and influential Jewish community'.

'The multitude of Jews all over the world on the eve of the Roman invasion of Palestine,' writes Rabbi Raisin, in his book *Gentile Reactions to Jewish Ideals,* 'was not the result of abnormal fecundity. A very large proportion of them were converted Gentiles.' The Greeks and Romans, with all their intellectual triumphs, were suffering from spiritual starvation and were profoundly attracted by the personal and spiritual appeal of Judaism. Philo, the Jewish philosopher of Alexandria shortly before the time of Christ, claimed that half the human race were Jews.

Renan (1823–92), the historian and philosopher, states that Jews arrived very early in Gaul, long before the birth of Christ. There were Jews, he continues, who did not have a single ancestor in Palestine. A Jew of Gaul, he says, was more often than not only a Gaul who had adopted Judaism.

But while the Jewish religion was thus spreading all over the Mediterranean world, Nehemiah (who had been cup-bearer to Artaxerxes I, King of Persia) was made Governor of Judaea by his master, in about 440 B.C.

About 397 B.C., Ezra was made governor by the King of Persia, and inaugurated the separation of Jews from the rest of mankind. This was a complete innovation. Even Rabbi Raisin condemns Ezra's narrow bigotry. He forced all professing Jews to divorce their non-Jewish wives. It may here be emphasized that, even in Judaea, Jews were not an ethnic group or a 'race'. They were those who worshipped Yahweh, as opposed to the other gods of the ancient world.

Consequently, from about 397 B.C. onwards, Judaism assumed a new pattern. A narrow fanatical community was established in Jerusalem, while outside Judaea 'half the human race' in Europe and North Africa were Jews by religion. In addition great numbers of people were attracted by the spiritual appeal of Judaism, but were unable or unwilling to observe all the dietary laws. These persons were classified as 'god-fearers', or half-Jews. Their numbers have been estimated as equal to that of the full adherents of Judaism. Far from being persecuted, Jews enjoyed many privileges under the

Romans and exercised far-reaching influence.

Thus, for more than 500 years from the Babylonian conquest to the time of Christ, Judaism was the leading spiritual religion of the West, and continued to make more and more converts. The Jews were passionate missionaries. In *Matthew* XXIII, 15, Christ states that the Pharisees cross land and sea to make one proselyte.

It is noticeable that when the Jews in Judaea rebelled, and Titus took Jerusalem in A.D. 70, the Romans treated the affair as a local revolt. No action whatever was taken against the millions of persons professing Judaism all over the Roman Empire.

Unfortunately, today the general public is so ignorant of history that political movements can invent their own versions of history and gain credence. The myth that the Jewish 'race' was living in Palestine until A.D. 70, and that the Jews were then driven from their homeland by the Romans, is completely untrue. The Romans did not expel the Jews. Jerusalem as a rebellious city was destroyed, but Rabbi Johanan ibn Zakkai was allowed to establish a rabbinical school at Jamnia in Palestine, where spiritual Judaism reached new heights.

Christianity, which Christ declared was a spiritualization of the Law and the Prophets, gained converts in the West even more rapidly than Judaism had previously done, and superseded it in the Mediterranean basin.

At the time of the Muslim conquest of Palestine in A.D. 633–8, there are said still to have been 200,000 persons there practising Judaism. A few years later, there were only 100,000. This was a normal pattern in countries conquered by the early Muslims. The latter did not persecute other religions, but any adherent of another religion who was willing to say, 'There is no god but God and Muhammad is the messenger of God,' was automatically accepted as an Arab. Thus in the 'Arabs' of Palestine there is doubtless a considerable hereditary strain of Judaism.

Eight hundred years after Christ, the rival super-powers were the Byzantine Empire of Constantinople and the Muslim Khalifate of Baghdad. In contact with both lay the powerful Khazar Kingdom on the Volga, north of the Black Sea and the Caucasus. The Khazars were of Turkish origin and their alliance was sought by both the Byzantines and the Khalifs. Meanwhile the Khazars were

Shamanists, a religion of which they had become ashamed.

Fearing that if they became Christians they would become a satellite of Constantinople and, if Muslims, followers of Baghdad, the great Khan of the Khazars with all his people accepted Judaism. In the tenth century, however, the Khazar state was overrun by more barbarian invasions from the east, and its people scattered to Hungary and Poland, carrying their Judaism with them. Thus Eastern Europe was peopled by great numbers of Jews of Turkish and Slavic origin who were not descended from the ancient Israelites.

The people of Europe, Western Asia and North Africa who professed Judaism were called Sephardic Jews, while those descended from the Khazars of Eastern Europe were named Ashkenazis.

Later generations of 'Jews', from Judah, Egypt, Africa and Spain, reached Britain, Holland and America, where they early enjoyed freedom. But the East European 'Khazar Jews' were bitterly persecuted in Russia, on the grounds that they had crucified Christ, although in fact they had never had any connection with Palestine. Truth is indeed stranger than fiction. No author of tales of mystery and imagination could have invented so wildly improbable a story.

During the period of Arab rule in Spain, Jews were wealthy and powerful; but with the Christian *reconquista* they were evicted and persecuted. Some of these Sephardic Jews escaped to the Netherlands, then to Britain and later to America. By the mid-nineteenth century, Jews in Western Europe had become normal citizens, but East European Jews were still persecuted in Russia, and many Ashkenazis migrated to Western Europe and then to the United States.

There can be no doubt that in past centuries many Christians looked askance at Jews as having been the crucifiers of Christ. They forgot that Christ Himself had been a Jew, and that the apostles and the first Christians had been Jews also.

Jews tended to draw closer to one another in order to maintain the purity of Judaism. This attitude incurred the resentment of Gentiles, as also did their dietary laws, which prevented social intercourse between them and non-Jews.

When Christ drove the merchants from the temple, He was thought to be showing support for the poorer Jews against their oppressors, the rich ruling classes of Pharisees and Sadducees. As a result, Christ came to be thought of as the advocate of the poor, who were converted in large numbers to Christianity. The wealthy Jewish ruling classes remained Jews. Thus, from the very earliest times, the rich merchants were normally Jews, while the poor became Christians. 'Hath not God chosen the poor of this world rich in faith, and heirs of the kingdom which he hath promised to them that love Him?' asks James in his very early epistle, written from Jerusalem.

It appears, therefore, that from the earliest Christian times, Judaism was associated with wealthy merchants. Subsequently the Christian church denounced usury, as did also in due course the Muslims. As the Jews were already rich merchants, and usury was not forbidden under the Mosaic Law, they automatically also became money-lenders. All these developments, many of which still persist in our modern world, can thus be traced right back to the time of Christ.

The endless and tragic history of Jewish–Christian antagonism might have been ended during the second half of the nineteenth century, for Jews had everywhere become normal citizens in Western Europe and the United States. Unfortunately, however, persecution still continued in Russia. As a result, ironically enough, the Zionist movement originated in Russia, demanding a 'return to Zion', although the Russian Jews were Ashkenazis or East European Jews whose ancestors in most cases had never known Palestine but were the descendants of the Turkish Khazars.

The first Zionist Congress was held at Basle in 1897, under the direction of Theodor Herzl, and stated as its object the creation for the Jewish people of a home in Palestine. It will be seen, then, that the Jewish people are not an ethnic group, being indeed descended from innumerable racial stocks. The unifying influence between them is solely religious. But they have been drawn together by the unfriendly attitude which they have often encountered from the outside world.

The Zionists took advantage of the First World War to obtain from Britain a confused statement, known as the Balfour Declaration, to the effect that the British government 'viewed with favour the establishment in Palestine of a national home for the Jewish people'.

The whole confusion of the Jewish question is now impossible to unravel. Even Western Jews were almost entirely converts from Egypt, North Africa and Western Europe. The East European Jews had little or no hereditary connection with Palestine, yet had been far more intensely persecuted than those of the West.

It was Hitler's persecution which caused great numbers of Jews to wish to escape to Palestine, into which they forced their way, evicting as many 'Arabs' as they could in the process. As we have already seen, there may well have been more ancient Jewish blood in the veins of the 'Arabs' of Palestine than there was in the East European Turko-Slavic 'Jews' who forced their way into Palestine.

It is quite impossible to take labels of today like 'Jew' or 'Arab' and claim that they are descended from people bearing those names a thousand or two thousand years ago. There was and is, however, no reason why all these peoples should not live peacefully together, were it not for the orgy of hatred, violence and intolerance which dominates our unhappy modern world.

After the end of the Second World War, the Jewish immigrants in Palestine embarked on a campaign of terrorism against British officials and soldiers, many of whom were murdered. Although it was Britain who had issued the Balfour Declaration and had facilitated the immigration of Jews to Palestine, the Jewish terrorists now denounced her as an imperial power occupying the 'Land of Israel'.

The Arab states – Egypt, Syria and Iraq – were completely unpractical. Syria had only just been declared independent and had enjoyed no time to form a government or an army. None had any conception (as we had in Trans-Jordan) of the power and organization which the Palestine Jews had attained. Most Arabs visualized Jews in general as usurers or shopkeepers.

In these circumstances, everybody demanded a British withdrawal – the Jews, supported by the U.S.A., and the Arabs because they had not taken the trouble to go into the matter. Britain, exhausted by war, was faced with a universal demand for her withdrawal. Both the Soviet Union and the United States were loud in demanding the withdrawal of Britain from Palestine. For the first time on record, America and the U.S.S.R. spoke with one voice.

They did so for different reasons: the President of the United States, Harry S. Truman, because he was anxious to secure Jewish

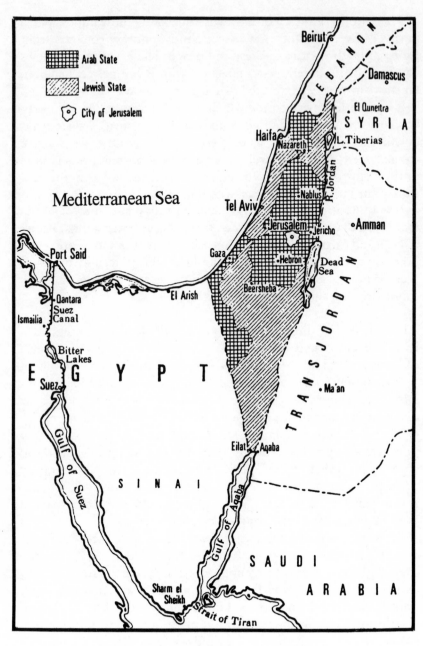

United Nations partition plan, 1947.

*Note its impractical nature, with cross-overs south of Nazareth and Tel Aviv; also that the Arab
Legion did not 'attack Israel', but took up defensive positions well inside the area allotted to Arabs.*

support in the U.S.A. for his re-election; the Russians because the Middle East had hitherto been a Western sphere of influence. The Soviets doubtless foresaw that a British withdrawal would lead to chaos and civil war, from which Russia might reap some advantage and, in any case, had nothing to lose.

Britain accordingly notified the United Nations of the surrender of her mandate, to take effect on 15 May 1948. After various commissions and a period of intense intrigue in New York, the United Nations passed a plan to partition Palestine. The plan, which allotted provinces to the Jewish and Arab states in inter-crossing areas, was quite impracticable. The city of Jerusalem was to be an international area, administered by the United Nations which, however, appointed no officials or police to control it.

Two months before the end of the mandate, Taufiq Pasha, the Prime Minister of Trans-Jordan, went to London and took me with him. We had an interview with the British Foreign Secretary, Mr Ernest Bevin, at which I interpreted. Taufiq Pasha said that the British mandate for Palestine was about to end. The Jews had an army and a government ready; the Palestine Arabs had nothing, but were appealing to Jordan for help. What would be the view of the British government if the Arab Legion were to cross into the areas of Palestine allotted to the Arabs to help them? 'It seems to be the obvious thing for you to do,' said Mr Bevin, 'but on no account enter any area allotted to the Jewish state.' We could help forward the United Nations plan, he added, but under no circumstances were we to go against it. At that time, we had no idea that any other Arab country would intervene.

The Trans-Jordan government accordingly decided, with British government approval, to assist the Arabs of Palestine to defend the area allotted to them in Judaea and Samaria, north of Jerusalem, as soon as the mandate ended. No clash with the Jews was anticipated since they had accepted the United Nations Partition Plan. King Abdulla was prepared to come to a peaceable agreement with them on the lines of the U.N. plan.

The Trans-Jordan government was unaware of the fact that the Jewish Agency had accepted the partition plan in order to achieve the end of the mandate and the withdrawal of Britain. As soon as the

British were gone, the Jewish Agency proposed to conquer all Palestine.

General D'Arcy, who commanded the British troops in Palestine, was better informed, however. He gave it as his opinion that the Jewish forces would overrun all the areas allotted to the Arabs and reach the Jordan in a week.

The Trans-Jordan government was too simple-minded and accepted at its face value the Jewish agreement to the partition plan. It accordingly anticipated no complications.

On 13 May 1948, however, two days before the end of the mandate, Azzam Pasha, secretary of the Arab League, arrived in Amman. He informed us that the Arab League had decided to fight and that the Egyptian army would invade Palestine. This announcement destroyed King Abdulla's plan of an agreement with the Jewish state on the lines of the partition plan. (In fact, however, we now know that his plan would have been still-born, because the Jews had already made up their minds to conquer all Palestine by force of arms.)

Azzam Pasha asked how many men we had. I told him that, without the police, we had some 4,500 officers and men. 'I thought you had far more,' he commented. He then enquired how many the Jews had; I replied, 'Perhaps 60,000, but in several different categories.' He was surprised and said, 'I did not know they had so many.' I could not but be impressed by the fact that the Arab League had decided to fight without even asking how many men they had, or how many constituted the enemy.

The intervention of the Arab League upset all King Abdulla's plans. Nevertheless, the Jordan government decided to continue with its intention to send troops to the areas allotted to the Arabs in the Partition Plan, and not to enter any area allotted to the Jewish state. The Arab Legion was strictly forbidden to enter Jerusalem, which the U.N. had proclaimed to be an international enclave.

Taufiq Pasha informed me that, whether or not we became engaged in battle, we could expect no money. We must fight without overspending our peacetime budget! The total forces engaged by the Arab League were:

142

Egypt	10,000
Arab Legion	4,500
Syria	3,000
Iraq	3,000

giving a total of 20,500. The Israeli forces may have amounted to some 60,000, but this figure included every sort of man with a weapon. Their spearhead, the Palmach, were approximately equal in numbers to the Arab Legion. They were the 'Jewish Brigade' which had been trained by the British to fight in Europe during the Second World War, but who never actually saw any fighting. Next came the Hagana, a partially trained underground militia. Finally there were the civilian garrisons of Jewish colonies, who were armed to defend their colonies.

In addition, the Jews had spent large sums of money – all their colonies were fortified with trenches, dugouts, barbed wire and minefields. They had established factories which manufactured mortars and mortar-bombs.

Some persons have argued that, as the Jews were so much more efficient than the Palestinians, they deserved to have the country. But often those same people are furiously opposed to the white South Africans, whose superior efficiency is not accepted as justification for domination. In fact, Jewish aggressiveness in Palestine was a typical example of a European invader conquering a 'native' population.

Meanwhile a ship, laden with ammunition loaded in Suez harbour for us by the British army, was seized by the Egyptians and all the ammunition confiscated, leaving us with reserves for only about one battle. Hitherto the British army had supplied us with ammunition and we had never had the money to build up our own reserves.

Amid such violent passions and such total inefficiency and folly, I could only fall on my knees and pray for God's help, for I felt myself totally incapable of solving such chaos.

I think it was Disraeli who once said that the Jews were the cleverest people in the world but the least wise. Their action in 1948 was a case in point. The Jewish immigrants in Palestine came principally from Germany, Poland and Russia. Many were scientists, doctors and businessmen with a European standard of education. Behind them stood the immense wealth and power of world Jewry, especially the Jews in the United States.

If the Jewish immigrants in Palestine had shown themselves friendly and tolerant towards the Arabs, first in that country and then in Syria, Iraq and Arabia, they could have taken over almost all the wealth and business of the Middle East.

Before Hitler, they had enjoyed a leading position in business in Germany. They were pre-eminent in finance, in business and in controlling the public media in the United States. If their business acumen could give them such power in Germany and America, how could the Arabs have resisted it, if they had exerted it with tact? They could have allowed the Arabs to retain the visible positions of power while the Jews, as their subjects, inconspicuously took over financial and commercial control. But the Jews were supremely clever but lacking in such calm wisdom.

Not only so, but they were determined to seize Palestine by force. Perhaps such action fulfilled for them a psychological need. Having suffered so long from the bullying brutality of others, they were determined to behave with equal brutality to another race weaker than themselves, thereby proving – at least to themselves – that they were likewise a military conquering race, like the Germans and the Russians who had previously oppressed them. People with a secret inferiority complex are often the first to resort to violence.

As I write these lines, I have on my desk a letter which I have just received from an English Jewish lady. 'As time goes on,' she writes, 'the Zionists in Palestine become more and more brutalized, and the Palestinians in the occupied territories are being treated as the Jews were treated by the Nazis.'

I do not believe that the Jews of the world are aware of the brutalities of the Zionists in Palestine, or that they would for a moment condone it. But human nature is such that kind, moderate, well-intentioned people (and such are most Jews) feel unhappy at reports of human cruelty, but take no action to prevent it. Meanwhile extremists and fanatics seize power, monopolize the propaganda and actively and violently trample on their fellow human beings.

Love, I was convinced, was the lubricant which made all life run smoothly and happily. It seemed to me that I had proved this in my eighteen years in Jordan. The English language is so lacking in words that love has many meanings. Love seemed to me to be a (pale) imitation of the attitude of God to men – a universal attitude of benevolence. Yet it was more than an intellectual policy – it was a warm personal emotion.

I had arrived alone in Jordan, and had succeeded in ending desert raiding (and even stealing) without firing a shot or sending a man to prison. The tribes, previously the bitterest enemies of the government, had become its most loyal adherents. Even the tribes of the Jebel Druze, officially Syrian subjects, had pressed into Jordan and begged to enlist in the Arab Legion.

On 15 May 1948, the day the mandate ended, the Arab Legion crossed the Jordan. We drove up a steep spur of the Palestine mountains, the same spur up which Joshua had led the Children of Israel three thousand years before. We took up a position at Bethel.

Jerusalem was not only a holy city, but was the strategic key to all Palestine. Occupying the top of the only low pass across the Palestine mountains between Hebron and the Plain of Esdraclon, the road from Tel Aviv ran through it and straight down to Jericho. Jewish forces were pouring up the road from Tel Aviv to Jerusalem, from which they could drive down to the Jordan at Jericho. The first step, therefore, seemed to be to block the Tel Aviv–Jerusalem road, which we did by placing one of our three regiments at Latrun.

(Meanwhile, on 15 May, the State of Israel had been proclaimed. Henceforward we shall refer, not to Jews, but to Israelis.)

Latrun was well within the zone allotted to the Arabs in the partition plan, and our occupation of it was therefore entirely legitimate. Our regiment there was, however, attacked night after night by Israeli forces, but in vain. We had no intention of attacking Jerusalem, which the United Nations had declared to be under its own administration.

The policy of the Jordan government at this stage was mistaken in one direction: it believed that the United Nations included all the great nations of the world and, as such, that its authority would be supreme. It took us some time to realize that the United Nations was located in New York, the largest concentration of Jews in the world. Atmosphere counts for a great deal. We were only slowly to discover that the Israelis took no notice whatever of the United Nations.

The invasion of Palestine by the Egyptian army confused the

whole hysterical situation. (The Syrian army took virtually no part, and there was no Lebanese army.) If the Egyptians had not intervened, the situation would have been clearer. The Arab Legion was trying to defend the main area of Palestine allotted to the Arabs, but was respecting the international status of Jerusalem. We could not, however, defend Galilee, which had also been awarded to the Arabs, but which was immediately overrun and annexed by Israel.

Meanwhile, however, inside the city of Jerusalem, the Israeli forces already there had started energetically to conquer the whole city, half of which was Arab. The inhabitants appealed in frantic terms to King Abdulla and the Jordan government to save them. Amman was in a state of passionate emotion.

I had only some 4,500 men to face a much greater number of Israelis and to defend an area of some 3,000 square miles. I could ill afford to break into the city of Jerusalem, where our small numbers would immediately be swallowed up. Street fighting is extremely expensive in men and a waste of regular trained soldiers.

The Israelis inside Jerusalem were methodically taking over the Arab half of the city, street by street. For five days we waited, while the Trans-Jordan government appealed passionately to the consuls of the Western nations in Jerusalem, to the United Nations who had allotted the Holy City to themselves, and to the British government. It was obvious that, in a matter of hours, the Israelis would have occupied all Jerusalem and would be able to drive down to the Jordan at Jericho.

At dawn on 19 May we were therefore obliged to break into the city of Jerusalem, as the Jordan government ordered. We moved along the line of junction between the Jewish and Arab cities, without attacking any Jewish quarter, until we made contact with the old city. With a force of 300 men we entered Jerusalem, a city which contained more than 100,000 Jews.

A Jewish writer, reporting from Jerusalem, wrote shortly afterwards, 'The Legion launched the attack with four batteries of heavy guns, smaller artillery units, two infantry regiments and large units of tanks and armoured cars. After the artillery barrage, they advanced in massed strength, tanks in the lead.' The force which actually entered Jerusalem consisted of one company of infantry and a squadron of four armoured cars.

The Israelis, however, enjoyed world publicity, and their version

146

was soon broadcast all over the world.

Twenty years later, when lecturing in the United States, I was asked on more than one occasion, 'How *could* you attack the peaceful Holy City with all your guns and tanks?'

14

A War of Peoples

As already explained, the Arab Legion had crossed the Jordan on 15 May, with the approval of the British government, to help the Arabs defend the area of Judaea and Samaria allotted to them. We were strictly forbidden to enter Jerusalem, which had been declared by the United Nations to be an international enclave, or to enter any area allotted to the Jewish state in the partition plan. Our plans were therefore strictly in accordance with the orders of the United Nations and the approval of the British government.

The Jordan government was simple-minded enough to believe that the Jewish state, having accepted the partition plan, would abide by it.

Jerusalem, declared an international zone, was the strategic key to Palestine, being the junction of the main roads from Tel Aviv to Jericho, and from Hebron to Nablus. The new state of Israel fully realized this and proceeded to seize the whole city as soon as the British left.

For four days of anguish, we remained between Ramallah and Jerusalem, passionately hoping that the U.N. or other diplomatic forces would stop the Israeli conquest of the city, but finally we were forced to enter the city. The unforeseen invasion of Palestine by the Egyptian army had produced the impression of a concerted Arab attack on Israel as set up by the partition plan.

I have been often vilified as the man who led an army wantonly to attack the innocent newborn state of Israel. I can only state in my defence that military commanders do not start wars. To do so is the prerogative of governments.

In any case we had no intention of clashing with Israel, who had accepted the U.N. plan with which we were conforming. Eventually we were obliged to break into Jerusalem with 300 men, although the city contained a population of 100,000 Jews.

When we were obliged to intervene to stop the attempted Israeli breakthrough in Jerusalem, we found ourselves holding about a thousand square miles of territory with four regiments, one regiment and a half having eventually been drawn into Jerusalem. Of the remaining two and a half regiments, one whole regiment was at Latrun, closing the road from Tel Aviv to Jerusalem. (Our regiments were approximately 700 strong.)

An armoured-car regiment had meanwhile arrived from Iraq, and took over the Nablus sector from the Arab Legion. On 30 May 1948, an order was received recalling all regular British officers from the Arab Legion, as a result of a resolution of the Security Council. I had resigned from the British army in 1926, and could not therefore be ordered to leave. But when our British officers were withdrawn, we were surprised to hear that a colonel in the United States army was commanding the Israeli forces attacking Latrun!

On 1 June, Count Bernadotte arrived in Amman, as United Nations mediator. He was a member of the Swedish royal family, an international figure who had devoted himself during the Second World War to the rescue of refugees, including many Jews. He immediately impressed me as a man who could be entirely relied upon, one whose life was devoted to duty and service. Shuttling backwards and forwards, he worked untiringly for a truce, which he eventually succeeded in arranging on 11 June. It was to last for a month.

I went to see the Jordanian Prime Minister, Taufiq Pasha. I pointed out that we had a month's breathing space to strengthen our forces and repair the losses we had suffered, and asked for his sanction. He replied that that would be quite unnecessary, as there would not be any more fighting. I replied that the Israelis were desperately engaged in increasing their strength. Contrary to the

149

terms of the truce, they had received arms and equipment from Czechoslovakia, for the Soviet Union at this stage was supporting Israel. In spite of the Prime Minister's prohibition, I did my best to recruit and train more men. Weapons and ammunition could not be obtained, for our source of supply was Britain, and she rigorously applied the ruling of the Security Council against supplying munitions of war to the combatants. Meanwhile Court Bernadotte set himself to draw up a revised partition plan, as a basis for a permanent settlement.

The Jewish quarter in the Old City was inhabited by old-fashioned and completely Arabicized Jews, most of them intensely devout and with no sympathy for the German or Russian Zionists. Before we intervened in Jerusalem, however, the Israelis had sent a detachment of Palmach, the *corps d'élite* of their army, into the Jewish quarter. When, therefore, the Arab Legion entered the Old City, it was fired on by these Palmach. Some unpleasant close fighting resulted, in a rabbit warren of poor houses, but finally the Jews surrendered. I immediately visited them myself, and found them a delightful community of poor, simple, pious folk. Their mother tongue was Arabic.

We arranged with the International Red Cross to send the old persons, women, children and non-combatants across the lines to the Israeli side. The sad little caravan hobbled through the narrow streets of Old Jerusalem, Arab Legion soldiers supporting the sick and old and carrying their little bundles of domestic possessions. 'Well, that is what I call chivalry,' a European press correspondent remarked.

The truce was due to end on 11 July. The Arab armies were in no position to renew hostilities. Only Egypt and Jordan were in close contact with the Israelis, and neither had any reserve ammunition or any outside source of supply. Both armies had originally been equipped by Britain, who was conscientiously applying the ruling of the Security Council and refused to supply them with any warlike stores.

Before the end of the truce, the Arab governments assembled in Cairo. Both King Abdulla and I begged the Jordan Prime Minister to extend the truce, which he promised to do. No news was received of the deliberations in Cairo until Taufiq Pasha returned and reported that Nokrashi Pashi, the Egyptian premier, had insisted on terminating the truce.

'But how can we continue to fight without ammunition?' I asked the Prime Minister.

'Don't shoot unless the Jews shoot first,' he replied.

I wondered if any commander had ever been faced with such a position. The Israelis had agreed to prolong the truce; the Arabs, at the instigation of Egypt, had refused. But, in view of the fact that we had scarcely any ammunition, we were told not to shoot if it could be avoided. Taufiq Pasha reiterated his orders to spend no money. King Abdulla was as unhappy as I was.

I made a note in my diary regarding the Prime Minister's orders to renew the war, but not to shoot or spend any money:

The Arab Legion has received strict orders to perform the impossible. But after all, Napoleon Bonaparte said, *'Impossible n'est pas un mot français.'*

I could not avoid some surprise at the fact that, while hundreds of thousands of refugees were being driven, penniless, from their homes in Palestine, the British House of Commons was hotly debating a law to prohibit foxhunting. I could not help deprecating that British sentimentality towards animals, which is at the same time indifferent to the suffering of hundreds of thousands of fellow human beings.

It is true that the United States and Russia, the Jews and the Arabs alike, were loudly demanding a British withdrawal, and that the British themselves were sick and tired of war. But I could not help feeling that Britain should at least have warned the United Nations of the chaos which would follow, or have left a division in Jerusalem to prevent a war, until the proposed Arab and Jewish states had been able to establish themselves.

We were now aware that we were engaged in a war of the new type – a war of a whole people fighting to exterminate another whole people – a struggle far more ruthless and savage than any war between the old kings and emperors. This was a total war, in which one people sought to drive out or destroy another people and seize their homeland.

The first period of fighting had been occupied solely with Jerusalem, with preventing the Israelis from taking the whole city, and with blocking the road from Tel Aviv at Latrun, to prevent the passage of more Israelis up to Jerusalem.

The Israelis, however, had used the first truce to replenish and reinforce Jerusalem. In the second period of fighting, they decided to take Lydda and Ramle, and outflank Latrun by advancing on Ramallah. Lydda and Ramle were completely Arab towns, allotted to the Arabs in the partition plan. But they were in the coastal plain only a few miles from Tel Aviv. We had not a man to defend them.

Against the Arab Legion, the Israelis had mustered the Palmach. It consisted of some 6,500 men, organized as a division of three brigades, and well equipped with jeeps, armoured troop-carriers, armoured cars and field artillery. The Israeli plan was to overrun Lydda and Ramle, and then to outflank Latrun by taking Beit Sira and then Ramallah, cutting off and surrounding both the Iraqi army and the Arab Legion.

The Palmach began by passing two brigades round Lydda and Ramle and attacking them from the east. The encircling movement also surrounded a company of one hundred men of the Arab Legion which, however, fought its way out.

The Jordan government had agreed on the impossibility of holding Lydda and Ramle, and behind the two towns there was a fifteen-mile gap between a company of ours at Beit Sira and the left of the Iraqi army at Majdal Yaba. Our 1st Regiment was charged to defend this fifteen-mile sector.

When they entered Lydda and Ramle, the Israelis rounded up all the civilian men as prisoners of war. They then used the women in a ruthless manner so as to emphasize their order to them to leave the towns immediately. Some 30,000 women and children fled across the open fields to our post at Beit Sira, followed by bursting mortar-bombs. Then, more slowly, they dragged themselves up the hills to Ramallah. No one will ever know how many children died or were abandoned. The International Red Cross, a splendid organization, picked up a number of abandoned children whom their mothers had left.

A storm of fury broke out against the Arab Legion, accused of treacherously abandoning Lydda and Ramle. I myself was stoned in my car. The men of the Arab Legion, fighting against heavy odds, were loaded with abuse as traitors and cowards for not having defended the two towns. Although the government had agreed not to try and hold Lydda and Ramle, they now joined in the hue and cry.

The politicians announced that Britain wished to help Israel and that I had received secret orders from Mr Ernest Bevin to evacuate Lydda and Ramle. I was summoned before a full meeting of the king and the cabinet and charged with treachery.

Meanwhile the Palmach, having mopped up Lydda and Ramle, re-formed their columns for a grand attack on Beit Sira and Latrun. On the morning of 15 July 1948, the Israeli columns advanced against Al Burj, Bir Main and Beit Sira, while other columns renewed their unceasing attacks on Latrun.

Only three companies barred the way to the advancing Palmach columns at Beit Sira. Heavy fighting with attack and counter-attack lasted all day of 16 July, but the line held. There was a lull on 17 July, while both sides reorganized. During the day we were told that all parties had agreed to another cease-fire, to begin at 5 p.m. on 18 July. The Israelis put in all they had, in order to take Latrun and Beit Sira and break through to Ramallah in the last twenty-four hours of the fighting.

Two brigades of Palmach advanced against the Latrun–Beit Sira front. In addition, the Israelis produced an armoured force of five tanks, ten bren-gun carriers and a number of armoured half-trucks, which advanced on Latrun. The 2nd Regiment was holding Latrun and had a single six-pounder anti-tank gun on the roof of the old police station. This little gun engaged and knocked out all five tanks. All the men on the gun were killed but, as each man fell, he was replaced by another.

Another Palmach brigade advanced on Beit Sira, but was counter-attacked from the north by one company of the 1st Regiment and driven back. At last it was 5 p.m. and fighting ceased. Our frail front had held!

Before fighting had begun on 15 May 1948, Azzam Pasha, the Secretary-General of the Arab League, had come to Amman and had promised the Trans-Jordan government £3 million from the League as war expenses, and had paid us an advance of £250,000. I must admit that during the weeks of fighting I had not stopped to check the accounts. When firing ceased, we found that we had overspent the advance of £250,000, and we applied to Azzam Pasha for more, but were refused.

In company with the Minister of Defence, I went to see the Prime Minister. Taufiq Pasha was angry. 'I warned you not to exceed your budget heads,' he said. 'Where am I to get the money from?'

I was annoyed – after all there had been a war, and militarily we had been extraordinarily successful. 'You had better deduct it from my pay,' I said sarcastically. I was wrong to be angry but we were all overstrained.

Taufiq Pasha drove straight to the palace, and offered to resign. King Abdulla was in a difficult position. Eventually peace was restored and I was given a month's leave to England as a rest. On arrival at London Airport, a detective took me aside and asked me to register at a London hotel as Mr Smith. 'We have reports,' he said, 'that Jewish terrorists are looking for you.'

While I was in England, Count Bernadotte returned to Palestine. Throughout June and July he had been tireless in shuttling backwards and forwards, chiefly between Cairo, Israel and Trans-Jordan and across the Atlantic to New York.

In reality, his task was a hopeless one. Israel did not want a final settlement because she hoped to expand much more. Trans-Jordan and Iraq stood more or less together, but Egypt was jealous of both. Syria played little part in the military operations, but was unwilling to co-operate with the other Arab states.

Of the many plans discussed by Bernadotte and his international team from the United Nations, the greater part favoured the annexation of what was left of the Arab areas in central Palestine to Trans-Jordan, and the worldwide recognition of Israel. King Abdulla, it was hoped, would be willing to settle with Israel on these terms.

There remained two problems. A large area of southern Palestine was in the occupation of the Egyptian army, but had been allotted to Israel. The major part of this area was inhabited solely by Arabs and should not, on a population basis, have been allotted to Israel who desired it in order to secure a port on the Gulf of Aqaba.

The other problem was the city of Jerusalem, sacred alike to Jews, Muslims and Christians. In the partition plan, the United Nations resolution of 1947 had rightly declared Jerusalem an international city under its own U.N. administration, but had then refused to spend any money to set up its administration there. Bernadotte likewise personally favoured an international Jerusalem.

The area of Western Galilee had been allotted to the Arabs, but had been occupied by the Israelis. The Neqeb, or Beersheba area, had been awarded to the Israelis but overrun by the Egyptian army. Bernadotte made the reasonable suggestion that the Israelis be allowed to retain Galilee, which was good farming land, but that the Beersheba area, which was poor land and inhabited solely by Arabs, be left to the latter in exchange for Galilee. This solution would also consolidate both states and eliminate the impractical 'cross-overs' south of Nazareth and south of Ramle.

A disadvantage of these proposals was that the Arab state would have no harbour on the Mediterranean, unless it could retain Gaza, which at that time, however, was under Egyptian occupation. Bernadotte suggested that Haifa be a free port for Israel and the Arab state, but plans which involved co-operation risked producing sources of friction.

It will be seen that all Bernadotte's proposals were eminently reasonable and showed no signs of the Machiavellian imperialism attributed to them. His only error occurred when he allowed himself to be persuaded by his United Nations staff to recommend that Jerusalem be an Arab city, but in the end it is not certain that he retained the idea of an Arab Jerusalem.

In conversation with Mr Shertok, the Israeli Foreign Minister, on 10 August 1948, Bernadotte stated that the Israelis had shown nothing but hardness and obduracy towards the Arab refugees. If the Jewish people, which itself had suffered so much, had declared instead that it understood the feelings of the refugees and did not wish to treat them in the same way as it had itself been treated, its prestige in the world at large would have been immeasurably increased. In his final recommendations, he included a paragraph to the effect that the Arab refugees should be allowed to return to their homes.

This proposal, however, was totally unacceptable to the Israelis, who had deliberately driven the Arabs out. The Zionist ideal was to create a Jewish state solely and entirely inhabited by Jews. Bernadotte felt acutely the sufferings of refugees, having devoted himself throughout the Second World War to rescuing such unfortunates. In August 1948 there were about 300,000 Palestinian refugees.

On the morning of Friday, 17 September 1948, Bernadotte had taken off from Damascus and landed on the airstrip of Kolundia, north of Jerusalem. He called at the headquarters of the Arab Legion division in Ramallah, where he heard a report of increased Israeli sniping in Jerusalem. The Count intended to cross to the Israeli side through the city, but one of his staff suggested that the visit be postponed. 'No,' said Bernadotte, 'we cannot allow ourselves to be frightened out of doing our work.' An Arab Legion armoured car accompanied him until he crossed to the Israeli side.

The Count's convoy consisted of three cars, with himself and his United Nations staff and an Israeli liaison officer. As they drove through the Katamun quarter, they were stopped by a jeep parked across the road. Three men dressed in Israeli army uniforms jumped off the jeep and walked to Bernadotte's car. One of them pointed an automatic pistol through the window and fired at point blank range, killing the Count and the French Colonel Serot, who was a member of the United Nations staff.

The leaders of the Israeli Lehy terrorist organization, in a later interview, stated: 'The Lehy central committee decided to kill him. There is no discussion about that . . . I am proud of the killing of Bernadotte. I have no second thoughts about the killing of Bernadotte – we saved Jerusalem.'*

I had formed quite a friendship with Count Bernadotte, as a man. Being a member of the Swedish Royal Family, he had an assured position and was not continually struggling for money, power or publicity as politicians do. His life had been largely dedicated to works of compassion and of benevolence, partly through the International Red Cross. He was an earnest Christian, a very gentle perfect knight.

In Amman, we had made a fundamental error in our estimate of the situation. The United Nations included all the powerful governments in the world. We thought we could not go far wrong if we always obeyed their orders. Now the U.N. representative sent to mediate in Palestine had been brutally assassinated. We waited for the U.N. to rise in her wrath – but nothing happened. There was not even a protest or a complaint. The Israeli government made no

<hr>

*Israel Eldad, interview in Jerusalem, 10/1/1976, quoted by Sune Persson, *Mediation and Assassination*.

arrests. Suddenly the veil fell from our eyes. It was evident that the United Nations counted for nothing at all.

Although the state of Israel owed its existence to a resolution of U.N.O., it treated the local U.N. representatives with scarcely veiled hostility, not to say contempt. We realized that U.N.O. henceforward had no authority and no prestige whatever. The Israelis adopted the technique of the *fait accompli*. If they wanted to do something, they did it; if they wanted a piece of land, they seized it. The United Nations Truce Observers ordered them back, but they took no notice. The Security Council passed a resolution, but nothing happened and the Israelis remained in possession, realizing that no one was going to send an army to coerce them.

They were to adhere to this policy for the next thirty-two years. But in their defiance of the U.N., they also relied on the Jewish population of the United States. The headquarters of the United Nations was in New York, the largest conglomeration of Jews in the world. Moreover, Jewish power in America was believed to sway presidential elections. Candidates for the presidency vied with one another in their promise of lavish support for Israel in arms and money.

Though 'brave little Israel' was ecstatically praised for fighting back against 'the millions of Asia', in fact her power immensely exceeded that of all her Arab neighbours put together. She owed her predominance solely to the United States. Almost unconditional American support was not, however, to be attributed to 'American imperialism'. It was all due to the peculiarities of domestic politics in the United States – such sometimes are the unforeseen results of 'democracy'.

During the early stages of the Palestine conflict, the Soviet Union regarded the Arabs as bound to the West, and consequently gave energetic support to Israel. In November 1948, the London *Daily Telegraph* reported that Czechoslovakia had supplied Israel with a hundred Messerschmitt fighters. As many as four transport planes a day left Czechoslovakia laden with warlike stores for Israel.

All members of the U.N. had undertaken not to supply any war material to either side involved in Palestine. Britain rigidly observed this pledge, with the result that Jordan and Egypt, who both used British arms, could obtain nothing. The Russians, however, in spite of their pledge, poured weapons and aircraft into

Israel. While thus building up their forces for a new offensive, the Israelis did not want peace to be established. They consequently kept the situation lively by constantly firing with machine-guns or mortars, or sniping, especially in Jerusalem.

For several days before 15 October 1948, the Israelis refused to allow U.N. observers near their front with the Egyptians. During this period they built up a force of some 15,000 men. Then, on 15 October, they launched a massive attack on the Egyptians, supported by the considerable air force which had been smuggled in from Czechoslovakia.

The Egyptians resisted strongly for five days, but then their front collapsed and the Israelis broke through to Beersheba and Gaza. The Egyptians had previously been holding Bethlehem and Hebron, but these units had now vanished, and Bethlehem and Hebron were empty.

The Arab Legion had no reserve units available, but we scraped together a column of a squadron of armoured cars and two companies of infantry and, on 22 October, passed east of Jerusalem, and down to Bethlehem and then Hebron. While the Israelis and the Egyptians had each used some 15,000 men in their battle on the coastal plain, the Arab Legion column consisted of 350 men. On the same day, the Egyptians and Israelis both accepted a renewed U.N. cease-fire. Little help, however, could be expected from the U.N. as an American presidential election was due in a month, and all the candidates were anxious to obtain Jewish support.

Our 350-strong Arab Legion could scarcely engage 15,000 Israelis in the plains of Beersheba, but the ridge of the Palestine mountain range continued southwards to beyond Dhahiriya, where it ran out into the plain of Beersheba. Having occupied Hebron, an Arab Legion force of seven armoured cars drove down through Tarqumiya on 27 October to reconnoitre Beit Jebrin, where the mountains disappeared into the plains.

The Israelis were unaware that our little column had moved south of Jerusalem to Hebron, and on 28 October they sent a column from Beit Jebrin to go up the Tarqumiya road and occupy Hebron. The Israeli column was about five times as strong as that of the Arab Legion, which met it between Tarqumiya and Beit Jabrin, and drove it back to the latter.

The Arab Legion armoured cars, however, could not emerge on the open plain, but returned to the foot of the mountains between the two villages, where a post was established. Ten miles north of Beersheba, we established another position. By these lively operations, a column of 350 men of the Arab Legion had saved 600 square miles of Arab territory for its inhabitants. We could not have done this, had not the country been mountainous. We could fervently repeat the words of the 121st psalm: 'I will lift up mine eyes unto the hills, from whence cometh my help.' Indeed, we found ourselves in much the same position as the Children of Israel in Old Testament times who held the mountains of Palestine, but who never really held the coastal plain which belonged to the Philistines and then to the Greeks and Romans. The new state of Israel now held the Greek coastal plain, while we held the kingdom of David.

Meanwhile, however, fresh waves of refugees were flooding back through our lines, for it was now the regular policy of Israel, whenever they occupied a town or village, immediately to drive out all the inhabitants with just the clothes they stood up in. Everything else they owned in the world was seized. Any who delayed their flight were roughly handled – sufficiently to hasten their flight – or, in a few cases, massacred.

During the Second World War, Rosemary's mother, Mrs Graham Forbes, had managed Lady McMichael's Convalescent Home for Officers in Jerusalem. After the war, she moved to a small house in Amman. The influx of refugees from Palestine in 1948 called her once more to service. In Amman, she organized a milk centre for the children of refugee families from Palestine. Rosemary organized a system under which she bought material and paid refugee women to sew it into garments, which were then distributed to other refugees.

Mrs Forbes later received a medal from the International Red Cross Society, showing the head of Count Bernadotte and inscribed: '*Muriel Forbes, en souvenir de l'oeuvre de la Ligue des Sociétés de la Croix-Rouge en faveur des Réfugiés Palestiniens. 1949–1950.*'

The Arab peoples are passionately anxious for education, which they believe to be the key to Western superiority. Even in Iraq in the 1920s, I can remember village boys running after me, calling, 'Please sir, I want to go to school.'

In the West, boys are not particularly anxious to go to school, nor to acquire knowledge when they are there. We never appreciate those privileges which we have long enjoyed. But those who have never possessed our advantages covet them passionately. Thus when boys from Middle Eastern countries succeed in entering Western schools or universities, they often prove to be the most successful students because they have a passionate desire to learn.

The same considerations apply to work. Those who emigrate to the West are prepared to work for twelve or fourteen hours a day, though the citizens of Western nations constantly demand shorter hours and more pay. As a result, Middle Eastern immigrants to Britain and the U.S.A. often meet with rapid success and fortune.

In my later years, when lecturing in the United States, I several times encountered wealthy Jordanians. Some had been soldiers or N.C.O.s in the Arab Legion, but were now prosperous shop-keepers or businessmen. Whey they had arrived in America, they had worked day and night until they became wealthy.

Thus a natural rotation comes into play. Those accustomed to wealth and knowledge grow idle, while those deprived of both work day and night to acquire them.

At times, this Arab thirst for academic knowledge was embarrassing. I remember, at the end of the fighting in Palestine in 1949, the Jordan Minister of Defence saying to me, 'The Egyptian army is really splendid. Every officer in it has a university degree. I wish we in Jordan could achieve even half their high standard.'

'That is all very well,' I replied, 'but after all we have held a great part of Palestine for its Arab inhabitants, but the Egyptian army saved nothing.'

The Minister brushed my comment aside. 'Yes, yes,' he said, 'but don't you think we could aim at achieving equality with the Egyptian army?'

15
The Shooting Truce

In January 1949, Ralphe Bunche, an American who had succeeded Count Bernadotte, arranged a meeting between representatives of Egypt and Israel on the island of Rhodes. The two sides signed an armistice on 24 February 1949. On 23 March, Lebanon signed an armistice, though she had virtually no army and had played little or no part in the fighting. At the end of March, the government of Iraq notified Amman that it would withdraw its forces which for ten months had been holding sixty miles of the line. Meanwhile the Israelis had occupied the Neqeb as far south as the Gulf of Aqaba.

The Arab Legion was thus left alone facing the Israelis on a front of some 300 miles. We had by now some 10,000 men, as against a far greater number of Israelis.

In February 1949, the Jordan government received an invitation from Dr Bunche to send a deputation to Rhodes to negotiate an armistice with Israel under the auspices of the United Nations. On 11 March 1949, Jordan signed an armistice with Israel on the island of Rhodes.

Meanwhile the Iraqi army had declared its intention to withdraw its forces without negotiating with Israel. The latter announced that the armistice she had signed with Jordan did not apply to the Iraqi front and that, if the Iraqis withdrew, the Israeli army would occupy their area 'to keep order'. On 13 March, the Israeli government cabled Dr Bunche that, if the Arab Legion took over from the

Iraqi army, Israel would consider such action a breach of the armistice.

The anxiety and tension of those days cannot be described in words. Israel was everywhere victorious. On 11 March 1949, she was admitted as a member of the United Nations. Although she had everywhere rejected the orders of the United Nations and had assassinated their special representative, Count Bernadotte, she was given an enthusiastic welcome. The admission of Jordan to the U.N. was vetoed by Russia, she being an ally of Britain.

Eventually the Israelis demanded the cession of a further 400 square kilometres along the Iraqi front, promising (if this were granted) to sign the armistice with Jordan for the Iraqi front. If not, they would renew the war against Jordan on all fronts. Israel was still bound by the Security Council Truce of 18 July 1948, so that if she had (as she threatened) resumed hostilities with Jordan in order to annex more territory, she would once more have been openly defying the United Nations, who had just welcomed her as a member.

The Jordan government cabled the governments of the United States and Britain; the former replied refusing to intervene. Eventually on 3 April 1949, the Israel–Jordan armistice was signed, including the Iraqi front, which we took over with 2,000 men, replacing 19,000 Iraqi troops.

The Arabs themselves have a proverb which says, 'The Arabs are only agreed on one point and that is never to agree.' A considerable area of Palestine had been saved for its native inhabitants by the Arab Legion alone which, however, had never attacked any area allotted to Israel by the U.N. partition plan.

Neither Egypt nor Syria had saved anything. Yet, in the course of the following two or three years, the facts were everywhere turned upside down by political propaganda. Egypt and Syria were the heroes of the Arab cause, but had been betrayed by the treachery of Jordan. This treachery was, of course, conveniently blamed on the British commander of the Arab Legion who was said to have received secret orders from the British government to help Israel or, alternatively, who had been bribed by the Israelis with large sums of money.

From 1948 to 1956, I was responsible for the 300 miles of frontier between Jordan and Israel. The Zionist objective had been to create

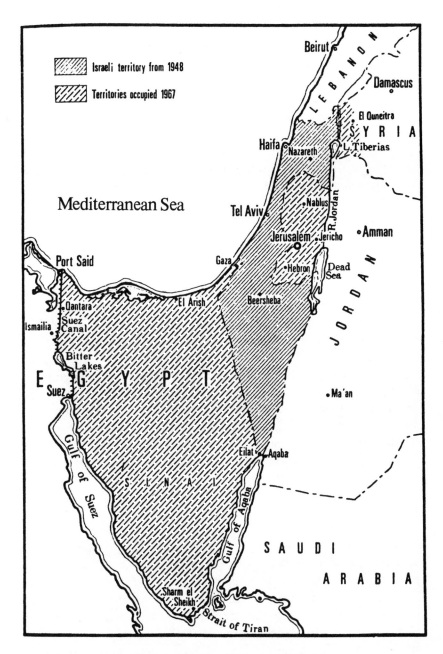

Boundaries around Palestine, 1948-67.

a state which would be solely inhabited by Jews. From the end of the mandate, they had systematically driven out all native Palestinians from the territory they occupied with such violence that they were obliged to flee as they stood, leaving behind all their possessions, which were seized by the Israelis.

Whole villages were bulldozed down and then ploughed over, so that the refugees would have no homes to which to return. After the armistice, some of these refugees attempted to return to their homes at night to see if they could retrieve any of their possessions. All such persons caught by Israeli patrols were shot dead on the spot, without arrest or trial.

As a result, the infiltrators began to carry weapons and a little sub-guerrilla war developed, which need never have happened. The Jordan government instructed me to prevent refugees from crossing the demarcation line, not out of consideration for Israel, but because the majority of them would be killed, and there was nothing to be gained. For this reason, I made every possible effort to co-operate with the Israelis to keep the border quiet. My efforts were completely unavailing.

There was little doubt that the Israelis were dissatisfied with the demarcation line and were still anxious to seize all Palestine down to the Jordan, as they have since freely admitted. If, for the moment, the international situation was not favourable to an immediate renewal of the war, they desired at least to keep the situation fluid, so that fighting could be renewed when a suitable occasion arose.

The second principle on which their action was based was that of ten-fold reprisals. If one Jew were killed by a refugee infiltrator, ten Arabs must be killed in revenge. For this purpose, a platoon of Israeli soldiers would be sent across the line to kill ten Arabs in a border village.

We accordingly erected wire fences round our frontier villages, issued each village with ten rifles and posted an Arab Legion soldier to organize the defence of every village.

Israeli spokesmen claimed that the Jordan government was solely responsible for border shooting because it did not prevent its subjects from crossing the demarcation line into territory held by Israel. No such principle has ever been heard of in international relations. If an undesirable person enters France from Britain, the French government does not protest that the British government should have prevented his departure.

The infiltrators were not ever on any occasion Jordanian subjects, nor the inhabitants of the border villages on whom the reprisals fell. All were destitute refugees, in many cases from refugee camps many miles behind the border or, in some cases, still living in caves in the hills.

But more significant was the fact that I made every possible effort to co-operate with the Israelis in avoiding incidents. I offered trans-border telephones between Israeli and our own police posts, or joint patrols of Israeli and Jordan soldiers. No offer I made was ever accepted.

An interesting episode occurred on the line just west of Jenin where for some time no incidents ever occurred. We eventually discovered that the Israeli police officer on this sector had been in the Palestine police during the mandate and was friendly to the Arabs. After a time, however, the Israeli authorities realized what was happening. The police officer was transferred elsewhere and incidents immediately commenced on the Jenin sector also.

Half a million destitutes, most of them in Jordan, had been driven penniless from their homes in Palestine. Our border with Israel was over 300 miles long. It was utterly impossible to prevent one or two men creeping across the line at night, usually to visit their old homes. Many such were entirely innocent – for example, in some cases the infiltrators went back to pick their own oranges in their own orchards. But any caught doing so were shot out of hand by Israeli patrols.

On other occasions, Israeli soldiers broke into frontier villages, carrying small explosive charges which they placed against the doors of houses. The charge was then fired, the door blown in and an Israeli soldier sprayed the dark interior of the house with a sub-machine-gun, where men, women and children lay asleep.

To multiply examples of these incidents would be wearisome. Suffice it to say that the Israelis seemed to be motivated by two considerations. First, they were dissatisfied with the demarcation line and aspired to occupy all Palestine down to the Jordan. They therefore wished to keep hostilities alive until an opportunity to renew the fighting presented itself. Second, Israel relied solely on force and sought to protect its own citizens by ten-fold reprisals. For every Israeli killed, ten Palestinians must die, completely regardless of whether the ten persons killed had the slightest connection with the killer.

I should like here to emphasize the fact that these methods were purely political. Jews are, as we have seen, not a race but the followers of the religion of Judaism – one of the world's most noble religions, and that from which Christianity sprang. The leaders of Israel in the 1940s and 1950s were not in general the descendants of the biblical Children of Israel, but were East European Jews who had themselves suffered undeserved persecution in Germany, Poland and Russia. Their brutality and ruthlessness – for I can use no milder words – were not therefore the product of Judaism but of Nazism or Russian autocratic methods under which they themselves had suffered.

I have heard Jews say that Christianity is the most cruel and savage of religions, basing their accusations on persecution or pogroms which Jews have suffered in nominally Christian Europe. But fortunately the New Testament is available, with its commands to love our enemies and to do good to those who persecute us. We cannot blame the cruelty of Europeans on Christianity, nor can we blame the brutality of some Israelis on Judaism.

I do not, however, think that there can be any doubt that the state of Israel has been built on reliance on force and a disregard of either humanity or justice. My experience of eighty-four years of life has convinced me that this is a mistaken line of action, even from a purely worldly point of view. Kindness, generosity and mutual understanding have always produced vastly better results than violence. Sometimes, when others use violence against us, we are obliged to resist, but only to defend persons who are under our protection. But as soon as we get to know our attackers and can talk to them, we should endeavour to reach an understanding with them.

One Friday in July 1951, I was walking through the shopping centre in Amman with my family, for Friday was our Sunday. The children were in a toy shop, when a police officer dashed up. 'The Prime Minister wants you in his house at once,' he gasped. 'Something has happened to the king.' I drove quickly to the house of Sameer Pasha who was then Prime Minister.

Inside the house, the cabinet was assembled, all weeping unashamedly, the tears running down their faces. 'Our lord is dead,' Sameer Pasha blurted out between sobs. 'Call the army to stand by in case of emergencies.'

King Abdulla had gone to pray in the mosque in Jerusalem – the Mesjid al Aqsa. A man hiding behind the door had shot him through the head as he crossed the threshold.

In Turkish times, there had been two leading families in Jerusalem, the Husainis and the Nashashibis. The British, during the mandate, had appointed Haj Ameen al Husaini to be the Mufti – the Muslim religious head in Jerusalem. But during the war, Haj Ameen had gone over to the Nazis and was unable to return to Jerusalem after the war. The Arab Legion entered Palestine in 1948 to defend the central area allotted to the Arabs, and that area, as already explained, had been annexed to Jordan. The Mutfi, who aspired to be the leader of Arab Palestine, saw himself supplanted by King Abdulla. Another member of the Husaini family was arrested for the murder of King Abdulla and was condemned to death and executed.

The king's eldest son, the Ameer Tellal, was in a mental hospital in Switzerland, suffering from schizophrenia. He was a charming young man, devoted to his family, though he had not been on good terms with his father. On 5 September 1951, he returned to Amman to mount the throne. The streets were gaily decorated and he received an enthusiastic welcome, many people shedding tears of joy and emotion.

Meanwhile the sub-war continued on the Israeli demarcation line. Palestinian refugees still infiltrated across the line at night to visit their old homes. Israeli troops constantly crossed the demarcation line to shoot Arabs, allegedly in reprisal for refugee infiltration. No case of Arab Legion troops crossing the line was ever reported. The staff of United Nations Observers, army officers from neutral countries, had virtually abandoned any hope of controlling the situation. If they reported incidents to head-quarters in New York, no action ever resulted.

As the force holding the demarcation line, the Arab Legion and myself were the constant victims of vituperation. The other Arab countries, Egypt, Syria and Saudi Arabia (none of whom had saved a square yard of Arab Palestine), never ceased to proclaim the 'treachery' of Jordan. One Egyptian newspaper stated that I was in the pay of Israel and that they were in possession of a photograph of myself sitting in conference with Israeli military commanders in Tel Aviv, plotting the overthrow of the Arabs. The paper announced that they would publish the picture in a forthcoming issue, but it never appeared.

King Tellal was a charming man and very easy to work for. He was in his early forties – the ideal age for a new king: old enough to be experienced but young enough to be still energetic. During the year of his reign, July 1951 to July 1952, Jordan seemed still to be as stable as ever. The Israeli army constantly raided across the border. There was a military *coup d'état* in Syria and rioting in Baghdad. Martial law was proclaimed in Teheran. Cairo had been half burnt down in rioting. There had been fighting in the streets in Beirut. The Israeli police had fired on rioting crowds. But in Jordan a general election had taken place without a single arrest. Never was a single shot fired by either the police or the army against a Jordan citizen. Once again, love had been shown to be more powerful than coercion. King Tellal was beloved, he was deeply conscientious, his private morals were faultless and his personality charming.

But in April and May 1952, his mental illness became aggravated. The king was living in his palace but was not exercising his sovereign rights, which were in the hands of a council of regency. On 11 August 1952, the Jordan parliament was called into secret session, and the king's medical documents were laid before it. After several hours' debate, parliament decreed the deposition of King Tellal and the succession of his eldest son, the Ameer Husain.

King Tellal first went to Egypt, but then moved to Turkey, where he lived sadly and alone in a villa on the Bosphorus until his death a few years later.

Meanwhile the Ameer Husain was at Harrow. He returned to Amman on 25 August 1952 and received an enthusiastic popular welcome. But he was legally unable to exercise his royal duties, being only seventeen years of age, whereas he would not come of age until his eighteenth birthday. He accordingly returned to England, where he did a six months' abbreviated course at the Royal Military Academy at Sandhurst.

During these years of increasing anxiety, we achieved one heartening success, in that we won the almost universal loyalty of the villagers of Palestine. 'Reprisal' raids by the Israeli army on Arab frontier villages had led to the formation by us of the National Guard. This involved the enrolment of the young men in the villages and their training to defend their homes by N.C.O.s or soldiers of the Arab Legion who were posted in the villages. We also obtained limited quantities of barbed wire (for we had no money to buy more) with which the frontier villages were surrounded.

On several occasions, attacks by Israeli infantry companies on the villages were repulsed. These failures seemed to anger the Israelis, who stepped up both the military inroads and the propaganda. In May 1953, there were fourteen incidents in four days. The Jordan government, in an official statement, claimed that 200 attacks had been delivered by Israeli troops from 1 January to 25 May 1953, resulting in the deaths of 165 Arabs, mostly women and children.

In vain we begged the United Nations Truce Supervision Organization to persuade the Israelis to conclude an agreement for the co-operation of the Israeli and Jordan police on the border.

When I was young, if we boasted of anything we had done, we used to be asked if our trumpeter was dead. I have several times blown my own trumpet in these pages by recording the testimonials which I have received.

One such incident occurred at this time. The wife of the President of the Lebanese Republic visited Jordan and went to see the ancient city of Petra. There was a police fort built at the entrance to the archaeological site. The distinguished tourist rested for a short time at the police post and talked to the sergeant in charge.

'How do you feel, being under the command of an English officer?' she enquired.

The sergeant looked puzzled. 'How do you mean?' he asked.

'I mean Glubb Pasha,' she said.

'He is not English,' replied the sergeant. 'He's one of us.'

16

Now Lettest Thou Thy Servant Depart

In April 1953, King Husain attained the age of eighteen, which was the royal coming-of-age, according to the constitution. He returned to Amman, where he was everywhere greeted with enthusiasm. His youth, his charm and the misfortunes of the royal family won the affectionate loyalty of us all.

For thirty years, Jordan had been the happiest and most stable of the Arab countries, though one of the smallest. Much of this stability, it seemed to me, had been due to the loyalty of the army to the throne, and I made every effort to reinforce this loyalty. I encouraged the king to visit army units and to get to know the officers.

It was soon apparent that the young king had a will of his own. He was extremely keen to learn to fly and went up to the aerodrome every day to receive lessons. As a result, the cabinet, urged on by the anxiety of the Queen Mother, passed a resolution to the effect that the king should not fly. His Majesty took not the slightest notice but continued to fly until he qualified as a pilot. Then, one day, he took his revenge and invited all the cabinet to fly with him. I joined the party and we took off from Amman airfield in a twin-engined aircraft – I think it was called an Anson but I cannot be sure.

Having gained height, the king made a steep dive towards the centre of the town of Amman, pulling out at the last moment in a steep climbing turn.

The Prime Minister was sitting in front of me. Judging by his wan complexion and the convulsive way he clung to his seat, he did not enjoy the trip. The cabinet passed no more resolutions to regulate the king's activities.

The summer of 1953 was strenuous in the extreme. There was the king's inauguration (Arab kings are not crowned) and the ensuing ceremonial parade. Jordan was suddenly overwhelmed by a plague of locusts, a major disaster in an agricultural country. The army was called out to fight the locusts.

On the Israeli border, we redoubled our efforts to prevent infiltration, and in April, May and June there was a marked diminution of incidents. Then, suddenly, on the night of 11 August 1953, the Israeli army delivered simultaneous attacks on three Arab villages: Wadi Fokeen, Sureef and Edna. We could not understand the reason for these attacks, as no incidents had occurred to provoke reprisals.

On 13 October 1953, the Israelis claimed that three Arab infiltrators had thrown a grenade in at a lighted window in Tirat Yehuda, killing a woman and two children. We immediately took every possible step to trace the offenders and offered our assistance to the Israelis, inviting their police to come over and work with us.

At 9.30 p.m. on 14 October, twenty-four hours later, an Israeli force of all arms broke into the village of Qibya, a mile and a quarter inside Jordan. The operation had been carefully planned. The village was first shelled and mortared; then the infantry moved in, firing indiscriminately down all the lanes with sub-machine-guns. At the same time, the neighbouring villages of Shuqba and Budrus were bombarded.

Behind the infantry came engineers, each with a pack of explosives on his back, and these he placed against a house. The inhabitants were all cowering inside their houses, terrified by the shooting. The engineers then fired all the charges and the whole village dissolved into mounds with the inhabitants buried underneath. The Israeli forces probably consisted of a battalion group, with added engineers and artillery.

Whether or not there had been an incident in Tirat Yehuda the night before was never settled, but it is certain that such a complicated operation could not have been improvised in twenty-four hours, but must have been carefully worked out and rehearsed. Sixty-six people were killed in Qibya and the whole village was reduced to mounds of rubble.

The disaster was followed by violent riots and demonstrations in the towns of Palestine and in Amman, accompanied by cries of 'Down with the Arab Legion.' In Amman, demonstrators gathered outside my office, yelling, 'Down with Glubb Pasha.' The Palestinians were difficult people to serve. Every inch of Palestine which had been saved for the inhabitants had been defended by the Arab Legion, and yet the slightest setback was always marked by street demonstrations, not against Israel, but against the Arab Legion.

This faculty for attributing Machiavellian motives to their rulers seemed to be a particular characteristic of the Palestinians. Every action one performed was analysed with a view to discovering the tortuous motive which actuated one. I do not know whether this quality is to be attributed to the considerable amount of Greek blood which flowed in their veins and gave them this intellectual subtlety.

Much of this situation was due to the inability of the Arab countries to agree – or, rather, to their intense jealousy of one another. The Arab Legion was especially the victim of this jealousy by the mere fact that it had saved so much of Palestine. Egypt and Syria, whose armies had saved nothing, never ceased to publicize their accusations of treachery against the Arab Legion.

This intellectual subtlety, which attributes to every action a tortuous ulterior motive, is not to be found among the original natives of central Arabia, whose minds seem to work openly and in a straightforward manner. Their tendency was to speak the truth and to accept what they were told at its face value.

The Jordanians were of mixed origins. The Decapolis (or ten Greek cities) was established in the north-western hills of Jordan, probably from the time of Alexander the Great (one of them, Beisan, was west of the Jordan), with the result that the people of northern Jordan still retain their subtlety of intellect today. The remainder of Jordan, however, was largely peopled by central Arabians, whose minds were more frank and straightforward.

The regular Arab Legion itself was paid for by a British grant-in-aid to the Jordan government; without the Legion the Israelis would have reached the River Jordan in 1948.

Incidents continued on the Israeli border in 1954. At 8 p.m. on 30 June 1954, for example, the Israelis suddenly opened fire with all their weapons in the city of Jerusalem. Commander Hutchison of the United States Navy was the local chief of the U.N. armistice commission. A calm and fearless officer, he lived with his wife in a house almost in the no-man's-land between the two armies. He called both sides by telephone and secured their agreement to a cease-fire. But a few hours later, the Israelis would open fire again; once more a cease-fire would be arranged and last for a few hours, and then fire would be reopened.

Charges that Jordan was the aggressor scarcely seemed convincing. The Israeli army was about ten times as strong as we were, and their military budget was ten times as large as ours.

But more alarming was the increasing build-up of the Israeli air force. Jordan had acquired one or two passenger aircraft for communications purposes, but to build an air force was out of the question. There was still a squadron of the R.A.F. on Amman airport, however.

The disproportion between the strengths of Jordan and Israel was so great that the principal hope for the survival of Jordan lay in her defensive treaty with Britain. No specific enemies were, of course, mentioned in the treaty but, if either Britain or Jordan were attacked, the other party bound herself to come to her assistance with all the means at her disposal. It was, of course, in accordance with this treaty that Britain paid for the regular Arab Legion. As long as this treaty remained, it was hoped that Israel would not attack.

Britain concluded this treaty with Jordan with a view to the possibility of another great war, Jordan having proved so valuable and loyal an ally in the Second World War. To Jordan, the treaty was her principal guarantee against attack by Israel. But the treaty was not limited to considerations of higher policy and strategy. A genuine, even an enthusiastic, friendship inspired both sides, extending on the one hand to the soldiers, officials, villagers and tribesmen in Jordan and, on the other, from the British Foreign Office to the many British soldiers and airmen who had served in Jordan and to their families.

Meanwhile events in the Middle East had assumed a new complexion. The Egyptian defeats in Palestine had given rise to revolutionary movements at home. On 23 July 1952, a *coup d'état* was staged in Cairo by the so-called Free Officers, led by Jemal Abdul Nasser. King Farouq left the country and the government was taken by a Revolutionary Command Council led by Nasser.

To account for Egypt's failure against Israel, Nasser laid the blame on Britain, which had hitherto been Egypt's supplier of arms. During the fighting in 1948, the United Nations had called upon its members to abstain from supplying arms to the combatants. Britain complied and refused to supply weapons or ammunition to Egypt or to Jordan. The U.S.S.R., however, which was then supporting Israel, supplied her with warlike stores from Czechoslovakia, even during the Bernadotte Truce. When he seized power, Colonel Nasser accordingly blamed the Egyptian defeat on Britain's refusal to supply munitions; and he placed orders for arms and ammunition with the Communist bloc. This measure received widespread propaganda in the Middle East as the solution to the Arab dilemma in Palestine.

In 1954 Britain concluded a military agreement with Egypt, under which British troops were to be gradually withdrawn from the Suez Canal Zone, leaving their heavy war material behind, in order that the personnel could return by air in the event of an emergency. Future military co-operation between Britain and Egypt was foreseen. At the same time, the United States and Britain promised Egypt a loan to enable the latter to build a new high dam at Aswan, to render possible the extension of irrigation in the Nile Delta.

In July 1956, however, the American Secretary of State, John Foster Dulles, suddenly announced that the United States had cancelled her undertaking to assist in financing the Aswan Dam. The American refusal could scarcely have been more rude or brusque. Nasser countered with the nationalization of the Suez Canal and with increasing co-operation with the Soviet Union, who agreed to complete the Aswan Dam on which the United States had defaulted.

President Nasser, whether or not his policies were wise, was a demagogue – a trait which caused him to be likened to Hitler. He not only had the power to rouse large audiences, but he made a speciality of broadcasting his speeches on the radio, for which purpose he erected a high-powered transmitting station which he named 'Voice of the Arabs'. His voice boomed through the bazaars in Amman in passionate political speeches.

The Middle East had its own acute problems, particularly that of Israel, but their solutions were rendered immensely more difficult by the intensified rivalry between the Western and the Communist blocs – or between the U.S.A. and the U.S.S.R.

While Egypt was co-operating more and more with the U.S.S.R., a new agreement was signed in 1955 to oppose the spread of Soviet influence. This was known as the Baghdad Pact, its signatories being Turkey, Iraq, Iran, Pakistan and Britain. The pact had been largely engineered by the U.S.A. to resist Soviet expansion, although America did not openly join it.

Egypt and Iraq have often been rivals for predominant influence in the Middle East, and the Baghdad Pact was immediately denounced by President Nasser in his most flaming oratory. He claimed, though with a remarkable lack of logic, that the Baghdad Pact was an intrigue to assist Israel, basing his accusation on the fact that Turkey, one of the signatories, had accorded diplomatic recognition to Israel.

Jordan found herself in the centre of this storm. Britain, her ally, was a member of the Baghdad Pact, but Nasser's accusation that the pact was an intrigue to support Israel could not but cause misgivings. Demonstrations against the pact marched through the streets of Amman, urged on by President Nasser's passionate voice on the radio.

King Husain, straight from Harrow and Sandhurst, found himself, at the age of nineteen, plunged into the midst of this cauldron. President Nasser invited him to visit Egypt. His cousin was the King of Iraq. In addition to the rival propaganda of Egypt and Iraq, he was also subjected to the emotional appeal of Arab nationalism in general, and its denunciations of British and Western 'imperialism'.

I was devoted to the Shareefian family, of which he was the fourth generation which I had known personally. But I was also of the opinion that Arabs in general were more at home with a government which had a personal ruler at its head. This was partly due to ancient if unconscious tradition and partly to the religion of Islam. No Muslim country had ever been successfully governed by elected parliaments, assemblies or committees. The principle followed had always been the appointment of one man for every responsible task.

The British and the Americans were convinced that their system of elected bodies was the ideal form of human government. Similarly the French had bequeathed republican institutions to Syria and Lebanon. While Jordan had remained completely stable during, and for ten years after, the Second World War, Syria had been the victim of a succession of *coups d'état*.

I was visited at about this time by a Frenchman, who had lived most of his life in Syria. I asked him why, since the war, Syria had had so many revolutions, while Jordan had remained so stable. He replied that the Syrians were too intelligent. 'A certain amount of stupidity is necessary to political stability,' he added. 'The British, for example, are famous for their stability!'

There may well have been some foundation for his opinion, for historically Syria and, even more, Lebanon and the 'Arabs' of Palestine have been heavily interbred with Greeks – a nation famous for acuteness of intellect but not for political stability.

Until the Second World War, these Arabic-speaking peoples of the eastern Mediterranean coast were generally known as Levantines. There was nothing derogatory in such an appellation which merely meant 'eastern' – the east end of the Mediterranean. But the spread of Arab nationalism gave rise to the impression that all the peoples who spoke Arabic belonged ethnically to one race – a completely erroneous belief. In reality, the term 'Arab' resembles rather the word 'European' – a jumble of many races which resemble one another in certain cultural fields but differ widely from one another in temperament. So widespread, however, had been the propaganda, that many Arabic-speaking people really did believe that the Arabs were a single ethnic people. This illusion encouraged Nasser to dream of making himself leader of the whole Arab world.

Meanwhile the Israelis themselves were growing more aggressive. They had withdrawn from the U.N. Mixed Armistice Commission, so that there was no longer any neutral ground on which we could meet them under the auspices of the United Nations.

On the night of 1/2 September 1954, an Israeli force of battalion strength attacked the small village of Beit Liqya, four miles on our side of the demarcation line. The operation, as usual, had been most carefully planned. Two companies attacked the village, while the other two companies of the battalion each mined one of the two approach roads by which Arab Legion reinforcements might come.

The village was held by the National Guard, that is to say the young men of the village who had received a limited amount of training. They were commanded by a regular Arab Legion N.C.O. and succeeded in repulsing the attack. Arab Legion reinforcements hit both the land-mines on the two approach roads, two men being killed and one wounded, but the remainder attacked and drove off the Israeli companies which had been in ambush above the land-mines.

Another encouraging feature was that the National Guard from the neighbouring village of Beit Nuba, hearing the firing at Beit Liqya, took the initiative under their regular N.C.O. and set out across country in the dark, attacking in the rear the Israelis who were attacking Beit Liqya. The retreating Israelis abandoned considerable quantities of ammunition, grenades and explosives, making it appear that they had planned a major demolition raid like Qibya.

In a subsequent debate in the Israeli parliament, the government openly admitted its policy of ten-fold reprisals, although it had in fact been pursuing it for four years. 'Force is the only argument which Arabs understand,' the Israelis frequently claimed. I had already spent thirty-four years among Arabs, and had proved again and again that they could be won by love and trust, when force was unavailing.

It was now five years since the armistice which ended the active hostilities of 1949. One-third of the people in Jordan were destitute, driven from their homes in Palestine by the Israelis. The latter continued to attack Palestinian frontier villages. Jordan had taken the most energetic measures to prevent refugees infiltrating across the line, but her requests for Israeli assistance were refused.

Meanwhile, the Arab Legion had grown from 6,000 in 1948 to 23,000 in 1955, while an almost equal number of villagers on both banks of the Jordan had received elementary training in the National Guard.

The new revolutionary government in Egypt under President Nasser had begun actually to encourage infiltration and guerrilla raids into Israel. This enabled Nasser to pose as a true patriot, boldly resisting the Israeli invaders. By contrast, we, who endeavoured to keep the peace, were held up as traitors, acting on secret orders from London.

Soon after the king's inauguration, he had appointed Fawzi Pasha al Mulqi to be Prime Minister. Fawzi Pasha was a young man who had been a student at a British university and had inbibed British ideas of democracy and freedom of speech. When he took office, he introduced legislation establishing freedom of speech and of the press.

It is rarely advisable to introduce into one country the political ideas and institutions of another. Fawzi Pasha's widely advertised freedoms did not allow a safety-valve for the public to express their pent-up feelings, but merely gave an opportunity for professional extremists to collect in Jordan. For the first time, the word Communist was heard. The self-styled Freedom Party, founded by a Palestinian religious teacher, was violently xenophobic.

The marked deterioration in stability caused by Fawzi Pasha's 'liberalizing' policy resulted in his fall. Taufiq Pasha returned to office and called a general election. Determined to secure a majority, Taufiq Pasha asked me to arrange for the soldiers to vote for his candidates. I protested but eventually agreed to his supporters being marked 'government candidate' on the lists of persons standing for election.

Meanwhile the elections had to be held under the laws providing for free speech, as passed by Fawzi Pasha. The Communists, who had suddenly appeared from nowhere, were led by a doctor, Abdul Rahman Shgair who came to Jordan from Damascus. His every speech was an incitement to rebellion.

On the morning of the election, 6 October, shots were suddenly heard in the town. The police moved out to investigate and were immediately overwhelmed by a hail of stones from the flat roofs of a number of large buildings. We were obliged to call in two regiments who restored order in a few minutes when they arrived. The police succeeded in guarding the polling booths and no ballot boxes were tampered with. Large accumulations of stones were found stacked on the flat roofs of several buildings. The riot had obviously been carefully planned. Meanwhile Dr Abdul Rahman Shgair had arrived back in Damascus.

The members of the government and the politicians were entirely ignorant of military affairs and were not interested in them. I could not persuade them to listen. But they never interfered and they allowed me a free hand in everything. Nevertheless, as the situation became increasingly threatening, I felt that they ought to know. Eventually the king consented to a top-secret meeting in the palace, to be attended only by His Majesty, the Prime Minister, and the Ministers of Defence and Finance.

When we arrived at the palace, however, the king brought with him his young A.D.C.s and a number of palace hangers-on. I spent an hour explaining our military situation *vis-à-vis* Israel, pointing out that, in the event of war, we would have to withdraw from positions in the flat coastal plain and hold certain defensive positions in the hills.

When I had completed my explanation, the king stood up and read out from a piece of paper in his pocket. 'I do not agree with any of the plans we have heard. I will never surrender one hand's breadth of my country. We will defend the demarcation line. Then we shall attack.' The palace servants applauded loudly. We rolled up our maps and withdrew.

A few days later, I again saw the king in the palace. He was smiling and charming. I invited him to spend three days with me in the frontier area, examining the positions of the troops. He readily agreed and we spent three days together, after which he admitted smilingly that he was convinced.

In April 1955, a conference of Asian and African nations took place at Bandung, attended by President Nasser, at which he made up his mind openly to join the Communist bloc. As a result, in September 1955 he signed an arms deal with Czechoslovakia, by which the Communist Powers agreed to supply Egypt with arms. In this year, Iraq signed the Baghdad Pact supporting the West, while Egypt concluded the arms deal which allied her with the Soviet bloc. Nasser appeared as the hero who, assisted by the U.S.S.R., was to defeat Israel.

To sustain this heroic pose, Nasser encouraged guerrilla raids into territory held by Israel on the Gaza sector. He also attempted, through the Egyptian Embassy in Amman, to encourage infiltrators to cross the demarcation line from Jordan into Israeli territory. In one case, even an Arab Legion officer was invited to the Egyptian Embassy and given a sum of money to organize infiltration into Israel.

The revolution led by Jemal Abdul Nasser in Egypt, which had dethroned King Farouq, had been carried out by a group who called themselves the Free Officers. In 1955, pamphlets began to appear in Amman signed 'Free Officers', posted in Amman to various addresses. At first we were puzzled, but then we noticed that they contained various military terms which were used in Egypt but not in Jordan. The origin of the pamphlets was thus revealed.

One morning in February 1956, we received in Arab Legion Headquarters letters from various units enclosing 'Free Officer' pamphlets, each with the office stamps of some other unit on it. The impression conveyed was that Free Officers in all units were corresponding with one another. We asked all units to send in their office stamps and, on comparing them, we found that they were different. The office stamps on the pamphlets had been made in Egypt.

An Egyptian newspaper published a leading article on disloyalty in the Jordan army, together with one of the pamphlets. We sent someone to Egypt to investigate. He reported that the article had been sent to the paper by the Egyptian Ministry of Guidance with orders to print it.

Soon the whole conspiracy came to light. All the pamphlets and the office stamps had been produced by the government of Egypt, and posted to Arab Legion units by the Egyptian military attaché in Amman. There were some 1,500 Arab officers in the Arab Legion, six of whom were involved in the plot. I took the names of the six and gave them to the king who, however, knew them already, for they had been in touch with him.

The Arab Legion was holding some 350 miles of demarcation line with Israel, the 'common enemy', a distance approximately equal to that from Southampton to Edinburgh. It was remarkable to what lengths the Egyptian government would go to destroy the Arab Legion. But perhaps this is incorrect; the plot went much further, as we shall see.

Since the stream of vituperation had been turned against me, I had on several occasions told the king that I was ready to resign any time he wished, but he always replied most cordially that such a thing was out of the question. I think, when he said this, he really meant it, but he was under strong pressure from different directions.

I was subsequently informed that an article appeared at this time in a British periodical which has since disappeared, describing me as the strong man of Jordan, and implying that the king and the government were without power. This article was shown to the king by the six officers and was the chief factor in persuading him. It was the exact opposite of the truth. Any influence I possessed in Jordan was solely due to my policy of love and trust. I had always been punctiliously obedient to the king and the cabinet ministers.

On 1 March 1956, the king attended a meeting of the full cabinet and told them that I was to be dismissed at once. When His Majesty left, the Prime Minister telephoned to me to ask me to come to his office, where he informed me of the king's orders. He asked me to leave in six hours. I said I could not do that, as I had a wife and two children in Amman where I had lived for twenty-six years. We compromised for the next morning.

The urgency was due to the fact that the king and the six young officers were afraid that I would order the army to march on Amman and would overthrow the government. I was grieved that, after I had devoted half my life to absolutely dedicated love and service to Jordan, it should be expected that I would plunge the country into civil war. The day after my departure, the British Ambassador saw King Husain. The former subsequently informed me that the king and the young officers who were advising him believed that I would take the bedouin-recruited units and would march on the capital.

The young officers who believed such a thing only revealed their own lack of scruple – we attribute to others the intentions which we harbour ourselves. These same young officers who advised the king to dismiss me were themselves pledged to President Nasser to betray the king.

I had sworn allegiance to King Husain. I had promised his grand-father, King Abdulla, that I would serve Jordan as my own country, unless Jordan should ever become an enemy of Britain, in which case I would be free to retire from my command in Jordan and remain neutral.

King Husain's commission was the sole authority under which I exercised my powers in Jordan. It was unthinkable that I should resist the authority of the king and of the Jordan government, whom I had faithfully served for twenty-six years. Indeed to this day, twenty-four years after these events, I still feel myself under an obligation of loyalty to the king and the people of Jordan.

After my interview with the Prime Minister, I left the office and drove to my house. My personal secretary, Molly White, courageously put the secret files in a bag and walked out a few minutes later.

I arrived home at midday and told Rosemary that I was dismissed. 'There have been troubles before,' she said. 'Won't this one blow over too?' I replied that this one seemed to be final.

We spent the rest of the day deciding what to take with us, as we were limited to what we could carry, though we had two small children and a house in which I had lived for twenty years. Rosemary said, 'If the house were on fire, what are the possessions I would grab to escape with?' She eventually took a suitcase of clothes and a basket of toys and teddy bears.

The next morning our Sudanese cook, Juma, served us with coffee and the tears were streaming down his face. He had been with me for more than twenty years, since before I was married.

After our departure, the Jordan government auctioned our furniture – which produced some unexpected results. Our mahogany dining table fetched only £2, but a Moses-basket made of reeds, which we had used as a cradle, was sold for £8. Arab friends who wrote to me from Amman told me of the general surprise at the fact that our house contained nothing of value. Havng occupied a senior post for so long, the public imagined that I must have lined my pockets.

Our portable possessions were most honourably collected and shipped to England, even down to a box of paper chains which we had used at Christmas.

Thus ended my long and happy service to Jordan, a country of which I had grown inexpressibly fond and to which I am still devoted.

Mr (later Sir Charles) and Mrs Duke, the British Ambassador and his wife, saw us off at the airport and promised to look after our tame gazelle. We then boarded an Arab Legion aircraft for Cyprus.

Years later, when re-reading the diary which I had kept during the First World War, I found an entry: 'A new officer has just been posted to us. He is twenty-seven years old. I cannot imagine why they have to send us these old men for service in the front line.' I was twenty-one when I wrote those words, as was King Husain when he ordered my dismissal. I was then fifty-nine, my hair was white and I must have appeared to him incredibly old.

I had devoted twenty-six years of my life to Jordan without any hesitation or afterthought, and my dismissal seemed to be the end of my useful career. But I have often taken courage from the repetition of Robert Browning's famous lines:

> One who never turn'd his back but marched breast
>   forward,
> Never doubted clouds would break,
> Never dream'd, though right were worsted, wrong
>   would triumph
> Held we fall to rise, are baffled to fight better,
> Sleep to awake.

No man can ever know the results of his life's work. The material results may be obvious – he made a million pounds, founded a great commercial company or commanded an army. But very often such successes are the least part of his life's work. The most important effect of our lives – though the most difficult to assess – may well be the influence we have had on other people. Perhaps some casual word we have spoken, remembered by chance by someone after we are dead, may light a spark which will flash across the world. How many men, now hailed as men of genius, died unknown and received a pauper's funeral? It is waste of time, therefore, for us to worry whether we have really rendered any services at all – it is a secret known only to God.

Yet it is gratifying to our human weakness to know that our efforts have been appreciated if only by the poor and the humble. In January 1981, I received an Arabic poem, signed by Hasan ibn Mutlaq al Ghanim of the Huwaitat tribe. It began:

> 'O Kloob, by God, we have not forgotten you,
>   O Kloob,
> Your conduct was always in the way of generosity
>   and honour.'

There is no G in the Arabic alphabet, so my name became Kloob.

17
A Second Career

In fact, my dismissal was only the first step in President Nasser's plot. The second was to get rid of the king himself.

Soon after my departure, a semi-Communist government assumed office. Ali abu Nuwar, the A.D.C. who had persuaded the king to dismiss me, was promoted to commander-in-chief. Both the new government and Ali abu Nuwar were agreed on a plot to dethrone the king. Every detail of the 'Jordan Republic' had been prepared, even to the republican flag and boxes of new cap-badges made in Egypt.

On 14 March 1957, Jordan denounced the Anglo-Jordan Treaty, thereby cancelling Britain's obligation to come to her aid if attacked. It is extraordinary how often small countries have an inferiority complex which causes them violently to reject an alliance with a more powerful nation. Medium-sized nations do not seem to suffer from this psychological handicap and are normally only too pleased to have the additional security of a powerful alliance.

When I was responsible for the defence of Jordan from 1948 to 1956, I was fully aware that we were not strong enough to resist an attack by Israel, which was armed to the teeth with the latest weapons by the United States. This American support for Israel was not due to moral considerations of justice or to the true interests of the United States, but was motivated by internal American politics, for it was generally believed that Jewish support was necessary to win a presidential election.

In view of this situation, it seemed to me that Jordan's only hope of survival was to retain her alliance with Britain to counter American support of Israel. This British alliance cost Jordan nothing, as the British government did not interfere in Jordan's affairs. On the contrary, Britain paid £12 million a year as a grant-in-aid to Jordan as an ally, to enable her to keep her army up to date.

The presence of a squadron of the R.A.F. in Amman was an added guarantee of British support against Israeli attack. The areas of Judaea and Samaria inhabited solely by Arabs had been recognized internationally as being part of Jordan. If Jordan had retained her alliance with Britain, these Arab areas of Palestine might have still been part of Jordan and might still today be inhabited by an 'Arab' population, as they had been for thousands of years.

But her unfortunate inferiority complex caused Jordan to denounce her alliance with Britain, enabling Israel, eleven years later, to occupy all the Arabic-speaking areas of Palestine. The chief issue at stake here was not the aggrandizement or the shrinking of Jordan, but the freedom of the Arabic-speaking Palestinians who had been living in their own country for thousands of years but who, since Israel conquered all Palestine in 1967, have been living under Israeli military rule, constantly evicted from their homes, deprived of their lands or 'exiled' from the country of their ancestors.

If King Husain disliked me, he was free to dismiss me. Britain did not protest, nor would she have protested if he had appointed an Arab officer to succeed me. But Britain's military alliance with Jordan would have continued to protect her against Israeli attack and would have allowed the Arabic-speaking Palestinians to go on living in their homes under Arab rulers.

By denouncing her treaty with Britain, Jordan also lost the British grant-in-aid of £12 million a year which Egypt, Syria and Saudi Arabia jointly agreed to pay. Once Jordan had denounced the British treaty, however, none of these countries paid anything. A more complete series of betrayals and false promises it would be hard to find.

By April 1957, the country was in chaos and the situation seemed to the conspirators to be ripe for the overthrow of King Husain. The machinery was therefore set in motion. In Zerqa, the Aldershot of Jordan, the artillery officers ordered their men to open fire on the infantry. The king, who was always fearless, decided to go himself. His personal appearance produced a triumph, all units receiving him with wild enthusiasm.

Both Egypt and Syria were behind the plot to dethrone King Husain; on this day of crisis, the Syrian army occupied the northern province of Jordan. But King Husain's personal courage alone had won the day. From April 1957, he emerged from a year of chaos during which, at any moment, he might have lost his throne and his life.

After the year of anarchy which succeeded my departure, Jordan recovered her stability. The pseudo-Communist government had been replaced by a cabinet led by Ibrahim Pasha Hashim, the elder statesman of Amman. I wrote to congratulate him and at the beginning of July 1957, I received his reply.

> Office of the Prime Minister
> Amman
> 29/6/1957

My dear Glubb Pasha,
I have received with great pleasure your letter dated 24/6/1957. I fully appreciate your feelings of devotion to Jordan. In this connection, I would like to inform you that the recent events which were fomented by those who sought to destroy our dear country are over. The situation is now stable once more, life has resumed its normal course, and we hope that public security will remain firm if God wills.

I was delighted to receive news of you and to know that you are now enjoying a quiet life in your new house in the country. This in my view is the best reward a man can earn by his life's work.

I am looking forward to the publication of your book which will certainly be of great value, for we know that all you write will be true concerning the events through which you lived and experienced, in spite of anything the enemy and their like may say.

In conclusion I would like to emphasize to you how often I think about the happy days we passed together and I hope that I may be so fortunate as to meet you once again.

With all good wishes to you and all your family and may God keep you.

Yours sincerely,
Ibrahim Hashim

Perhaps we may justifiably claim that King Husain was able to survive – partly at least – because the country and the army had been built up by thirty-five years of steady, honest government. In spite of the wildest plots and most violent subversion directed from outside the country by Communist and extreme elements, the heart of Jordan had remained firmly loyal.

All the plots to dethrone King Husain had been directed by President Nasser of Egypt, who aspired to become dictator of the Arab world. The king, who had at first admired him, was now disillusioned. The six 'free officers', on whose advice he had dismissed me, had all been in the pay of Nasser and had attempted to dispose of the king as soon as they had used him to dispose of me. King Husain defeated all his enemies by his sheer personal courage.

Thus ended my long and happy service to Jordan, but perhaps it may be helpful to mention the denouement in 1967. President Nasser's career seemed to go from triumph to triumph. Supported by Russia and the Communist bloc, he increased his army and completed the high dam at Aswan. His wild demagogy, delivered over his so-called 'Voice of the Arabs' radio station, thrilled the Arabic-speaking world. But he was himself carried away by the exuberance of his own verbosity.

In 1967, he established a garrison at Sharm ash Shaikh, on the southern tip of Sinai, and began to molest ships bound for the Israeli port of Eilat. In fact, Israel had little or no commerce down the Gulf of Aqaba and the gesture was little more than symbolic, but it provided Israel with a pretext.

Nasser did not attack Israel, as has often been claimed. It was Israel who attacked Nasser, justifying her action by his threats. King Husain had no reason to love Nasser but, in this crisis, his generous emotions caused him to fly to Egypt and pledge himself to stand by him.

When Israel launched her attack on Egypt, President Nasser telephoned King Husain, asking him to attack from Hebron the flank of the Israeli forces moving into Sinai. The king, with

187

uncalculating courage, led all his armoured forces in person through the mountains of Hebron, where they were attacked from the air and destroyed on the narrow mountain roads, being without air cover or anti-aircraft artillery.

Meanwhile the remainder of the Jordan army was still scattered in small pockets along the demarcation line. No studies had been carried out by the staff of the Jordan army and no battle plans had been considered. As a result, when the armoured column was destroyed in the Hebron mountains, the Israeli forces everywhere poured over the demarcation line against the dispersed Jordan units which were without orders. Some units put up desperate isolated resistance, but the Israelis swept past and down to the Jordan.

If the king had maintained his treaty with Britain and had kept a group of British officers who could have planned operations in advance, something might have been saved. But the king was defeated by his own virtues – his generous emotions and his fearless courage.

After the *débâcle*, King Husain came to London, and I paid him a courtesy call at the Dorchester Hotel. He received me with open arms, admitting generously that I had been right in warning him that Israel, with her lavish build-up of American aircraft and weapons, was too strong to be tackled.

It is possible now to write candidly of the king's youthful mistakes, because he has since become one of the shrewdest statesmen in the Middle East.

The real victims of these miscalculations were the Palestinians, wave after wave of whom were driven destitute from their homes. All of them were living in areas allotted to them in the U.N. partition plan. Those still living on the West Bank of the Jordan have been under Israeli martial law for the past fifteen years and enjoy no civil rights. Many have been evicted from their lands which have been seized by Israelis. Under international law, the West Bank is still 'occupied enemy territory', in which such changes of status are illegal.

Let us, after this digression, return to my dismissal in March 1956. Having been put down in Cyprus by an Arab Legion aircraft, we went down for a day or two to the Dome Hotel in Kyrenia, where we had twice before stayed on local leave. Then we obtained seats on British Airways and flew to London.

On landing at Heathrow, we were immediately overwhelmed by a horde of journalists, who surrounded us and bombarded me with questions. Brigadier Robert Elliot, who had at one time commanded the Arab Legion artillery and was living at Camberley in Surrey, had come up to meet and to help us. In co-operation with the police, he eventually smuggled us out of the airport building and into his own car, and we drove out. But the press were not so easily to be eluded. It was already getting dark and, as we looked back, we could see a long line of car lights following us.

Unable to shake them off, we decided to stop at an inn by the roadside and face the music. Once more we were surrounded by a crowd of journalists, and stood answering questions till even they were tired out. Then finally, after a long day of physical and emotional exhaustion, we dragged ourselves and two small children into the hospitable Elliot house in Camberley. In times of utter physical prostration, journalists sometimes seem to be without pity!

Nothing could have exceeded the kindness of the Elliots, who turned their house upside down to accommodate us and our children. As long as we live, we can never repay the debt we owe to them.

The Prime Minister, Sir Anthony Eden, telephoned to inform me that the Queen had been graciously pleased to make me a Knight Commander of the Bath, and I went up to Buckingham Palace, where I was knighted and most graciously received by Her Majesty.

We found somewhere to stay at South Godstone in Surrey, and I was cross-questioned by a committee of the House of Lords without much success. I can never speak impromptu, and had not thought out in advance what I wanted to say. Eventually the tension eased and we were left to face the future.

The most urgent problem was that we had very little money. I had never been able to save and my salary in Jordan had not been too generous. Moreover, we already had two children at paying boarding schools in England. I wrote to Mr Selwyn Lloyd, who was Secretary of State for Foreign Affairs, and asked him if I could obtain some financial assistance. He replied that the British government had no responsibility for me, and that there were no budget heads from which I could be assisted. However, he instructed the British Ambassador in Amman to ask the Jordan government to help me. The latter, however, replied that they were under no obligation to do so.

This was true. Although I had served the Jordan government with all my soul and strength for twenty-six years, I had never troubled them for a contract or for terms of service. We were, however, saved from immediate destitution by an unexpected windfall: the *Daily Mail* offered me £6,000 to write a series of articles. No one had ever offered me £6,000 in all my life!

My lack of money was, of course, entirely my own fault. I had never given money a thought. No one in his senses would have served Jordan (or any other government) without first obtaining a contract with terms of service and provision for a pension on retirement, or at least a gratuity.

During the Second World War, John Attenborough, the director of Hodder and Stoughton, the publishers, had served in G.H.Q., Middle East; at that time he had suggested to me that I write a book. As a result, I wrote *The Story of the Arab Legion* in spare moments in Amman. The book had been published in England in 1948.

Now once again, I was approached by Hodder and Stoughton to write another book, for which they offered me a handsome cash advance. Thus, by the generosity of the *Daily Mail* and my publishers, we were saved from immediate bankruptcy. The book, *A Soldier with the Arabs*, was published the next year, 1957.

The next step was to find a house to live in. Rosemary had lived in Tunbridge Wells, and my father and mother nearby, at Pembury. So we naturally looked in that direction. We looked at a small house in Mayfield, but the roof proved to be infested with dry rot. A local agent, however, took us to see a large house nearby called West Wood St Dunstan, which had been empty for three years. The price asked was less than that for a small cottage in the village.

Unfamiliar with life in England, I could not understand why it was so cheap, and we bought it. It was only later that we discovered the amount of the rates and the cost of heating a large house, and realized why it had been sold at a low price. In the next few years, it nearly ruined us again.

When my father had died in 1938, I had taken by mother back with me to Jordan, having meanwhile married Rosemary Forbes in the registry office in Tunbridge Wells. When Rosemary later joined me in Amman, after our church marriage in Beirut, my mother moved to Jerusalem where she lived in the American Colony hostel.

In 1948, when the Arab Legion entered Jerusalem, it so happened that the American Colony found itself in the front line of the Arab-held portion of the city, and my mother's bedroom window looked out over no-man's-land. A few days later, when she was asleep at night, a belt of machine-gun bullets hit the wall just above her bed, missing her by two or three inches. However, she refused to change her bedroom, but moved her bed across the room to beneath the window sill. 'The bullets cannot hit me here,' she explained. 'They will pass over and hit the wall on the other side of the room.' She was then eighty-three years old.

When we returned to England, my sister Gwenda flew to Jordan and put my mother on an aircraft for England, and she came down to us in Mayfield. She was a little annoyed at being hustled out of Jerusalem and back to England without warning. Not appreciating the reason, she felt she should have been told that I was moving. One of her favourite sayings, when anyone tried to push her around, was: 'Hurry no man's cattle! Maybe you'll have a pig of your own some day.'

She lived with us in Mayfield for some years, but eventually moved to a hostel for retired missionaries called Troutstream Hall, at Rickmansworth in Hertfordshire, where she found the religious atmosphere congenial.

Crossing London through the traffic is a tiring drive, and we did not go to see her as often as we should have. (So often, after the death of our parents, we regret that we did not do more for them.) When she finally collapsed in 1962, I reached the hostel while she was still alive, but she did not know me. She was then ninety-seven years old, a woman of great character and a dedicated Christian. I owe more to her than to anyone else. The last time I visited her, she said to me several times, 'Isn't God wonderful! Isn't God wonderful!'

She had taught herself to speak French, Italian and German, and when younger she used to play the piano and paint in oils. Our house is still full of paintings by her and by her mother, who had studied painting in Rome. But above all my mother possessed character, that indefinable quality which distinguishes a great personality.

As must inevitably occur to anyone who lives to the age of ninety-seven, she was out of touch with the modern world, its social life, its music and its painting. In her forthright manner, she would sweep it all away as 'filthy modern rubbish'.

The next method to support a wife and four young children which was offered to me was lecturing. Foyle's Lecture Agency engaged me to lecture all over Britain. The financial benefit was small, but it enabled Rosemary and me to explore a great part of Britain by car.

Having only spent one complete year in England – 1919 – since I left school, I knew scarcely anything of my own country. We explored a large area of Britain, as far north as Edinburgh and Glasgow, though we never reached the Highlands. We were particularly attracted by the churches in East Anglia, said to have been built under the influence of Flemish weavers, with all the angels – a multitude of the heavenly host – carved under the roofs.

We revisited both Salisbury and York where I had lived as a boy, Wales where I had never been before, Preston where I was born, and Liverpool where everything was sooty black but the people were kind and cordial. Shrewsbury, Hereford and Winchester completely won our hearts, and I was glad to visit Melton Mowbray which, in my early days of hunting enthusiasm, I had dreamed of as the earthly paradise.

But this is not a guide book to the beauties of Britain which I discovered for the first time when I was over sixty. Suffice it to say that we found it enchanting, in spite of the fact that we could not get a cup of tea until after 7.30 in the morning. . . In Jordan we had made our morning tea at 5 a.m.

Our two daughters were weekly boarders at a girls' school in Eastbourne, some twenty miles from Mayfield. Every Saturday afternoon, when we were at home, we would drive down to collect them. On the way back, halfway between Eastbourne and Mayfield, there was a teashop called Green Shutters beside the road. Here the weekly routine included a stop for tea. Rosemary and I ordered tea and scones, but the girls, in the reaction from school food, would ask for Welsh rarebit or baked beans on toast with a poached egg. Early on Monday morning I would drive them back to Eastbourne in time for the first lesson.

It was a relief to be no longer a public figure. One of the chief drawbacks of being in the public eye is that the fact undermines one's character by causing one to think of one's self – a preoccupation destructive of the spirit of service. 'Self is the root, the tree and the branches of all the evils of our fallen state. We are without

God, because we live for self,' wrote William Law. Self is the cause of our constant restlessness, grumbling and discontent. If our preoccupation is with ourselves, we can never all our lives be satisfied or at peace. It is, indeed, almost impossible to prevent our thoughts turning constantly to ourselves, but once we realize that self is our chief enemy, we can at least mitigate our self-preoccupation.

For public figures, this is much more difficult, particularly perhaps for politicians under our system of government. Their retention of office depends not so much on the honesty or efficiency of their work, as on whether people will like them and vote for them. Almost inevitably, to be popular is their chief preoccupation, and to malign their characters or their intentions the objective of their opponents.

Democracy, that magic word, sounds so ideal a system of government – 'the people are free to choose their own rulers'. But what an unsavoury mass of intrigue, libel and misrepresentation it conceals. Politicians are almost inevitably led to attach chief importance to the winning of popularity by every form of device or deception. People complain that politicians are insincere, but it is difficult to expect anything else when their success seems to depend so much on public caprice.

When I left Jordan so unceremoniously, my useful career of service seemed to be at an end. My first objective was limited to earning enough money to support my family and to educate our four children, until they could earn their own living. But as time passed, I gradually became aware of the possibility that a new and entirely different career might still be open to me.

I had long forgotten that meditation on the object of my life which I committed to paper in 1920 in the Old Serai in Baghdad, and in which I had weighed the alternatives of a life of action and a life of authorship. The thirty-six years of constant action which had ensued had completely erased from my mind all idea of a literary career.

But Providence was to recall me to these long-forgotten ideas. I was amazed, when talking to educated people in England, to find how little they knew of the history of countries other than their own. One intelligent and educated woman said to me quite amicably, 'We at least have the Old Testament in common with the

Jews, but we have absolutely nothing in common with the Arabs who are just savages, riding about the desert on camels.'

For two hundred and fifty years, the Arabian had been the greatest empire in the world, not only in military power but also in culture, science, wealth, art and learning. I consulted John Attenborough, the director of Hodder and Stoughton.

'Elsie and I,' he said, 'may understand what you mean when you say that history must be the history of the human race. But the reading public do not.' (Elsie was Miss Elsie Herron, who was then the chief 'reader' of the scripts offered to Hodder's for publication.)

Mr Attenborough agreed to publish any books on Arab history which I might write. 'But,' he added, 'you won't make any money that way. If you wish to make money, you should write about growing roses in suburban gardens, or breeding Siamese cats.'

Professor William Barclay of Glasgow University has written somewhere, 'Things happen to us which look like disaster. Let us remember that nothing is a disaster unless we make it so, and everything is an opportunity if we believe in the God who is working all things together for good.'

It began gradually to dawn on me that my ability to serve had not been terminated by my expulsion from Jordan. In fact, that apparent disaster was to open for me a second and entirely different career, and fresh opportunities for service.

Foyle's Lecture Agency suggested to me a lecture tour in the United States, but I was reluctant to leave Rosemary and the children for so long a time. Eventually, however, my objections were overcome and Foyle's put me in touch with a lecture agency in New York. Lecturing in the United States, which I undertook with so much reluctance, was to open to me a new world, to give me some of my dearest friends and financially to tide me over the difficult years until the children had all finished their education.

How providential it is that we cannot know the future. If, as a young man, I had known all the crises and dangers which were in store for me, I could never have faced my life. As each crisis arose and passed, every disaster opened the way to a new opportunity of service, until ultimately I gained confidence that such would always be the case. Even when suffering was involved, the power to endure it was given, whenever the need arose.

18
The New World

I communicated with the New York lecture agency, the name of which had been given me by Foyle's Agency in London. With remarkable efficiency, they undertook to book me for a two-month lecture tour of the United States, including a daily (almost hourly) schedule, all aircraft flight tickets and railway and hotel reservations, and instructions regarding how to meet the representatives of the societies whom I was to address. The whole package would be handed to me on my arrival in New York, so that I could not possibly go wrong.

One communication, however, somewhat surprised me. The lecture agent, a man of British origin, asked me if I would object to giving a press conference on arrival at the airport of New York. At this press conference, I was to read out a prepared statement which was attached to his letter. The statement said that I wished to express my profound admiration for the heroic people of Israel, who had reconquered and defended their ancient homeland against such immense odds.

If I agreed to read this statement to a press conference, the agent said that he could book me to speak before all the wealthiest clubs in America at very high fees. If, however, I was unwilling to read out this statement, the financial expectations of my tour would be approximately halved. Nearly all the rich clubs, he explained, had one Jewish member on their selection committee, who would blackball me unless I had read out the statement on my arrival.

I replied that I had no feelings whatever for or against Jews, but that I preferred to state my own beliefs and opinions rather than read statements written for me by other people. He replied regretfully that, in that case, the financial results of my tour would be considerably reduced.

In view of these preliminary exchanges, I decided to speak only on Arab history and the centuries during which the Arab empire had been the world's leading great power. In the United States, even more than in Britain, the general public believed Arabs to be wild savages riding about the desert who had never been civilized in any sense of the word.

American clubs are extremely addicted to luncheons or dinners, followed by a talk from a speaker, especially if the latter bears a name which they have read in the press. The lecture agency's programme consisted almost entirely of such fixtures.

I offered a selection of subjects, of which the principal were as follows:

1 The Bedouins: a historical and sociological study.
2 The Arabs in History: a historical narrative from A.D. 600 onwards, but excluding modern politics.
3 The Middle East – Key to World Power.
4 The Arabs – our Teachers: the debt of the modern world to past Arab civilization.

These subjects were chosen as being positive and imparting information. There was no mention of Israel or of modern politics and no negative criticism of anybody.

Some cynical wit has remarked that, in the old days, people in general were uninformed, but that now, thanks to the progress of modern science, the whole world can be misinformed. That this epigram is profoundly true has been forced on my attention more and more. Indeed I would go so far as to say that hate propaganda is the chief danger to human life on earth today.

Of course, since childhood, I had always known Christ's command to love our enemies. I had been involved in many wars, and have never felt any personal animosity against the other side. But I had never realized, as I do now, the depth and significance of this order. Today, at the age of eighty-four, I believe that it is the solution of most of our modern problems.

If we were inspired by a spirit of tolerance and broad-minded goodwill towards all mankind, all our struggles, hatreds and fears would vanish. For we react to one another. Hate arouses hate, suspicion breeds suspicion, and friendliness produces friendliness in an opponent. I am not a starry-eyed idealist; I do not suggest that we abolish our armed forces in the hope that our potential enemies will follow our example. But I do suggest that we should all – including our governments – always deal with one another in a spirit of open, frank and simple friendliness.

To return to my lecture tours in America: on one occasion I was to speak at a businessmen's luncheon club. When I arrived, the chairman warned me that a strongly worded protest against my being allowed to speak had been received from the chief rabbi of the city. 'This man,' the rabbi had written, 'has been declared by the Society for the Protection of Human Rights to be an enemy of the human race.'

I did not know if a society for the protection of human rights existed, though I certainly felt no enmity to the human race! The chairman told me that all the rabbis in the city were to be present, and that I had better be prepared.

I gave the talk on Arab history which I had prepared, and there were no hecklers. The chairman subsequently received a letter of apology from the chief rabbi saying that he had imagined me to be quite a different type of man. The chief rabbi was obviously an honest man who had been persuaded by propaganda that I was some kind of brutal torturer and massacrer of Jews. This was one of the earliest incidents to impress me with the power of hate propaganda across the world.

I had never received the impression of being hated in this manner by the people of Israel with whom I had tried to deal for eight years. Since I left Jordan, I have occasionally received letters from Israelis, or excerpts from their newspapers, which have never impressed me with a spirit of hate. But in the United States the spirit was more virulent, though I found no difficulty in being friendly with any Jews whom I could meet personally.

Although I had originally been reluctant to go to the United States to lecture, I was deeply grateful that I had done so. First, of course, it opened up an entirely new world to me. It is impossible to generalize about the American people which include so many different groups and communities. Speaking, in my early tours, principally to luncheon or dinner clubs, I naturally met the middle-class English-speaking community, but among them I made some of the closest friends I have had all my life.

Everywhere in America I met with unfailing kindness and cordial hospitality. I have since regretted that I did not keep a diary of my lecture tours, as I have at some other periods of my life. As a result, I am obliged to write largely from memory. Lecture tours planned by the agency were strenuous. They included a talk every day and sometimes two a day.

The normal daily routine was: an early start to the local airport, a flight to a fresh city and a talk, probably at a luncheon club, but possibly in the evening or sometimes both. Next morning, another flight to the next city.

As a result, I saw little of the countryside. Only rarely did I succeed in having a train journey – one a memorable trip from coast to coast across the continent. Panic situations sometimes arose when the weather was unfit for flying, and I had an appointment to speak a few hours later in a distant city. On one occasion, I was due to speak in Washington (was it in the Mayflower Hotel?) in the evening. The same morning I came down to breakfast in a distant city, to be told that the weather was unfit for flying. Someone, however, remarked that there was a train in twenty minutes. I raced out of the hotel without paying the bill, and just caught the train; and I arrived in Washington in the nick of time.

For the rest, I must confine myself to such memories as still come to mind. My most hilarious flight was from Rochester to New York, when the only available seat was in the luxury class and we were served with champagne the whole way!

One of the remarkable experiences I enjoyed was a visit to the capital of the Mormons, Salt Lake City. I had a vague impression that Mormons had great numbers of wives, but found that they no longer do so. They proved, however, to be a delightful community. Their history was not without romance when, in 1846, Brigham Young led them into the wild west to found Salt Lake City in Utah.

I fell in love with Arizona and New Mexico, owing to their close resemblance to the scenery of the Middle East. In Montana, I visited the site of General Custer's famous last stand, an incident perhaps rather more romanticized than it deserved.

As a young officer, I had studied the life of 'Stonewall' Jackson and his splendid campaigns in the Shenandoah Valley, and had come to regard him as one of my personal heroes – memories which were revived by a visit to Richmond, Virginia. I was surprised, however, when I spoke of this experience to be told by an apparently wealthy and sophisticated lady in New York that Stonewall Jackson was one of the worst presidents the United States had ever had. . . She was confusing him with Andrew Jackson.

Another memorable visit was to the Alamo in Texas. In 1833, Texas was still pioneer territory under the influence of Mexico, but largely settled by United States and British nationals. In that year, General de Santa Anna carried out a *coup d'état* and made himself dictator of Mexico. He then prepared an army with which he proposed to discipline the Anglo-American pioneers in Texas. In February 1836, Santa Anna attacked the fortress of the Alamo which was defended by 187 Anglo-Americans, whose object was to delay the Mexican advance until Sam Houston could organize a Texan army. On 16 March 1836, the Alamo was carried by assault and all the defenders killed, including such famous frontiersmen as Jim Bowie and Davy Crockett. But the Alamo had served its purpose. On 21 April, Sam Houston defeated Santa Anna, and the Republic of Texas became independent. In the Alamo today, the Stars and Stripes and the Union Jack hang side by side.

Altogether I visited the United States twelve times, each time for two months or more, so that I must have lived there in all for more than two years. During this time, I visited every state on the continent with the exception of Alaska and, I think, Wyoming.

As I grew to know the country better and made more and more friends, I abandoned the lecture agency, and began to make my own plans and engagements. This took up a certain amount of time in England during the summer. I went to the U.S.A. every autumn.

As time passed, the nature of my tours began to change. I had by then written a number of books on Arab history, many of which had been published in New York. As a result, I obtained more and more engagements in colleges and universities, where I often spoke to student audiences. My engagements with society clubs grew fewer, though I still sometimes talked to Rotary Clubs or to branches of the English-Speaking Union.

As I passed through my sixties and approached my seventies, I became less anxious to undertake a daily flight from one city to the next, and eventually began to accept invitations to stay for longer periods at universities to give a series of lectures.

I also introduced two new lecture-subjects. I offered a lecture called 'A New Look at the Arab-Israeli Confrontation', which was chiefly devoted to an ardent plea for the U.S.A. to use her influence in the promotion of peace. In this I failed. Jewish influence is so powerful in internal politics in America, that politicians and presidents seeking election almost always support their candidacy by promising support for Israel regardless of justice or peace or, indeed, of the interests of the United States or its reputation for morals and justice.

Democracy sounds such a fine word. 'America is a free country,' visiting foreigners are told with pride. But the world is now so small that, to win votes in an American election, politicians unintentionally sow wars and disturbances in other continents. This is especially so in a presidential election.

I particularly remember speaking on the Arab-Israeli confrontation at a large college. After my talk, the president of the college said to me that it was the first time in his life he had ever heard it suggested that there could be a single point or argument in favour of the Palestinians. Every exposition he had heard hitherto had emphasized that Israel was one hundred per cent right in all she did.

After 1965, I offered an additional lecture topic: 'The Rise and Fall of Nations'. My continued historical studies in England had impressed me with the regularity of the life-histories of the dominant nations of the past.

On different occasions, I spent several days giving lectures at both Harvard and Yale. On one occasion at the former, I was specially invited to an all-Jewish reception, where everyone was most pleasant and cheerful.

A memorable visit was that which I paid to the Virginia Military Academy at Lexington and to the neighbouring Lee and Washington University. I was much impressed by the spirit of cadets at the Military Academy. The students at Lee and Washington have a pleasant tradition of always saying good morning to any stranger whom they see on their campus.

The cadets of the Virginia Military Academy are still proud of the battle of New Market in the Civil War. When a Union army was marching southwards, the cadets turned out and formed up to give battle. In perfect dressing and with precise drill, the cadets marched against and repulsed the Union Army.

When I had passed the age of seventy, I was pleased to accept invitations to teach Middle East history for a term at a time in one place. In 1970, I spent the autumn term – or, as they called it, the Fall Semester – at Lewis and Clark College in Portland, Oregon.

I was given a tiny bungalow to live in on the campus. By day I lectured on Middle East history, while in the evenings I gave a course of talks in my private sitting-room on the Arab-Israeli problem.

Colonel Jim Davis had been American military attaché in Amman when I was commanding the Arab Legion. He and Mrs Davis were now living in the neighbouring state of Washington. While I was at Lewis and Clark, they took me out every weekend and showed me something of the incredible beauty of the north-west corner of the United States. I was even able to cross into British Columbia and visit Victoria, on Vancouver Island, a town more English than England, which reminded me of the Britain I had known as a boy.

I had already given a lecture on one occasion at Troy State University in Alabama. In 1971, I received an invitation to spend part of the Fall Semester there, to give a series of talks on Middle East history. While there, I was asked to give a lecture at Auburn University, also in Alabama. At the end of my talk, I suddenly fell down unconscious. A doctor examined me, could find nothing wrong, and advised a stiff glass of whisky.

Returning to Troy, I continued to have occasional fainting fits. At the end of my stay at Troy, I had a series of lectures booked in a number of cities all over the U.S. Leaving Troy, I gave a talk in Montgomery, Alabama, and the following day flew to Birmingham, Alabama.

In the evening, my kind hosts drove me into the town, where I was to speak at a dinner of the English-Speaking Union. They stopped at a filling station to fill up the car and we all got out, when suddenly I fell unconscious in the street. They picked me up and took me to the nearby hospital of St Vincent – called after St Vincent de Paul, a saint who worked among the poor in Paris in the seventeenth century and founded the Order of the Sisters of Charity, some of whom were in charge of this hospital. The sisters were surprised to hear that I knew of the life of St Vincent de Paul in France.

I had a long list of lecture engagements in front of me, while I lay helpless in bed. The Dean of Women Students at Troy University, Miss Diane Hanson, came to my rescue as the result of a telephone message. I gave her the list of my lecture engagements and she most kindly and laboriously telephoned all those who were expecting me, cancelling my appointments and explaining what had happened. But for her, all these people would simply have been let down by my non-appearance for my engagements. We have remained close friends ever since and Diane has come over and stayed with us in England.

The heart specialist in Birmingham decided that it would be best for me to return home – even if I were to faint on the way, it would not be fatal. So they put me on an aircraft, Rosemary met me at Heathrow Airport, and we got home safely.

Lying in bed in Mayfield, my heart stoppages became more frequent. At last I obtained a bed in the National Heart Hospital in London. It was none too soon. The day I was admitted, my heart stopped twice and I was taken down at night for an emergency operation. While they lifted me on to the operating table, my heart stopped for the third time that day. The surgeon quickly ran a wire down a vein from my left shoulder into my heart, attaching it to an outside battery, and this prevented my heart from stopping again. A few days later a battery was inserted in my right breast from which a wire ran down through another vein into my heart, which henceforth it drove. The pace-maker must surely be one of the most amazing inventions of modern medical science.

My attack of heart-block, as it is commonly called, put an end to my annual lecture tours in America, by means of which I had been able to pay for the education of our children. These tours had also introduced me to a new world which I would never have seen if I had not been so providentially dismissed from Jordan.

Although America was indeed the new world, I found it old enough to be full of the glamour of human heroism – not to mention the staggering beauty and variety of its natural scenery.

I was warmed and enchanted by the generosity and hospitality of the American people. At the same time, however, I could not but sense somewhere a certain hardness in some aspects of American life. Perhaps this factor may be due to the early struggles of the pioneers against nature and the Red Indians, or to the coarse crudity of the old Wild West.

Yet I, on the whole, found the United States a land of cordial hospitality and warm friendships, whatever other aspects so vast a nation may conceal.

In America, during the last five or six years of my annual visits, my lectures were principally delivered in universities. Yet in Britian, I have never been asked to speak at a university, an honour, it would appear, reserved for persons with academic degrees.

On one occasion at an American university, I happened casually to remark that the Germans seem to be more musical than the British. 'You cannot say things like that in the U.S.,' I was told. 'We believe all races to be equal.'

This remark, which at the time surprised me, seems to typify a good deal of modern thinking. It illustrates the common confusion of thought to the effect that 'equal' means identical. Everyone should doubtless be equal before the law, but otherwise people can only be equal in one particular characteristic. Two men may perhaps be equally good painters or runners, but otherwise they are entirely different characters. There are no two identical persons in the world.

Yet absurd confusions of thought arise as a result of the idea of universal equality. Women, it is said, are equal to men, and therefore they aspire to be jockeys, truck drivers or speed track riders. Of course women are equal to men, but at the same time they are a different creation. They alone can train young children and thus ensure the morals and the health of the next generation.

I hope that my female readers will not be angered by anything I have said. It is because I admire women so much more than men that I cannot understand why women wish to demean themselves by imitating men.

All human beings may perhaps be equal, but behind this equality they conceal an endless variety of gifts, powers and capabilities.

19
A Mind to Embrace the World

The whole world today is faced with the same problems. Such is the speed of communications that a crime committed in one country is, within a few hours, reported all over the world, and within a matter of days is imitated by the commission of similar crimes on the other side of the globe. (The media rarely report virtues for imitation elsewhere!)

The entire world is menaced by the possibility of nuclear war, which would at the best eliminate the results of thousands of years of civilization, and at the worst would exterminate all life on earth.

Yet, at the same time, modern science could infinitely alleviate the sufferings of humanity, if its discoveries could be used for constructive purposes, instead of for the destruction of life.

Suffice it to say that the speed of modern communications has so reduced distance and isolation that the whole world has become a single province.

If we are to handle such a situation with wisdom and success, it is obvious that we must consider the interests of the whole world without fear or favour.

But granted that our minds must grasp the world situation as a whole, sheer idealism is not enough. Every detail of human life must be envisaged in a strictly practical manner.

As nuclear warfare is the most urgent and pressing danger which confronts us, we are obliged first of all to consider the factors which make for war between the Great Powers. As any such war will inevitably become nuclear, the first principle we must establish is that *wars must be abolished now and for ever. There is no other means to avoid the extermination of the human race.*

What then are the means to be adopted to ensure the abolition of war and what are the causes which give rise to wars?

The first step to ensure the abolition of war, it seems to me, is for the leaders of all states openly and repeatedly to announce that another war will entail the extermination of the human race; that war is no longer a feasible proposition, and therefore we should put it out of our minds.

The first cause which is liable to give rise to wars is, in my opinion, habit. The public media and the politicians constantly discuss wars, the dangers to which we are exposed by the evil intentions of other powers, and the state of our own defences.

Obviously the answer to such a precarious situation is not to reduce our own armaments and to hope that other nations will follow suit. Such a course is more likely to tempt others to attack us.

Negotiations to reduce certain types of weapons are of no value as long as fear and suspicion continue. The only remedy must be much more radical: to eliminate the fear and suspicion. If that could be accomplished, a genuine reduction in armaments could be achieved, all countries, *pari passu*, moving in the same direction.

Diplomacy

I can personally remember the days when the public demanded 'open diplomacy'. Such a demand was based on the supposition that the secret machinations of emperors and kings gave rise to wars. Since then we have discovered that wars between whole peoples seeking to destroy one another can be far more cruel and savage than wars between rulers.

'Open diplomacy' is impracticable. Even two commercial firms negotiating a deal do not announce to the world how much each of them is prepared to pay, though they may keep their partners informed.

One dangerous feature of Western democracy arises when a government in office publicly discusses the actions of another nation. When President Carter denounced the Russian invasion of Afghanistan in 1979 and announced his intention to boycott the

Olympic Games, he made it impossible for Russia to withdraw. No Great Power will change its policy as a result of threats by the leader of another country.

If, on the other hand, the United States had made secret diplomatic representations in Moscow, an agreement might have been reached enabling the Soviet Union quietly to ease up on its policy towards Afghanistan without loss of prestige.

In the West, party politics are often a threat to foreign relations. If the government adopts some line of foreign policy, the opposition contradicts it; in the ensuing debate, critical and offensive remarks are made about other nations. It is essential to remember how sensitive other countries can be and to avoid insulting them publicly.

I have been told that courtesy towards other nations is impossible owing to the freedom of speech which exists in Britain, but I imagine that appeals by the government to the media would produce some effect. There would still remain the last resort of secret diplomacy to assure the country insulted of the government's regret.

It is so easy in life to reprove other people when we believe them to be at fault, but to forget to thank them when they do well. During the Second World War, Jordan rendered sincere and dedicated service to the Allied cause. When the war was over, I endeavoured to persuade the British government to offer some public sign of gratitude to Jordan. An answer at Question Time in the House of Commons would have been enough, and would have been reported in the local press. But I was unable to achieve anything.

In brief, the first step towards a better world-order seems to be courtesy and tact, the use of secret diplomacy, and never to use criticism of other nations as a weapon in party politics.

Causes of National Rivalries
Having dicussed the effects of fear, suspicion and habit, let us examine more closely the causes of national rivalries.

One of these is undoubtedly competition for the natural resources which exist in other countries. Of these, at the time of writing, the principal is oil. To guard the countries from which we obtain oil and the pipelines and sea routes from them, fleets and bases have to be maintained all over the world.

I cannot understand why we are content to remain in so vulnerable a situation. Should we not have set ourselves long ago to produce our own sources of energy?

Switzerland, even in my schooldays, made all her own electricity and was always clean, efficient and self-supporting in energy. She, of course, was blessed with mountains supplying water energy, but I can never understand why we have made no attempt to become self-supporting in energy. Could not we make full use of such rivers and mountains as we have? Why cannot we develop such purely natural sources of power as the wind, the tides or the sun to free us from the cost and the danger of imported fuel?

If we were successful, other nations would be quick to imitate us, and the world would be spared the constant fear and rivalry, fleets and bases, caused by the necessity of importing energy.

It may, however, be well to emphasize that it is the habit of hatred, fear and suspicion which makes the importation of oil a possible cause of war. If fear and suspicion were eliminated, all nations could buy oil wherever they wished in an open market.

Teaching the Nations how to Live
The British and their offspring, the Americans, have an annoying habit of trying to teach all other nations how to live, a characteristic perhaps inherited from the Puritans. We have already noted that the Americans, living in isolation, are unaware of the existence of other cultures, founded upon often unconscious traditions, thousands of years old, which have become second nature.

The British, with their long association with Asia and Africa, should know better, but often do not seem to do so. When we say today ecstatically that all the world is one, we forget that ten or twenty thousand years of development in isolation have produced immense differences in the various branches of the human race. Our endeavours to persuade or coerce them all to adopt our customs or our institutions are doomed to failure.

We would do far better to leave them alone to develop in their own way and to abstain from insulting them by labelling them 'backward', and treating them with condescension.

Many countries, like South Africa, are faced with problems of which we have no experience. Yet we are quick not only harshly to condemn them but to endeavour to coerce them to conform with our own ideas. If we wish to influence them, could we not do so far more effectively as friends and allies than by trying to boycott them?

One of the bases of civilized society is to mind our own business. If we were to tell our neighbours that we disapprove of the way in which Mr Smith in our street treats his wife, should we help to solve his domestic problems or merely divide our community into rival factions?

Forms of Government

> 'O'er forms of government let fools contest,
> Whate'er is best administered is best.'

Thus wrote Alexander Pope in 1733, in an age wiser than our own. Today we act in an exactly contrary manner. We insist that every nation in the world adopt what we call Western democracy. In every colony which Britain evacuated she installed a copy of her institutions before leaving. In almost every case (except of course the dominions peopled by Anglo-Saxons and Europeans), the system thus installed collapsed.

Never did we, or do we, allow for the immense differences in cultures and traditions. In every case, we attached importance only to the outward forms. Western democracy is not suitable to the whole world. Forms which have grown out of their past traditions are likely to be more successful.

We are equally in error in supposing that Communism can sweep the world, even apart from the fact that the U.S.S.R. herself is becoming decreasingly Communist.

When China declared herself Communist, the Western world was taken aback. But Communism in China proved to be quite different from the Russian variety, and soon the two countries were at bitter enmity.

When Vietnam was thought to be 'going Communist', the United States felt bound to intervene. But if she had not done so, Vietnam's Communism would soon have taken a local form, quite different from the European variety. Local cultures and traditions are always stronger than imported foreign systems.

Of course, all human beings are born equal, but we have to recognize that they differ widely from one another. Most of their differences are superficial.

If we were at sea in an open boat with four or five people of different nationalities, we should soon all be brothers. Thor Heyerdahl provided proof of this when he sailed the Atlantic in his reed boat. He deliberately selected a crew of seven, consisting of one Norwegian, one Italian, one Mexican, one man from the United States, one Egyptian, one Russian and one from Chad in Central Africa.

But in fact most of us live in superficialities. We dislike the way others eat or talk or sit. It is essential to realize this fact. Single persons, or small numbers, may live in a foreign country and completely absorb its culture. I often felt myself more at home with Arabs than with British people. Persons who thus become acclimatized to foreign cultures are of great value. They interpret one people to another and render international commerce smooth and mutually profitable.

But as soon as two different races or cultures come in contact with one another in considerable numbers, rivalry develops. How many problems and hatreds which increase the instability of the world today are due to the clash between different cultures and communities in one country?

Idealists who welcome immigrants from other continents into Britain are playing with fire. Of course all men are equal, but differing cultures and races do become rivals and enemies if they form large communities in one country. To boast that we have a multi-racial society in Britain is therefore dangerous.

The reverse is of course equally true. Large communities of Europeans in Asia or Africa are likewise liable to give rise to hatred. Let us admire and praise those enterprising persons who facilitate international understanding by living in other countries and absorbing their cultures, but let us use extreme caution in encouraging the build-up of large foreign communities in any country.

It is curious how any extreme tendency in any age builds up its own opposite. Periods of violence and hatred in history have often produced the greatest saints.

In a similar manner, rapidity of travel, which tends to mingle all races together, seems to have given an intense fillip to local fanaticisms and to smaller and smaller fragmentations.

The Roman Empire of two thousand years ago (when travelling was on foot or by horse or mule cart) is now divided into some twenty-four independent nations, each with its own government, its own laws, language, currency and armed forces. Only a few hours are required to fly from one end of the former Roman Empire to the other, yet many of the present successor states are on bad terms with one another.

But this is not all. Many of the twenty-four countries are themselves threatened with further disintegration: Corsica desires independence from France, the Basques seek to separate themselves from Spain, French-speakers and Flemish-speakers dispute in Belgium.

Languages

Language is one of the great barriers to human intercourse. In 1905, Zamenhof, a Pole, published his project for Esperanto, the language of hope, to be used all over the world. But now, every year sees more determined efforts to revive languages, dead for centuries if not millennia, with the result of further isolating men, one from another. Some claim that these revivals are purely cultural, but nevertheless they are often supported by arson, the pistol, or the time-bomb.

God Loves the World

I am happy to be a Christian, because Christianity is the religion of love and, if properly lived, lays more emphasis on love than does any other religion. But it does not seem to me that we can claim that God only loves Christians. 'God so loved *the world*' we are told – not the Jews or the Christians.

In any case, Abraham, allegedly the ancestor of the Children of Israel, lived only some 1,800 years before Christ. Archaeologists tell us that there were towns and villages in Palestine for 7,000 years before Christ. Did God not love his creation before the birth of Abraham?

For that matter, most of the rest of the earth seems to have been inhabited many thousands of years before Abraham. Was God indifferent to mankind during those long ages? Even today, there are hundreds of millions of persons in the world who have never heard of the Gospel. Does He not love these?

God, it seems to me, is a Spirit filling the universe and capable of inspiring the souls and minds of men. Does it not seem probable that He has always done so and that every good action and noble thought has been inspired by Him since the beginning of the world?

Let us then, to the best of our ability, develop our minds to regard all the races of mankind with equal affection, respect and courtesy. But let us also remember that the differences between races extend back through thousands of years of varying experiences and cultural development.

Let us remember that the idealism which claims that there are no races but the human race – and which advocates the free inter-mixture of all peoples everywhere – often leads only to bitter hatreds, internal feuds and savage terrorism. It is, moreover, to be noted that violence in speech or exaggerated criticism of others are often used by people who would not dream of resorting to pistols or bombs. Yet they go far to produce that intolerance which ends in physical violence.

Let us then love all the nations of the world, but at the same time make patient and tolerant allowance for their vagaries. Where their varying backgrounds make them objectionable to one another, let us allow for their foibles and not urge them to intermingle, thereby giving rise to internal quarrels. Let us not expect or hope that all the world will be like us, or criticize those who come from different cultures and backgrounds.

20

A Return to Greatness

When I was a child, I used always to pray, 'O Lord, I beseech Thee that Britain may always be the greatest power in the world, and the greatest power for good in the world.' Britain before 1914 was indeed the greatest power in the world, and I think also a very great power for good. Her decline in the last seventy years has been due to her moral weaknesses, not to external circumstances.

It was probably these weaknesses which gave rise to mistaken theories causing us to claim as virtues the abandonment of our role to serve and help others.

The Servant of All
In the nineteenth century, many persons in Britain realized that empire was a stewardship. 'He that would be first among you, let him be the servant of all,' is one of the basic principles of human life. My father, who was born in India during the Mutiny, was fully convinced that the British people were under a moral obligation to serve and help all the peoples of the empire. To do so involved many hardships, including long periods of exile in remote countries, the separation of husbands, wives and children, and exposure to dangers and privations. Yet such labours are all joy when undertaken as service.

Self-Persuasion
The human mind is a versatile instrument, which we can use to

persuade ourselves of the rightness of any action to which we are drawn by our feelings. From about 1897 onwards – the year of Queen Victoria's Jubilee – the feeling of stewardship grew weaker. First, it seemed to turn into a feeling of pride that we 'owned' the empire.

But after the First World War, it was changed into a feeling of lethargy – we could not be bothered to go on serving other peoples. This, we easily persuaded ourselves, was a virtue – what right had we to go on 'bossing' other races. The fact that such ideas could take shape proves that we had already lost the moral basis of the empire which was founded not on domination of other peoples but on serving them.

Precedents

History confirms these theories. Great empires of the past have normally abdicated their responsibilities when the moral fibre of the leaders has weakened. The colonies and the provinces have often begged the imperial government to remain, and have rarely rebelled and sought to break away. This was the case with many British colonies, which were compelled to become independent.

Equality

The basis of empire being service – he that would be first must be the servant of all – meant that Britain's role in the empire was to serve the other members. This principle necessarily assumed that the interests and traditions of all members would be equally respected and promoted.

This principle was automatically applied in the early days, for example in India. The government of India was almost entirely Indian, with a few, largely Indianized British officials in key positions who kept the peace between local rivalries and ensured the co-operation of the whole.

But, with the improvement of communications, the home government in Britain was able to interfere and to assert itself. Ignorant of Indian traditions and background, it tended to use its authority to Anglicize Indian institutions – a fatal mistake, for Indian culture was thousands of years old. In brief, the maintenance of the empire required mutual respect of the traditions of all the member states.

A Return to Greatness
The British Commonwealth still exists. All that is required to consolidate it and to make it once again 'the greatest power for good in the world' is for the people of Britain to follow the golden rule: 'He that would be first among you, let him be the servant of all.'

Epilogue

I was born in 1897 and cannot expect to live much longer. However stupid we may be, it must be difficult to live for more than eighty years without acquiring at least some useful experience. I should dearly love to help other people with the fruits of my observation. Young people tend to reject our efforts to assist them by saying that the world was different when we were young, and thus that our experience is without value for the world of today.

The changes which have occurred in the world, however, have been superficial, affecting such external and material factors as modes of travel and communication. But the most important factors in life are our relations to God and to our fellow human beings, and these, as far as we can judge, have changed little in the four thousand or so years of recorded history. I will endeavour, therefore, to summarize some aspects of my life, which I hope may be useful to others.

I was always a good boy, serious and obedient to my parents. Socially I was shy and spent most of my spare time with horses, to which I was devoted. I am always grateful for this period of my life which resulted in an affectionate family and a happy childhood and youth. I do not agree with the theory that adolescent boys should be wild or uproarious. They will meet enough trials in life to test their courage and initiative later, without causing pain and disruption to their families.

Even if I had not been of a serious nature, the experience of the front-line trenches in the First World War would probably have sufficed to sober me.

Although modern practice is to mix the two sexes at school, I consider myself fortunate to have had nothing to do with women when I was young. It seems to me that the adolescent intermixture of the sexes inevitably emphasizes the physical excitements produced. This factor, combined with the 'liberation' of teenage girls inevitably makes for early marriages, based on physical attraction.

Two or three years are sufficient to weaken the glamour of physical excitements, and the couple are divorced, leaving two or three children deprived of the happy security of family life.

During my twenties I was fortunate to live in faraway lands where there were no Englishwomen. But from about thirty-three years of age I found that my attitude had changed. I no longer desired physical thrills but I longed for a companion in life. As a result of my own experience, I do not think that, in most cases, men should marry before thirty, though, of course, no rigid rule can be laid down.

Young people often marry without realizing that marriage must involve sacrifices. At least half one's life has to be sacrificed or, at any rate, changed, in accordance with the wishes, tastes and interests of the other party.

But although I was always a good boy at home, I was often opinionated and disrespectful to my seniors in my twenties. All my work would have gone more smoothly, if I had been tactful and had taken more trouble to conciliate my superiors.

I had a remarkable facility for identifying myself with all sorts of communities with which I came in contact but, unfortunately, when I did so I tended to become militant and aggressive in their defence, especially towards the authorities who, in my opinion, were not doing enough for my protégés. I can see now that I would have been able to do much more for them if I had patiently explained their problems to my superiors instead of being defiant.

But though I was insubordinate to my seniors, I learned the priceless art of talking openly, honestly, frankly and reasonably to everyone. I became convinced that almost everything could be achieved by openness and sweet reasonableness, whereas force only increased trouble. Traditional enemies could be transformed into the closest allies by perfectly frank and friendly discussion. Even to this day, I feel most strongly that the Western Powers should engage in such frank interchanges with one another and with Russia, instead of exchanging long-range criticisms of one another in public speeches or in the press.

As commander of the Arab Legion, I continued the same process. I always spoke personally to every batch of recruits at the depot. I frequently visited units and addressed the officers or even the whole unit, frankly explaining the situation and the duties which were incumbent on us all.

I also explained to all ranks the necessity for discipline and a high standard of moral conduct, with the result that all ranks themselves voluntarily maintained the highest standards of discipline and smartness, almost without any disciplinary punishments.

When, however, I became involved in the hostilities with Israel, I encountered an enemy with whom I could not discuss our differences. King Abdulla would have liked to do so, but was unable. In any case, Zionism was a worldwide movement, and I occupied only a subordinate position.

I became involved in the bitterest kind of war – one in which one people wishes to destroy another people and drive it from its homeland. Even so, we endeavoured to fight honourably. After the Rhodes Armistice in 1949, I endeavoured with all my might to maintain peace along the demarcation line – but without success, for Israel was determined to renew the fighting and acquire more land.

After my dismissal by King Husain, my usefulness seemed to be at an end, but I gradually realized that all things work together for good, because all things that happen come from God.

In the twenty-five years which have elapsed since my dismissal, I have endeavoured, by lecturing and writing, to explain the Arabs and the West to one another.

Eighty-four years of life have convinced me that the basic element of the world is love. By this I do not mean the mutual attraction of the sexes, but a general atmosphere of benevolence and tolerance towards all creation. This, however, is not merely a cold intellectual conception, but is saturated with warm human emotion.

Men have been given Free Will, and it is open to them to spend their lives in hatred and fighting. But lives lived in such a spirit are restless, violent and unhappy.

On the other hand, a life spent in love, tolerance and benevolence is swimming with the stream of creation, and cannot fail to be peaceful and happy, in spite of the many trials and sorrows which it may experience. Such trials, we ourselves can see, are essential for the purification of our own personalities, for our tiny minds are inclined to become arrogant and self-centred when we meet with too much success.

Put in another way, we may agree that our aim in life should be to achieve a state of absolute selflessness, devoting our thoughts and efforts to service: the service of God, of mankind in general and of the neighbours whom we meet on our way.

Index

relations with Jordan, 185–6

Taufiq Pasha, 141–3, 149–51, 154,
    178–9, 181
Tellal, King, 167–8
Teneem tribe, 67
Teresa, Mother, 61
Tertullian, 106
Titus, 136
Trans-Jordan
    author in, 95–107, 115–22
    history of, 80
    relations with Britain, 131,
        141–2
    relations with Israel, 145,
        148–50, 152–4
Truman, Harry S., 139
Turkey, 175

United Nations, 156–7, 162
United Nations Partition Plan
    (Palestine), 141–2, 154–5, 188
U.S.A.
    and the Baghdad Pact, 175
    and mandates, 79
    and Palestine, 139–41, 151, 157
    and world politics, 206–8
    author in, 196–203
    relations with Israel, 162, 184–5
U.S.S.R.
    and Palestine, 139–41, 150–1
    and world politics, 206, 208–9

in the Second World War, 128–9
relations with Egypt, 174–5, 187
relations with Israel, 157–8

Vietnam, 208
Vigny, Alfred de, 55
Vincent de Paul, Saint, 201

Wahhab, Muhammad ibn Abdul,
    67
Wahhabis, 67–8
    see also Ikhwan
Wavell, General, 121, 126, 128
White, Molly, 181
Whittington, Mary Sarah
    Catherine, 2
Wilson, General Sir Henry, 122
Wilson, Woodrow, 61, 79
Women's liberation, 203, 216
Wounds, 33, 46–7, 84

Yaseen, Yusuf al, 91
Young, Brigham, 198
Ypres, 30–2

Zaid, Abdul Aziz ibn, 117–18
Zakkai, Rabbi Johanan ibn, 136
Zamenhof, Ludwik Lejzer, 210
Zillebeke, 32–3, 38
Zionism, 138, 144, 150, 155,
    162–4, 217